Who is Carl?

Carl Goes is named after an old friend with wanderlust who died too young. Carl was an avid collector of travel guides from the 1800s, a time in which a global standard for travel books was set.

Our friend Carl had only debts when he passed away, so everything he owned had to be sold at auction. We decided to pool our money and buy back everything we knew he loved — some antique paintings, family jewellery, and of course, his beloved travel book collection. Remarkably, when the antique traders in the room realised we were the friends and family of our dear friend, they stopped bidding, helping us save everything we could.

We wanted to pay tribute to our friend Carl by creating a modern-day series of books encapsulating a new type of travel, where work, play, creativity and curiosity combine. Capturing the spirit of the man *Carl Goes* is named after, our guides are for all the curious and creative folks on the planet. We hope Carl would be proud.

Foreword

Welcome to *Carl Goes Amsterdam*, a book that brings the local voices of Amsterdammers to our curious and creative travellers. *Carl Goes Amsterdam* is a lifestyle accompaniment. Many of our fans read our books from cover to cover before they travel to a destination, as an immersive experience before they leave home. They dip their toe in and out while they're in a city, taking inspiration from our interviewees and our recommendations, before veering off and crafting their own adventures. Unlike most other books out there, we've written and published the book within the same year. We think all of these things make *Carl Goes* a little different from other city guides, but we'll let you decide for yourselves.

Our readers are urban nomads and inquisitive entrepreneurs, but despite their love of tech, they find the tactile experience of a book to be a luxurious rarity amid the clutter of all the gadgets and apps out there. *Carl Goes Amsterdam* is for intrepid city breakers and seasoned globetrotters. It's for enterprising business executives and spirited start-up owners. And it's for everyone working in or interested in a broad spectrum of creative industries, motivated to slot in with the locals during their Amsterdam visit.

Every designer's paradise, whether in fashion, furniture or big budget adverts, the canal-adorned Dutch capital is a prime place to see and be seen in business and creative industries today. Amsterdam is aglow with a feeling of artistic freedom at this moment in time. Far from being just a city of red-lit windows and cannabis connoisseurs, Amsterdam has well and truly emerged as a serious and established city on the cutting edge of creativity, cuisine and original cultural happenings. Start-up entrepreneurs are flocking to the city to create new products and realise their dreams, co-working and creative exchange is becoming a way of life, and diversity is fiercely embraced, with more than 150 nationalities calling the city home.

While business life in the city involves big bucks and resolute attitudes, Amsterdammers love nothing more than to party in their spare time. Think picnics in Vondelpark as soon as the sun cracks a ray, rosé wine and beers while chugging along the canals — every Amsterdam citizen seems to have their own boat complete with outboard engine — and day trips to the trendy beach clubs just outside the city during summertime weekends. Craft beers, craft coffees and concept stores are all the rage, creating yet more opportunities for creative expression while enjoying the finer things in life. Blend that with brightly coloured clothing, the inevitable bicycles and fresh food sourced from the city's surrounding farms, and anyone can be an Amsterdammer for as long as they're in the city.

Amsterdammers embrace a healthy work-life balance and a refreshing directness; it's no accident that the Netherlands (or 'Holland' as the Dutch prefer to say) is consistently featured within the top ten in the World Happiness Report. Amsterdam is an easy city to blend into, with the majority of Dutch people speaking English too. Visitors feel quickly at home there, where everything is just a tram or bicycle ride away.

Through *Carl Goes Amsterdam*, we want you to become a citizen of Amsterdam for the time being. That's why we haven't created a directory of museums and landmarks, sightseeing tours and tourist hotspots. We know you're good enough at using Google for that. Instead, we let city residents describe their city in their own words. We tell you about co-working spaces and networking events, we hand-pick eateries and hotels with finesse and flair, and we give you inspiration for getting lost in the city, so you can discover Amsterdam on your own terms and in your own time.

Sascha Mengerink, Publisher
Sasha Arms, Editor

The locals

No-one knows Amsterdam like the people who live there, whether they've called the city home for a lifetime, or moved there and discovered everything for themselves. Throughout *Carl Goes Amsterdam*, we bring you interviews with well-connected Amsterdammers, who share their Amsterdam experiences and best bits of the city especially for you.

Adjiedj Bakas
page 22
Futurist and trend-watcher Adjiedj has received numerous awards and accolades, including Trendwatcher of the Year. He's also been named one of the most creative Dutch people and one of the most influential Dutch people. He works across the world to predict trends, and he speaks at a multitude of high-profile events, on everything from 'slowbalisation' to how today's creative class will become tomorrow's Alan Turings. When he's not working, Adjiedj likes people-watching near the Albert Cuyp Market.
Our favourite Amsterdam tip from Adjiedj: Go to Pakhuis de Zwijger, a cultural meeting place inside a revamped harbour building, for events designed especially for creative people.

Kenrick Vrolijk
page 40
This hair and make-up stylist to the rich and famous has a loyal following. Working his way to the top at a young age, Kenrick learned his trade in the prestigious Rob Peetoom salon in de Bijenkorf department store, and from famous stylist Mari van de Ven, who he appeared on TV shows with. He is now setting up his own hair salon brand KENVO Hair and Make-up. When he's not working, Kenrick hangs out in the chic Oud Zuid neighbourhood and enjoys gin and tonics at the Conservatorium Hotel.
Our favourite Amsterdam tip from Kenrick: Go to Milkshake for an open-minded festival where bisexual, transgender, gay and straight people can all party together.

Martien Mellema
page 86
The Creative Director for *Vogue Netherlands* has had an enviable career in the world of fashion, working for *Elle, Glamour, Mexx* and *Vogue Bambini* before taking up her current post at *Vogue*, launching *Vogue Man Netherlands* in 2015. She spends her days cycling around Amsterdam visiting her teams shooting on location, and conceptualising the next editions of *Vogue*'s magazines. When she's not working, Martien enjoys IJburg, ice-skating there in the winter and swimming in the summer.
Our favourite Amsterdam tip from Martien: Visit Sauna Deco, inside the decadent interior of a former 1920s Parisian department store, for relaxing on comfortable beds in the huge sauna.

Boris Veldhuijzen van Zanten
page 104
As an entrepreneur, CEO and co-founder of The Next Web, Boris is a familiar face around Amsterdam. He started out in circus school and went on to create successful companies from scratch. The Next Web is considered to be one of the most popular tech blogs in the world. He was also a member of the prestigious Startup Europe Leaders Club, shaping European policy. When he's not working, Boris enjoys entertaining friends in his former school-house home, and feeling like a king in the Amstel Hotel.
Our favourite Amsterdam tip from Boris: Buy your favourite magazine from The American Book Store and read it in the bar on Wolvenstraat with no name.

Ben Lambers and Tatjana Quax
page 128
This husband and wife team are look-and-feel-makers and the founders of Studio Aandacht. They work with established brands such as Brabantia and have networks and friendships with all the major design players in the city. They have authored and produced renowned design books and exhibited in the Stedelijk Museum in 's Hertogenbosch. When they're not working, they enjoy visiting the city's Blijburg beach and eating out in Amsterdam Noord with friends.
Our favourite Amsterdam tip from Ben and Tatjana: Visit Czaar Peterstraat for a lesser-known Amsterdam shopping experience.

Árpád Gerecsey
page 146
Entrepreneur and Chief Innovation Officer of A Lab Amsterdam, Árpád spends his days in 'Amsterdam's ultimate living lab' with creatives and technologists. Árpád is also the former CEO of World Press Photo and previously worked for Médecins Sans Frontières. When he's not working, Árpád enjoys the northern Amsterdam countryside with his family, rides his motorcycle and keeps 500,000 bees.
Our favourite Amsterdam tip from Árpád: Go to the cultural venue Melkweg, where you can watch everything from performances by well-known artists to air-guitar playing contests.

Yvette van Boven
page 172
Recipe writer, food stylist and TV chef Yvette is adored by Amsterdammers, who love her TV show *Koken met van Boven* and cookbooks. She has received awards for Dutch Cookbook of the Year and the ELLE Award for Best Dutch Food Photography. Her books have gained global notoriety, having been translated into many languages. When she's not working, Yvette enjoys exploring Amsterdam's creative food scene.
Our favourite Amsterdam tip from Yvette: Have a meal at Lighthouse Island for a truly memorable dining experience on an island only accessible by boat. The adventure begins on the journey across the water, when guests receive boxes of nibbles and drinks.

Richard Jones
page 194
The Welsh Founder and Managing Director of Jones Brothers Coffee Company has helped turn Amsterdammers into a nation of more discerning coffee lovers. After building a successful coffee business across the United Arab Emirates, Richard launched his products in Amsterdam just a few years ago. When he's not working on his business, he cycles around the city as 'The Espresso Hunter' blogger, tracking down the best coffee bars.
Our favourite Amsterdam tip from Richard: For people who know their stuff about coffee and a unique Amsterdam experience, visit KOKO Coffee & Design, a fashion shop with a beautiful coffee bar with a handful of seats.

Contents

Essentials

Work

Live

Getting away and getting lost

Amsterdam's DNA
A visual tour of the Amsterdam identity.

1. Bicycles
2. ...bicycles
3. ...and more bicycles
4. Canals
5. Summertime jaunts on boats
6. Being outside as soon as the sun cracks a ray
7. Sitting outside one way or another...even if you have to drag your sofa onto the pavement!
8. Orange
9. Pink
10. Rainbow
11. Casual but bright clothes
12. Open-minded
13. Saying it how it is
14. Design conscious
15. Creative
16. Amazing public transport network
17. Meetings in hotels
18. Great coffee
19. Craft beer
20. Concept stores
21. Organic, biodynamic, locally produced
22. Old is new
23. Speaking English
24. Turning industrial into creative
25. Creative entrepreneurship
26. That thing when you have to move your furniture into a canal house
27. Outdoor festivals
28. City of denim
29. You can look through my windows if you want to
30. A city of trade: as relevant today as it was centuries ago
31. Man-made islands
32. Water everywhere

26

Three days in Amsterdam

Get a feeling for the city and join Amsterdammers doing the things they love best during three fun-packed days.

Day one

Spend your first day in Amsterdam getting an overview of the city and some of the things it's most famous for. Kick this off with a canal cruise using a provider such as Amsterdam Canal Cruises (www.amsterdamcanalcruises.nl) or the Blue Boat Company (www.blueboat.nl). Cruises take just over an hour and get you acclimatised to the canal life in the city, while meandering past some of Amsterdam's most famous sights and buildings. After the cruise, hire a bicycle (p39) so you truly fit in with the locals, and take in some of the city's most beloved museums such as the Rijksmuseum and the Van Gogh Museum. Soak up the atmosphere afterwards in the buzzing Museumplein by the giant 'I amsterdam' sign (p55).

For lunch, head over to the Vietnamese eatery, Pho 91 (p168) and afterwards explore the Albert Cuyp Market (p64) — the most loved market in Amsterdam. While you're in De Pijp — one of the trendiest and liveliest neighbourhoods in Amsterdam — visit CT coffee & coconuts (p161), a favourite café of coffee guru Richard Jones found inside a converted theatre, or stop for a drink and a play on a retro video game in the Arcade Hotel (p190). Walk back towards the city centre along Utrechtsestraat, a favourite street of both trend-watcher Adjiedj Bakas (p22) and entrepreneur Boris Veldhuijzen van Zanten (p104).

Spend the afternoon wandering around the central streets of Amsterdam, taking in famous sights such as the Dam Palace (p49) and the oldest church in Amsterdam, Oude Kerk (p57), and exploring some of the less famous sights, such as The Cat Boat (p56) — a canal boat that previously homeless cats live on, and Wynand Fockink (p170), a 17th century distillery and tasting tavern. Have a casual dinner of chicken and self-serve beer in Bier Fabriek (p207), or a classier meal at Restaurant Johannes (p166) along an idyllic canal street.

Day two

If you're curious about Amsterdam's start-up and creative scene, spend your second day in the city exploring everything the city has to offer in this respect. Start the day by catching the free ferry across the water from Central Station to Amsterdam Noord, the emerging hub of creativity in the city. Go to The Coffee Virus (p126), the café inside A Lab (p116), to soak up the vibes from this hotbed of bleeding edge experimentation. Also visit the architecturally-impressive EYE Film Museum (p60) next door, where many of the city's creatives visit for inspiration.

For lunch, head a little further inland to De Ceuvel (p60) where landed canal boats have been converted into creative workspaces, and an on-site café that serves food TV chef, Yvette van Boven (p172) loves to eat.

For the afternoon, head back over the water and spend some time at a co-working space such as Impact Hub (p113) or at Seats2Meet (p117), a free co-working space where you pay in kind by contributing your expertise to the community.

If you need a venue to discuss business over a meal, visit De Ysbreeker (p126) brasserie by the water — a favourite of Creative Director of *Vogue Netherlands*, Martien Mellema (p86) — or visit Canvas (p71) at the top of the trendy Volkshotel. Canvas is also the ideal spot for a cocktail nightcap, or for a lower key affair, have a drink at Wolfje (p49), a favourite spot of the city's creative scenesters, including the well-known hairdresser and stylist Kenrick Vrolijk (p40).

Day three

Enjoy a little relaxation during your final day in Amsterdam and make the most of the open spaces the city is famed for. Spend the morning in the east at Blijburg Aan Zee (p72), Amsterdam's very own beach retreat and a favourite of local design heroes Ben Lambers and Tatjana Quax (p128). Starting the day there with a coffee and croissant is the ideal way to welcome the morning, whether it's on the beach in the summer or by the log fire indoors during the winter.

Before heading back into the city centre, stop off at the library (p57), Openbare Bibliotheek Amsterdam (OBA). On the top floor is a cheap café with stunning views over the city. KSNM Island (p72), near the city centre, is also worth a stop: it's a picturesque man-made island full of boutiques, making it an ideal place to take a stroll. Carry on and do the Western Islands Walk (p79) too: it's a series of interconnected islands full of quirky canal boats and creative happenings.

The only way to spend a final afternoon in Amsterdam is at Vondelpark (p64): the biggest park in the city and the most revered open space by Amsterdammers too. Pick up the ingredients for a picnic lunch from Small World (p54) or Hartje Bos (p76) before heading to the park and enjoying a lazy afternoon. For creative discoveries, check out the Vondelbunker (p64) while you're there: a venue for art and counter-culture events.

For an intimate dinner, visit Grand Café De Tropen (p164), squirrelled away in the imposing Tropenmuseum. It's yet to be discovered by many, making it feel like you've been let in on a local secret. For some evening entertainment, see what's going on at Melkweg (p156), a music and arts venue where entrepreneur Árpád Gerecsey (p146) is Chairman. Everyone from internationally renowned musicians to up-and-coming artists host events there.

Three weeks in Amsterdam

*Explore central neighbourhoods, dip your toe into life in diverse localities
and spend some time networking with the city's entrepreneurs.*

Week one

Get a feeling for the rhythm of the city of Amsterdam during your first week by
sticking to the most central areas and getting to know them really well. Spend
each day in a different locality of the centre. Visit Haarlemmerbuurt (p54) for its
boutiques, concept stores and casual cafés, and spend some time in the Jordaan
(p54) for a bohemian vibe and hidden courtyards, as well as an important part
of Amsterdam's past: the Anne Frank House (www.annefrank.org.uk). Visit the
Museum Quarter (p55) to soak up the culture from Amsterdam's museums of
international significance, and enjoy the Spiegelkwartier (p57) for the antiques
shops and collectibles hidden away in shops there. And finally, enjoy Nieuwmarkt
(p55) for its market and eateries in Chinatown, and wander around the streets of
the red light district (p56), which isn't as seedy as you'd imagine, and is actually
home to some of the best espresso cafés in the city (p205).

While exploring these central and much-loved neighbourhoods, enjoy some of
the best of Amsterdam's food, coffee and drinking scene. Go on the hipster Gs
'brunchboat' (p161), enjoy lunch and a coffee in the secret courtyard of Zuivere
Koffie (p162) and enjoy any mealtime in The Lobby at Hotel V (p186) on the Nes:
a favourite of many locals in the creative scene. Eat Mediterranean food at 5&33
(p30), enjoy truly innovative creations at Restaurant Kaagman & Kortekaas (p180)
and stop for wine and deli meat at Ibericus (p54).

Drink in one of the city's traditional brown bars such as Café Hoppe (p170), sample
beer from a local micro-brewery such as De Prael brewpub (p171) and enjoy a
throwback to times past in a pub such as In 't Aepjen (p56), where sailors used to
pay in monkeys instead of cash.

Week two

After your first week of fun, it might be time to do a little work during your
second week in Amsterdam. Hire a space at a co-working location for a week to
gain access to all the facilities you need, as well as to embed yourself in the local
working life for a while. The industrial-esque Mixtup (p115) is a good bet, with its
shared spaces, coffee corner and garden. Alternatively, hot desk at one of WeWork's
(p120) canal-side locations for access to the co-working space's weekly events and a
games room. Check out what networking (p142) and business events (p144) are on
during the week too, to get a true flavour of the city's entrepreneurial life.

In your spare time, soak up as much of the city's creativity as you can. Visit the Frozen Fountain (p185) shop for designs by established and new artists, stop off at Peter van Ginkel (p185) for a haven of art supplies and to enjoy the work of the artists in residence, and check out By AMFI (p185), the showcase store for the Amsterdam Fashion Institute. Visit an arthouse cinema such as The Movies (p54) or watch the EYE Museum's catalogue of films in quirky yellow pods (p177), visit concept stores and concept cafés such as KOKO Coffee & Design (p208) or Latei (p168), and enjoy cultural performances such as those at Podium Mozaïek (p76), or take a tour run by a local such as the Street Art Museum Amsterdam (p77).

Enjoy eating and drinking at the spots entrepreneurs and creative locals love to visit, such as the café attached to Werkplaats (p71) at the Volkshotel, Loetje aan 't IJ (p162) in the former harbour master's office and De Foodhallen (p162) for street food stands inside an old tram depot. Creative locals love tasting sessions at micro-breweries such as Butcher's Tears (p64) and Oedipus Brewery (p60), so join them there.

Week three

If you haven't already, hire a bicycle (p39) or get an OV-chipkaart (p38) so you can get around the city to explore some of Amsterdam's outer neighbourhoods. In northern Amsterdam, enjoy coffee in the Noorderparkbar (p60) made from reclaimed materials, visit Neef Louis (p185) to explore vintage and design furniture and watch a theatre performance at Tolhuistuin (p60). In the south of Amsterdam, visit the foodie hub of Amstelveenseweg (p64), enjoy festivals such as Amsterdam Open Air (p66), and visit Amsterdamse Bos (p65), the city's 2,500 acre forest, with its biodynamic goat farm and climbing park.

In the east of Amsterdam, soak up the vibrant culture of Javastraat (p70), enjoy summertime outdoor fun at Hannekes Boom (p72), and watch a skilled performance by easylaughs (p71), an improvised comedy group. In the classy western part of Amsterdam, gain creative inspiration from the galleries and artistic spaces along Witte de Withstraat (p77), catch a creative event at VLLA (p77) inside a converted funeral home, and take yourself on an architectural tour along Bellamystraat (p78).

Enjoy some of the more tucked-away eateries these neighbourhoods have to offer, such as secret Japanese restaurants in the south of the city (p89), Asian food in eastern Amsterdam, such as at Vijfnulvijf (p70), and Turkish coffee and baklava at Şerifoğlu Café & Patisserie (p77) in the west of the city. For a real treat, have a meal on Lighthouse Island (p138), only accessible by boat.

Three months in Amsterdam

Spend three months living the Amsterdam life based out of different localities in the city,
to experience the identity and vibe of locally-loved neighbourhoods.

Month one

Spend your first month in Amsterdam in a southern neighbourhood (Amsterdam Zuid) such as De Pijp (p64), which is fast becoming a more popular place for Amsterdammers to call home than central areas. Enjoy living and working according to the southern Amsterdam rhythm of life. This includes spending plenty of time in markets such as the Albert Cuyp Market (p64) and ZuiderMRKT (p65), buying foodie treats from Tjin's Toko (p64) and organic wine from Bar & Shop Glouglou (p30). Eat gluten-free and sugar-free food at The Meets (p161), munch on hotdogs while sipping champagne at The Fat Dog (p164) and taste Mediterranean dishes inside a former chapel in Restaurant As (p180).

Spend time outdoors in Sarphatipark (p64) or on the terrace of Café Gruter (p65), a traditional brown café, and drink in the Strandzuid (p65) beer garden or in Brouwerij Troost (p170), a micro-brewery in a former monastery. For entertainment, visit the Ziggo Dome (p65) or have more wholesome fun canoeing, horse-riding and surfing in Gaasperpark (p65).

If you need to work, go to the southern Amsterdam branch of Spaces (p120) for book-adorned comfortable areas and in-house baristas. Impress business contacts in Restaurant Jaspers (p30) for French fine dining, or in the Michelin starred Restaurant Sinne (p30). Gain creative inspiration by people-watching from the terrace of De Duvel (p30) or Pilsvogel (p64), or go further out and wander around the area of the Olympic Stadium (p64), built for the 1928 Summer Olympic Games.

Month two

Spend your second month in Amsterdam in an eastern Amsterdam (Amsterdam Oost) neighbourhood such as the culturally diverse Indische Buurt (p70) or the network of man-made islands at Zeeburg (p72). Combining diversity and a beachy feeling, this is a totally different neighbourhood to experience a new way of life. Enjoy outside space in Frankendael Park (p70), the previous estate of a wealthy Amsterdam landowner, or in the rural-feeling Diemerpark (p72), which comes complete with deer and kingfishers.

Eat at Café Kadijk (p92) for Indonesian food or World of Food (p92) for international cuisines inside a converted parking garage. Drink spirits in the tasting room at 't Nieuwe Diep Distillery (p70), inside a magical pumping station in Flevopark, and find entertainment in Studio/K (p70): a bar, cinema and club.

For a cool working spot, go to Zoku (p188), a hotel-workspace concept that is revolutionising life for visiting travellers in the city. Gain creative inspiration by wandering by the water villas (p134) designed by Dutch architect Marlies Rohmer and by shopping on Czaar Peterstraat (p138) in stores such as Dreamboat. If you need to wine and dine business contacts, take them to De Kas (p71) inside a former greenhouse, or to Bedford Stuyvesant (p70) for a coffee meeting.

Month three

Spend your final month in Amsterdam in the city's former industrial zone — now the pioneering creative hub of Amsterdam —Amsterdam Noord (p58). This is where the most creative new concepts are emerging and where an increasing number of Amsterdammers are flocking to in order to get more bang for their buck on the home front, before prices rise. This is also the place to enjoy time along the River IJ in hotspots such as Pllek (p60), especially popular during the summer for its beach, and at the lesser known Schellingwouderpark (p60), accessed by pull ferries.

A number of foodie hotspots are emerging in this part of the city: Café Modern (p138) inside a former bank and De Goudfazant (p92) inside a former industrial space are just two of them. There are plenty of places to gain creative inspiration in this part of the city, from cycling along the historic dykes (p60) to spending a night in the Faralda Crane Hotel (p190), inside an actual industrial crane. Be inspired or grab a bargain at Vlooienmarkt IJ Hallen (p60), the largest flea market in the Netherlands. And spend a day working at A Lab (p116) if you can, for an insight into the cutting edge creative and tech scene there, or hop across the water on the ferry to Pakhuis De Zwijger (p30), a cultural meeting place.

By the end of your third month in Amsterdam, you'll have lived, worked and breathed daily life in diverse neighbourhoods of Amsterdam. If you stay in Amsterdam for even longer, you're bound to have found the right neighbourhood for you by now. Wherever you end up, the entrepreneurial, creative and sociable spirit of Amsterdam pervades all corners of the city.

Globalisation will slow down;
it will become 'slowbalisation'.

Adjiedj Bakas

Futurist

Introduce yourself.

I'm a futurist and trend-watcher, based in the Netherlands having moved to the country to study about 30 years ago. I studied in Utrecht for two years, and then moved to Amsterdam. I was born in Latin America and my family is from India, so I'm from a bit of everywhere. Amsterdam is diverse in a very positive way, and that's one reason why I feel quite at home in the city.

You've received numerous awards and accolades, including Trend-watcher of the Year and Immigrant Entrepreneur of the Year. You've also been named one of the most creative Dutch people and one of the most influential Dutch people. How did you get into your line of work?

It's a small country so it's easy to get some of these accolades! I studied communications at university and went on to work for Dutch television and Royal Dutch Airlines, KLM. I had to communicate a lot of messages in those jobs, and I was always very aware about what was in line with reality today, and what was going to happen in the future. My manager at KLM told me I had a special talent that I should explore further, and I was given the time and budget to do so. That's when I found Wim de Ridder, who is now in his 70s; he's a Professor of Futurology at the University of Twente. He was previously the Chief Economist for ING Banking, the largest bank in the Netherlands. He taught me how to be a futurist. Although trend-watching starts with an instinct or intuition, you have to do it in a scientific way, because you cannot use a glass ball and tell people what it says. Trend-watching in a scientific way means applying research lines A, B, C and D to what is happening behind today's news headlines. I've been doing it for a couple of decades now and have seen some good successes with my work.

What is life like as a futurist?

It's a fascinating life. I'm always at work in a sense because even if I'm on holiday I may spot something interesting. I always have my notebook with me or use the voice recorder on my phone to note my observations, wherever I am and whatever I'm doing. I have had to teach myself not to become a workaholic, so I try to meditate twice a day. It's not always possible, but I try at least not to have my phone with me all the time, and I generally try not to be a slave to work. I think I manage a good work-life balance most of the time. The best thing about my work is that I meet the most fantastic people. For example, when I get invited to do a lecture, I am invited by people who are enthusiastic. They're people who want to do something with their lives, and not people who want to go on in the same way for the next 30 years until they retire. I meet so many inspiring people.

What trends are you predicting in cities?
There are about 30 mega cities in the world that in five or ten years' time are going to yield more power than 50 nation states. These cities are becoming extremely powerful. We're starting to see it in many countries: London is starting to suck up the rest of England, Berlin and Frankfurt are sucking up the rest of Germany, Paris is sucking up the rest of France. What we're also seeing is that smaller cities with populations of less than a million people are really coming up. Amsterdam is one of them, and you see it in other countries too. In Germany you see it in Dresden, in Britain you see it in Manchester, in Israel you see it in Tel Aviv, and in France you see it in Nice, with a lot of the new tech industries coming from there. I call these smaller cities 'city states', since they have a great deal of independence and their own dynamics.

How is this changing the shape of cities such as Amsterdam?
Beneath the city power houses are the smaller city states like Amsterdam, which are trying to do more to achieve the same status as the mega cities. But these city states are cosier and more intimate and it's the small scale that attracts different kinds of people. You see this tribe of people coming up; creative people working in creative industries who want a city that offers a combination of things. You see this in Amsterdam; it's greener, on a smaller scale, and you can handle it. The city is attracting a lot of new start-ups and people from creative industries. I like it.

What do you prefer — mega cities or city states?
I love the big cities and the energy of London and New York, but I don't necessarily need to live there. A lot of people feel lonely in bigger cities; that's why my husband left London. He wasn't born in the Netherlands, but Amsterdam is at a scale he can handle. The cost of living is a significant factor too and smaller cities are much, much cheaper than the big cities. The equivalent of my house in Amsterdam would be unaffordable in London, for example. Small is the new big nowadays when it comes to cities. There are sometimes suggestions that Amsterdam should merge with Rotterdam, Utrecht or The Hague to make it a city of four or five million, but why do we have to be big in the first place?

Are there any disadvantages to city states like Amsterdam?
The very rich influential people who lead the world — this global elite of a couple of thousand people — don't like these small cities. Madonna would never buy a penthouse in Amsterdam. This tribe, the super trendy and very rich crowd, is only interested in the bigger cities. They might visit the

smaller cities for a day or two, but that's about it. That kind of kudos and
the approval of the global elite is something these city states are missing,
but I don't think it stops them from thriving.

<u>You are often invited to speak at globally renowned conferences. What
is your favourite topic to speak about?</u>
I really like to speak about how technology is changing our lives, as well
as the social impact of the technology. Part of my job is to open peoples'
eyes to things they don't see or don't want to see. It doesn't always make
me popular, but I'm hired to tell these messages. For example, I recently
did a lecture for the Port of Rotterdam, who invited 300 of their biggest
clients from all over the world. They have built a 3D printer, which can
print spare parts of a ship in steel. It means that ships coming into harbour
can now get spare parts in a few hours instead of a week or more, and ships
can depart again more quickly. This will have a significant impact on every
port city in the world. But I warned that harbours traditionally employ
a lot of less educated men. They are the losers of the future; robots and
3D printers are much cheaper than any human being, and these men are
becoming unemployed. One of the things I tell my customers is that we
have to use all our creativity to create new jobs for these men. We have to
do something about that because the differences between the social classes
are becoming too big. I try to inspire my clients to think of what they can
do. That's one reason why I advocate tourism. Some municipal officials
think too many tourists in Amsterdam could be problematic, but if every
two hotel rooms create one full-time job for the lower educated man or
woman, it's good for the economy and for the structure of the city.

<u>What are you working on at the moment?</u>
I've recently been hired to do some work in Italy. My first book in Italian is
being launched soon, which I'm co-authoring with the director of an Italian
telecom company. I really hope that my ideas combined with the creativity
of my Italian counterpart can help the Italians.

<u>Is the urban nomad trend just a phase, or is it here to stay?</u>
That's my tribe; these are my people! In the next couple of years,
globalisation will slow down; it will become 'slowbalisation'. This is partly
because a lot of things can be manufactured locally, and partly due to the
fact that economic nationalism is on the rise. I do quite a lot of work with
the pharmaceutical industry, and something we're seeing is that more
bacteria and viruses are now uniting against us as human beings. The fear
of getting ill from things like Zika or Ebola is another reason why I think a
lot of people who are now travelling quite far will not do so anymore ten
years from now. In ten to 20 years, travel and urban nomadism will become
centred on regions. The European tribe will travel more within Europe

to do their thing, and I think fewer Americans and Asians will come to Europe. However, society really needs this tribe of creative people. They think outside the box, and they're mixing ideas from country A and region B. The economy needs people like this to bring it all together and come up with brilliant ideas.

Are there any negative aspects of urban nomadism?

These footloose people can be lonely and find it difficult to connect with others. It can make it less easy to have relationships and get a love life going. We've been seeing this difficulty in connecting for a number of years with children who go to international schools too. I think that's something that people who choose this lifestyle should pay attention to. Stress management can also be a problem for people in these creative and entrepreneurial tribes. This is because people are 'always on'. They also need to take time to relax, unwind, meditate and sleep better. Energy management is one of the things this tribe should learn a bit more about.

What does the future hold for the creative class?

We are going to need the creativity of the creative class for the military industry and to tackle the issues of radical Islam. The family on my father's side are Muslim, and the Muslim people I meet are liberal; they want to go forward, they want to have a life, they're energetic and they're creative. Radical Islamists are a small tribe dedicated to the destruction of western civilisation. The creative class are not aware of the role they can play yet, but it already happened in Britain in the 1940s when Alan Turing broke the enigma code of the Germans. He was one of these crazy creative people doing things outside the box. Everything Turing did afterwards was the start of the modern ideas industry. We are going to need people like that. When human beings are under attack, we become extremely creative. We have to survive. It's not by accident that Israel is home to so many break-through innovations; about 25% of everything in our smartphones was invented in Israel. They have the most start-ups per head per capita than anywhere else in the world. That mentality is what we're going to need in Europe, and we're going to get it in the coming years. We will see a transition in the creative industry to come up with brilliant ideas, not only to make life better, smarter, more efficient and fun, but also to help western civilisation to survive and win. You could call this trend the militarisation of the creative industry. We need new Alan Turings, and we're going to get them.

Where else should visitors to Amsterdam go to get a feeling for Dutch trends?

We're now seeing this 'retro' trend, in the Netherlands and elsewhere in Europe, where people are not always looking for modern things. One of our most famous architects in the Netherlands is Sjoerd Soeters, and he's completely refurbished the city of Zaandam, which is about 30km from Amsterdam. I work with him quite a lot; I tell him the trends and he tries to translate them into architecture. Previously in Zaandam, there were 1980s apartments which had no soul and no identity. He brought back the identity of the town through green wooden houses that reflected an older style, but were built in a modern way. He went back to the roots of the town and it's fantastic; it's so utterly creative. The residents are happy and they have become some of the most photographed buildings in the whole region.

Describe the neighbourhood you live and work in.

I live and work in De Pijp, the neighbourhood bordering the canal district. The canal district is the real city centre; it's the picture on the postcard and the image of Amsterdam. Funnily enough, in the 1970s, nobody wanted to live by the canals. The houses on the canals did not have modern sanitation back then and they were cold and old; it wasn't a very practical place to live. The situation was similar in the neighbourhoods surrounding the centre, including De Pijp. Then from the 1980s onwards, people started to move in, and in the last 20 years, all these areas have become sexy; people really want to live there now. Nowadays, visitors to Amsterdam even prefer to stay in De Pijp than in the canal district, for a more authentic 'neighbourhood' experience. I can understand that. I've been living in De Pijp for 20 years now and it's fantastic; I don't want to leave. It's lively and Amsterdam Zuid in general is a bit classier than other parts of the city. There are parts of the neighbourhood that are trendy and cultural, and other parts that are a little more conservative and boring. I like the fact there's a mixture of both.

What do you like to do in your leisure time?

In my local neighbourhood I like to go and sit with a coffee, enjoying a newspaper and people-watching. Close to the famous Albert Cuyp Market there is a nice place called De Duvel, where I like to sit on the terrace. There is such a fantastic diversity of people in Amsterdam and just watching people is a great way to spend time. It's inspiring to see what they're wearing, how they act and what they're doing. I also like to walk in the city centre along the canals. A lot of people cycle, but I always like to walk in Amsterdam, because then you discover all these new pop-up stores, new cafés and restaurants. There are new cafés and restaurants popping up all the time. They're going away all the time too, but that doesn't matter. The Utrechtsestraat is the street which goes from De Pijp right into the city centre. That's a very nice street that I love to stroll along for a couple of hours if I can, looking at the houses, little shops, restaurants and cafés.

How do you soak up the culture in the city?

I know all the museums and the regular collections well in Amsterdam, so I only go if there's a new exhibition. We have some great museums in the city. The Rijksmuseum was closed for ten years to be refurbished, so I've visited there again more since it re-opened. It's fantastic and for a city of Amsterdam's scale, it's big and you can see a lot. I also like Amsterdam's art venues, especially in the centre, where you can find very nice galleries with up-and-coming artists making beautiful paintings and sculptures. I like browsing the Spiegelkwartier too; it's where the antiques stores are and you can find some nice things there. De Negen Straatjes (Nine Streets) is a great place for soaking up local culture too.

Where should creative people hang out in the city?

Pakhuis de Zwijger is a great place to go. It's a revamped old harbour building that hosts many events, conferences and other meetings especially for creatives. The Lloyd Hotel is not far from Pakhuis De Zwijger. It is a so-called 'design hotel' and a 'cultural embassy' and has been designed as a home in Amsterdam for creative people. Amsterdam Noord is also a great place to visit. On the harbour front in this northern part of Amsterdam you find EYE, our film museum, and a lot of trendy venues where up-and-coming artists work and exhibit. It started out as a squatter area, but it becomes ever more established.

Where do you go for a special meal out?

In De Pijp, I really like Restaurant Jaspers, which is a classy, fine dining French restaurant. Restaurant Sinne, which has a Michelin star, is also a great choice. I also go to Restaurant Zaza's near Albert Cuyp Market for delicious French and international food.

Where is good for a casual meal out?

The west of Amsterdam has a few places I really like for food. Happyhappyjoyjoy has delicious Asian street food and is a buzzing and vibrant place to eat. Nearby is Foodhallen, which every visitor to Amsterdam has to try for all the different and delicious street food stands. There's also a cat café called Kattencafé Kopjes that is fun to visit — it was launched after a crowdfunding campaign, and you can be surrounded by cats while enjoying your coffee and a bite to eat. Near Central Station I like 5&33, which is a casual shared dining restaurant with lovely Mediterranean food. It's open all day and has something great for every mealtime. I also like The Seafood Bar near Vondelpark for great quality seafood in low-key surroundings. Whenever I go to Amsterdam Noord I Like to visit Bistro Noord for a good value meal in trendy surroundings. Further out of the city, I like Baut, which is a restaurant inside an old car dealership.

Where is the best place for a glass of wine in the city?
I have two favourites, both quite close to where I live. Bar & Shop Glouglou only serves organic wines. It's the perfect place to sit with a glass of wine and some cheese, but it's also a shop, so you can buy some wine to take home with you too. I also like La Viña, which is a wine bar and also a Mediterranean restaurant with a really cosy feeling.

What is Amsterdam's best quality?
Intimacy. It's a big city but concentrated on a very small amount of land. It has the feeling of being a much larger city than it really is.

How would you encourage visitors to Amsterdam to blend in and live like locals during their stay?
Explore the city by bicycle if you're able to, but if you're not a confident cyclist then don't! Cycling is wonderful in Amsterdam; it gives you freedom to just park your bike somewhere and explore a local area, or sit and enjoy what's happening there. People in Amsterdam speak good English because hardly anyone else in the world speaks Dutch! Quite a few people also speak German because Dutch and German have some similarities. Amsterdammers are very talkative, so it's easy for visitors to connect with the locals when they visit the city. When you're in a café having a coffee, it's quite normal to chat with others. Visitors to Amsterdam, especially those used to larger cities, should really enjoy that. Renting a room in someone's apartment is also a good way to blend in with the locals, although visitors should also enjoy the cheaper cost of hotels compared to larger European cities. Ten thousand new hotel rooms have been created in the city in the last five years, so there is a lot of accommodation to explore.

Is there anything you would change about Amsterdam?
There are some quite ugly buildings I would love to be torn down. In the 1970s the Dutch Prime Minister wanted to knock down the whole canal area and build skyscrapers. Thank goodness he didn't do that in the end. But a lot of the traditional buildings were still destroyed and replaced with some horrific 1970s and 1980s buildings, such as the City Hall and the Central Bank. The buildings had to be cheap because of the economic recession, and you can really see they're cheap and lack any grandeur.

Where's the best place for some quiet time in the city?
We've got a lot of smaller parks in Amsterdam, but the Vondelpark is a firm favourite, especially during the summer when I sit on the bench and read my newspaper or a book. My husband and I also like going picnicking in the parks. We just take plates, some sandwiches and sit there chatting with people.

Adjiedj's Amsterdam

Places to visit

Albert Cuyp Market
Albert Cuypstraat, 1072 CN
www.albertcuyp-markt.
amsterdam
Tram: Albert Cuypstraat

Amsterdam Noord
1020-1039
Boat: Veer Buiksloterweg, Veer
IJplein

De Negen Straatjes
Bus/Tram: Westermarkt

EYE Film Museum
IJpromenade 1, 1031 KT
+31 (0)20 589 1400
info@eyefilm.nl
www.eyefilm.nl
Boat/bus: Veer Buiksloterweg

Lloyd Hotel
Oostelijke Handelskade 34,
1019 BN
+31 (0)20 561 3636
post@lloydhotel.com
www.lloydhotel.com
Tram: Rietlandpark

Pakhuis de Zwijger
Piet Heinkade 179, 1019 HC
+31 (0)20 624 6380
info@dezwijger.nl
www.dezwijger.nl
Bus: Jan Schaeferbrug

Rijksmuseum
Museumstraat 1, 1071 XX
+31 (0)20 674 7000
info@rijksmuseum.nl
www.rijksmuseum.nl
Tram: Rijksmuseum

Spiegelkwartier
1017 JP
www.spiegelkwartier.nl
Tram: Keizersgracht (Vijzelstraat)

Utrechtsestraat
Utrechtsestraat, 1017
www.utrechtsestraat.amsterdam
Bus/tram: Keizersgracht
(Utrechtsestraat) or Prinsengracht
(Utrechtsestraat)

Vondelpark
Vondelpark, 1017 AA
www.hetvondelpark.net
Tram: J.P. Heijesstraat or Rhijnvis
Feithstraat

Zaandam
1500-1509
Train: Station Zaandam

Eating and drinking

5&33
Martelaarsgracht 5, 1012 TN
+31 (0)20 820 5333
reservations@5and33.nl
www.5and33.nl
Bus/metro/train/tram: Amsterdam
Centraal

Baut
Prinses Irenestraat 31-33, 1077
WV
+31 (0)20 465 9260
info@bautamsterdam.nl
www.bautamsterdam.nl
Bus/tram: Prinses Irenestraat/
Beethovenstraat

Bar & Shop Glouglou
Tweede van der Helststraat 3,
1073 AE
+31 (0)20 233 8642
www.glouglou.nl
Bus/tram: Tweede van de
Helststraat

Bistro Noord
Mt. Ondinaweg 32, 1033 RG
+31 (0)20 705 9906
bistronoord@gmail.com
www.bistronoord.nl
Boat: Veer NDSM Werf

Kattencafé Kopjes
Marco Polostraat 211, 1057 WK
+31 (0)20 737 0999
info@kattencafekopjes.nl
www.kattencafekopjes.nl
Bus/tram: Marco Polostraat

De Duvel
Eerste van der Helststraat 59-61,
1073 AD
+31 (0)20 675 7517
info@deduvel.nl
www.deduvel.nl
Bus/tram: Tweede van de
Helststraat

De Foodhallen
Bellamyplein 51, 1053 AT
info@foodhallen.nl
www.foodhallen.nl
Bus/Tram: Ten Katestraat

Happyhappyjoyjoy
Bilderdijkstraat 158HS, 1053 LC
+31 (0)20 344 6433
info@happyhappyjoyjoy.asia
www.happyhappyjoyjoy.asia
Bus/tram: Kinkerstraat

La Viña
Maasstraat 72, 1078 HL
+31 (0)20 662 0448
info@lavinaexperience.nl
www.lavinaexperience.com
Tram/bus: Maasstraat/
Rooseveltlaan

Restaurant Jaspers
Ceintuurbaan 196, 1072 GC
+31 (0)20 471 5233
contact@restaurantjaspers.nl
www.restaurantjaspers.nl
Bus/tram: Ceintuurbaan/
Ferdinand Bolstraat

Restaurant Sinne
Ceintuurbaan 342, 1072 GP
+31 (0)20 682 7290
info@restaurantsinne.nl
www.restaurantsinne.nl
Bus/tram: Tweede van de
Helststraat

Restaurant Zaza's
Daniël Stalpertstraat 103, 1072 XD
+31 (0)20 673 6333
info@zazas.nl
www.zazas.nl
Tram: Albert Cuypstraat

The Seafood Bar
Van Baerlestraat 5, 1071 AL
+31 (0)20 670 8355
www.theseafoodbar.nl
Tram: Van Baerlestraat

See also

KLM
www.klm.nl
Port of Rotterdam
www.portofrotterdam.com
Sjoerd Soeters
www.soetersvaneldonk.nl
Wim de Ridder
www.wimderidderfuturoloog.blogspot.nl

Find out more about Adjiedj Bakas at www.bakas.nl and on Twitter @AdjiedjBakas

Photo: Trend Office Bakas

chapter 1

Essentials

Amsterdam's neighbourhoods, how to get there and how to get around.

Facts and figures

Need to know
Currency
Euro (€)

Customs
Visit the customs website for the Netherlands: www.belastingdienst.nl

Electricity
220-240 Volts, 50Hz
Electrical sockets take the type C Europlug, and the type E and type F Schuko

Geographical location
5.45°E and 50.30°N

Language
Dutch

Local time
UTC/GMT +1 hours

Postal code areas
1011 AA to 1019 XH

Tax
A tourist tax of 5% is added onto accommodation costs in Amsterdam. 21% Value Added Tax (VAT), also known as BTW in the Netherlands, is added to many products you may buy in Amsterdam. Non-EU residents are able to claim a tax refund on eligible items, and this can be done at the Customs Tax Free Validation desk in Departure Hall 3 of Amsterdam Airport Schiphol.

Telephone country code
+31

Telephone area code
(0)20

Tipping
It is customary to add 5-15% onto the value of the bill as a tip when eating out. Some restaurants add on this service charge automatically.

Visas
Not required by EU, EEA and Swiss nationals visiting for tourism or work. Some other nationalities may require a visa when visiting for tourism purposes. Other nationalities hoping to work will need to apply for a visa and work permit. Visit the Netherlands Government website for more visa information: www.government.nl

Important phone numbers
Police, ambulance or fire brigade (emergencies): 112
Police (non-emergency): 0900 8844
Tourist Medical Service (ATAS): +31 (0)20 592 3355

Currency exchange
Major credit cards such as VISA and MasterCard are widely accepted. ATMs can be found across the city. Banks with currency exchange counters are also plentiful; you'll get the best exchange rates or lower transaction fees if you go to a bank affiliated with your own bank.

Etiquette
The people of the Netherlands are widely thought of as being liberal, laid-back and informal, but don't take this to mean any behaviour goes.

A well known example of the country's liberalism is the ability to smoke cannabis in the famous coffeeshops. If you want to visit a coffeeshop in Amsterdam to smoke cannabis or eat space cakes, remember it's not actually legal in the country; selling or carrying small amounts is simply tolerated. It is illegal to advertise that cannabis is for sale in a coffeeshop, so those looking to smoke a joint or eat a space cake will have to ask for a menu from behind the counter. You may also see cannabis seeds on sale, but remember growing cannabis is still illegal in most countries, so don't be tempted to try to take some home. In a peculiar twist, smoking tobacco cigarettes is banned in coffeeshops, and any other shop, bar or restaurant. Buying or drinking alcohol is also not permitted in coffeeshops.

Don't be tempted to take photos of the sex workers in the windows in De Wallen (the red light district) as it's seen as being disrespectful.

Given the prevalence of bicycles in Amsterdam, it always pays to double-check you are not walking in a cycle lane, as not to attract the wrath of the locals.

With only a few exceptions, Amsterdam's restaurant, bar and club scene is fairly casual, with trainers and jeans acceptable in most places. As long as you look well-groomed you should be fine. If you want to fit in with the locals, go bright with the colours of your attire.

The Dutch commonly give three kisses when greeting people, except when two men meet, when a firm handshake is the norm. It's polite to say 'hello' or 'good day' ('hallo' or 'goedemiddag') when you enter a shop, elevator or room full of people. It's also common to say 'goodbye' or 'have a nice day' ('dag' or 'fijne dag nog') when exiting similar situations. If you're invited to someone's house, bring a bottle of wine or a small gift to show your appreciation.

In general, the Dutch respect eye contact, and they're well known for their refreshingly direct and outspoken culture. The intention is not to be rude, but to demonstrate honesty and openness. Despite this, the Dutch are modest too, and don't appreciate big shows of wealth or brash behaviour. Amsterdammers also tend to be planners, organising social 'appointments' weeks ahead of time. Punctuality is important to the Dutch, so don't be late to an appointment!

Useful websites:

I amsterdam
www.iamsterdam.com

Discover Holland
www.holland.com

Time Out Amsterdam
www.timeout.com/amsterdam

Amsterdam travel guide
www.amsterdam.info

Photo: Cyril Wermers

Number of bicycles 🚲 **in Amsterdam: +1 million** Population of Amsterdam: 👥 815,000 **Length of cycle paths** 🚲 **and bike lanes in the city: 767km** Number of kilometres 🚩 cycled by Amsterdammers every day: 2 million **Number of bicycle parking spots** 🅿 **around Amsterdam Central Station: 10,000** Number of nationalities 👥 living in Amsterdam: 180 **Proportion of Amsterdam residents who are polyglots** Ola! Hallo! **(speak more than two languages): +85%** Proportion of the city built on 💧 water: 100% **Number of support poles** 🏛 **holding buildings up in Amsterdam: 11 million** Number of canals: 165 〰 **Bridges in the** 🌉 **canal ring: 80** Number of 🏠 houseboats: 2,500 **Number of bicycles found** 🚲 **in Amsterdam canals every year: 30,000** Number of 🌳 windmills: 8 **Number of** 🌻 **paintings by Van Gogh: 207** Number of concerts 🎪 and theatre performances every day: 25 **Number** 🍸 **of cafés and bars: 1,515** Average cups of coffee ☕ consumed per person per day: 3.2 **Number of** 🛏 **hotel beds: 37,627** Number of buildings 🏢 from the 16th, 17th and 18th centuries: 8,863 **Average height** 🧍 **of Dutch men: 184cm** Amsterdam was the first city in the world to allow same sex 💐 marriage

Getting there

By air
The Netherlands has a handful of airports serving the country, the main one being Amsterdam Airport Schiphol, which is also the most convenient airport for visitors to the city of Amsterdam itself.

Amsterdam Airport Schiphol (AMS)
The main international airport of the Netherlands is located 20km to the south-west of Amsterdam. Serving 55 million passengers every year, it's the fifth busiest airport in Europe. There's a single terminal and three departure halls. A number of the globe's major airlines fly to Schiphol, and the airport is the hub for the Dutch airline, KLM.
www.schiphol.nl

Travelling to Amsterdam city centre:

Bus

The Amsterdam Airport Express or the 197 line is the most commonly used bus line into Amsterdam city centre. The bus departs from bus stop B9 every 15 minutes and the journey takes around 30 minutes to the city centre. A return journey costs €10 and you can buy tickets directly from the bus driver. Alternatively, purchase an e-ticket online in advance for a small discount. Other bus routes that travel to locations around Amsterdam include 310, 69 and 300. The Schiphol Hotel Shuttle also serves almost 200 hotels in the Amsterdam area. The night bus N97 (or 'Niteliner') runs once an hour during the night and stops at a number of key Amsterdam locations.

See bus timetables on the Connexxion website.
www.bus197.nl
www.connexxion.nl
www.schipholhotelshuttle.nl

Train

Schiphol train station is underneath the airport terminal and there is a regular timetable of trains, with services running to Amsterdam Central Station in the city centre, as well as Amsterdam Zuid for the World Trade Centre and Amsterdam RAI for the conference centre.

Tickets are available from the yellow ticket machines near the platforms, or from staff at the service desks. Paper tickets are no longer sold, so locals and visitors now travel by OV-chipkaart, a chip card for public transport. It's possible to buy single (€5) and return (€10) fares, as well as one (€15), two (€20) or three (€25) day Amsterdam Travel Tickets. These tickets are valid on trains, trams, buses, metros and ferries.

The train journey from the airport takes around 20 minutes. Remember to touch your OV-chipkaart in and out as you enter and exit the platform.

There is also an hourly rail service from the airport to Amsterdam city centre during the night.

Check the Netherlands Railways (Nederlandse Spoorwegen) website for full timetable information.
www.ns.nl

Taxi

The airport's taxi rank is just outside the exit. Metered taxis cost approximately €45 to get to the city centre and

the journey takes about 30 minutes, depending on traffic.

Rotterdam The Hague Airport (RTM)
Located less than 100km to the south-west of Amsterdam, Rotterdam The Hague Airport is a much smaller airport serving around 2 million travellers per year. Flights from several European cities arrive at this airport, and with fast public transport links to Amsterdam, this can be a convenient option for some travellers to the city.
rotterdamthehagueairport.nl

Travelling to Amsterdam city centre:

Train

The train journey from the airport to Amsterdam takes approximately an hour and costs €45. Check the Netherlands Railways (Nederlandse Spoorwegen) website for full timetable information.
www.ns.nl

Taxi

The airport's taxi rank is just outside the exit. Metered taxis cost approximately €35 to get to the city centre and the journey takes about 25 minutes, depending on traffic.

By train

It is possible to travel by train to Amsterdam from numerous European cities, with international railway routes making train travel particularly easy from France, Germany and Belgium.

Check the Netherlands Railways (Nederlandse Spoorwegen) International website for full timetable and route information.
www.nsinternational.nl
www.seat61.com

By bus
Multiple coach providers run services from an array of mostly European cities to Amsterdam. Providers include Megabus and Eurolines. Fares can be cheap, but journey times long.
www.megabus.com
www.eurolines.co.uk

Getting around

Public transport
Amsterdam boasts an impressive public transport network of trams, buses and metros. Consult the maps on the Gemeentelijk Vervoerbedrijf (GVB) website or the 9292 website to plan your route.

The simplest way to pay for your journeys is by getting an OV-chipkaart, a chip card for public transport. Amsterdam Travel Tickets are valid for one (€15), two (€20) or three (€25) days, and allow unlimited travel on trains and ferries as well as trams, buses and metros. GVB day passes are valid for one to seven days, with prices starting from €7.50. These tickets are valid on trams, buses and metros operated by GVB in the city.

Trams, buses and metros run from approximately 6:00 to 00:30. The best way to travel by night is via the limited night bus services, which start at approximately 1:00.
www.gvb.nl/reizen/plattegronden
www.9292.nl
www.ns.nl
www.gvb.nl

Tram
There are four major tram routes in the city with multiple branches travelling to different neighbourhoods. There are two major tram stops outside Amsterdam's main train station, Amsterdam Central Station, where many of the city's trams terminate. Most locals and visitors touch in and touch out with their OV-chipkaart when travelling by tram, although it's also possible to buy a one hour ticket from the ticket attendant on-board.

Bus
The main bus routes in Amsterdam are run by GVB, Connexxion and EBS. Those who have the GVB day passes have all GVB services included in the fare, and those who have Amsterdam Travel Tickets can travel on transport by any of these providers. Otherwise, fares can be paid to the onboard ticket attendant.

Metro
Amsterdam's metro system operates four main routes that travel to Amsterdam's outlying neighbourhoods. OV-chipkaarts are needed to enter and exit Amsterdam's metro stations. Alternatively, you can buy a one-hour ticket from service desks or ticket machines inside metro stations. Travelling by metro is especially efficient for those

travelling outside Amsterdam city centre.

Train
Amsterdam Central Station is the city's main train station and most notable transport hub. There are various other train stations in important locations across the city, and train travel is an efficient way to reach locations in outlying areas in Amsterdam and the Netherlands in general.

Ferry
Amsterdam's ferry services are most commonly used by those who need to get across the River IJ; many locals take their bicycles and mopeds with them. These blue and white boats connect Amsterdam Central Station with locations north of the river. Ferries are free, regular and a countdown timer is displayed at ferry docks letting you know how long you'll need to wait. Ferries also run throughout the night.

Taxi
Taxis are a great option when many public transport modes stop working late at night. Depending on the time of day however, taking public transport can be quicker. Taxis in the city are not allowed to stop anywhere they like, so rather than trying to hail a taxi, queue at one of the many taxi ranks to be found across the city.

Taxi cars can take up to four passengers and have a maximum starting price of €2.83. The price per kilometre thereafter is around €2. Larger taxi buses, seating up to eight passengers, have a maximum starting price of €5.75, with the cost per kilometre thereafter at around €2.50. Licensed taxi drivers in

Amsterdam always have a meter switched on and provide receipts at the end of a journey. Taxi drivers are obliged to always accept short trips, and to take you to your destination via the shortest or quickest route.

If you want to book a taxi, there are various official operators in the city, including:

Taxicentrale Amsterdam
+31 (0)20 777 7777
www.tcataxi.nl

Stads Taxi Centrale
+31 (0)20 354 2232
www.stadstaxiamsterdam.nl

Taxistad
+31 (0)20 208 0000
www.taxistad.com

In true Amsterdam style, there are some quirkier taxi alternatives available, including:

TomTours
www.tomtours.nl

The Friendly Cab
www.thefriendlycab.nl

Water Taxi
www.water-taxi.nl

Disco Taxi
twitter.com/DiscoTaxi911

Yellow Backie
www.yellowbackie.org

Cycling

Amsterdam's bicycle culture is world famous. The flat landscape and network of cycle routes makes cycling the preferred option of many Amsterdammers, so you won't go for long without seeing a bicycle in the city. And as a relatively small city, everywhere is in easy cycling distance.

Hiring a bicycle in Amsterdam costs around €8 to €15 per day, with better deals available if you hire for more than one day. There's a multitude of bicycle hire

companies across Amsterdam; here are just a few:

MacBike
www.macbike.nl
5 rental locations across Amsterdam

Amstelfietspoint
Julianaplein 1, 1097 DN
+31 (0)20 692 3584
www.amstelfietspoint.nl
Bus/metro/train/tram: Amstelstation

Bike 4 U
www.rentbike4u.com
2 rental locations in central Amsterdam

By car

Renting a car in Amsterdam can be an easy way to get around the city, especially if you want to travel further out of Amsterdam during your trip too. Many of the internationally known car rental companies have offices in Amsterdam, or use a price comparison website before your visit to book a car in advance. Most areas of central Amsterdam have parking restrictions, so be aware of the digital parking system. This is where you enter your registration plate details into the parking meter when you pay for parking on the street. Payment cannot be made in cash; only international credit cards or Dutch bank cards are accepted. You don't need to display a ticket once you've paid, as the parking authority can scan their database to check this.

Car hire price comparison websites:
www.travelsupermarket.com
www.kayak.co.uk

Scooter

If you want a motorised vehicle but want to be more like an Amsterdammer, scooter hire is a great

option. To do so, you'll need a motorbike or regular driving licence, or a special scooter licence called a brommerrijbewijs in the Netherlands. Many scooter hire companies also offer electric scooters and electric bicycles.

Scooter hire companies in Amsterdam include:

Amstel Bikes
+31 (0)20 638 6392
www.amstelbikes.com

AmsterBike
+31 (0)20 419 9063
www.amsterbike.eu

Scooter Rent Amsterdam
+31 (0)20 810 02 03
scooter-rent-amsterdam.com

By boat

A city known as 'Venice of the North', Amsterdammers love nothing more than taking a boat out on the canals as soon as the sun cracks a ray. It's relatively straightforward to rent a boat in Amsterdam, since a licence is only required for boats longer than 15 metres or faster than 20kph.

The cost of hiring a boat starts from around €50 per hour, with better rates available for longer hire periods. Here are some boat rental providers:

Canal Motorboats
Zandhoek 10a
+31 (0)20 422 7007
www.canalmotorboats.com
Bus: 48 Barentszplein
Tram: 3 to Zoutkeetsgracht; last stop

MokumBoot
3 rental locations in the city
www.mokumbootverhuur.nl

Sloep Delen
Nassaukade 69
+31 (0)20 419 1007
www.sloepdelen.nl

Amsterdam's best quality is the fact it's like a village, but gives you a feeling of being in an internationally oriented city too.

Photo: Kenrick Vrolijk

Kenrick Vrolijk
Hair and make-up stylist

What was your first impression of the Netherlands?
I was born in Aruba, the Caribbean island near Venezuela. When I was six, I moved to the Netherlands with my mum, and grew up in Amsterdam. When I first arrived, I was in a car with the window open, and I said to my mum: "They have air conditioning outside here!" I was used to the weather always being warm in Aruba, and I was only used to cool air in the form of air conditioning inside hotels or homes!

How did you get into your line of work?
Growing up, I was a really creative person, and I was wondering how I could apply that to a career. I went to an acting school initially and loved it, but the chance of actually becoming a big actor in the Netherlands is tiny, since it's a small country and there aren't many opportunities for actors. I was prepared to work hard, but I wanted to do it for something that was realistic. A friend of mine was a hairdresser and she owned her own salon. I visited her there and I loved the feeling. She told me how she had achieved her dreams over the years, and it inspired me. I wanted to help make people beautiful, so I started hairdressing school in the southern area of Amsterdam when I was 18 years old. I did really well there; the teachers told me I was talented and was learning really fast. It made me want to develop my skills faster; I constantly wanted to be better.

What did you do next?
As well as studying for my diploma at the school, I started working at Rob Peetoom, one of the biggest hair and beauty salons in the Netherlands, inside the exclusive shopping mall de Bijenkorf. It's one of the more expensive salons in the country, with extra services such as waiters serving tea. Since it's a high-end brand, they invest in making it really chic and beautiful. They have their own academy, where I learned some commercial skills in relation to hairdressing. It helped me grow faster and become better at my profession. After a while I achieved my first diploma and although I was encouraged to go for a second diploma, I felt the connections and experience I was gaining in the salon were giving me better experiences than studying. I noticed a lot of my peers were working in a very systematic way — the way they learned through hairdressing school — whereas I would talk to my clients, look at them and understand them, and then come up with a really personal plan of what I wanted to do to make them beautiful. When I explained this to my professor at the hairdressing school, he agreed that branching out from the school would be good for me.

<u>Tell us about your experience of working with one of the most famous celebrity hair and make-up stylists in the Netherlands, Mari van de Ven?</u>
Around the time I left the school I met Mari van de Ven. He was also working in de Bijenkorf and he was impressed I was working at Rob Peetoom, especially at such a young age. He asked me what my aspirations were and I told him I wanted to have my own salon one day. He liked the fact I had big plans, and asked me to assist him doing the hair for a TV show he worked on. I said I would, of course! That was the first TV show I worked on and it was great fun; Mari told me I did really well. A week later, his management team called me and asked me if I wanted to assist Mari again, and I did a few more shows, including one starring Mari himself, who was giving hair and make-up advice to the audience. So I was on that show, doing the hair. Afterwards, I received a call from Mari's management team again, who asked to make it official; they wanted me to become Mari's right-hand man with a proper contract. So it all started from there.

<u>What did you learn from your experience with Mari?</u>
I worked with Mari for about two years, and I learned so much! Because of Mari, I have also been doing model shows, and I work with companies such as Elite Model Netherlands, to help with their portfolio of models. Through my experience with Mari, I learned that working in a salon is so different from working on TV, but I found that I was able to merge both worlds together. I learned you can have the quality of a salon, and at the same time give the image of a celebrity. That's the moment I started to define my own identity in my work.

<u>Tell us about establishing your own company, KENVO Hair and Make-up.</u>
I left Rob Peetoom after working there for five years. I wanted to become a name in my own right and not within another company. First, I wanted to gain some experience in a different salon, so I worked at Pierot in the Oud Zuid neighbourhood for a year after Rob Peetoom. I needed to see how a different salon worked before I set up on my own. After that, I started my own company, KENVO Hair and Make-up, starting out with a chair in the centre of Amsterdam on the Reguliersdwarsstraat. I found that a lot of my previous clients looked me up online and followed me. I've been investing all the money I've made into my business, so I can continue to demonstrate my vision to new and existing clients. It hasn't always been an easy journey; when you're young and you gain success fast, there are always people along the way who are jealous and who try to bring you down. I learned that people can be awful, and that people can have such hate because they see others doing well. I struggled with that for a while. But I realised this is something you will always encounter in business. I want to do things my way; I want to make people beautiful and at the same time, I want to feel free. I want to enjoy life to the fullest.

What is original about KENVO?

I have a particular vision that focuses on detail, and I create styles that take each individual client into consideration. I'm constantly thinking about how to offer a better service and what the customer needs. I use the best, environmentally-friendly products, which is very much in-keeping with the ethos of Amsterdam. I try to use natural colours, but colours which can be seen and respect the health of the hair. Colours I use are always suitable for the eyes and skin of the individual. I'm extremely inspired by the Italian attention to detail; I always notice how Italians have hair that suits their whole style. These are the kinds of clients I have: people who want to look amazing for work, but at the same time look modern when they go out. I don't want to give someone a haircut that doesn't suit them, or that is only appropriate for going out. Some people think having their hair done is a luxury, but I see it as a lifestyle. Your hair is part of your image and your own personal business card. I want people to come to KENVO to help them become a little bit more successful in their lives.

What is your relationship like with your clients?

My clients have a classic, chic style. They're paying for the detailed service I provide that goes beyond giving them great hair. For example, if they need an iPhone charger, I have it. My clients want to have a good conversation too. Small details make a big difference to an overall experience. I become so close to my clients that I want to do even more for them. We can talk about anything. Since I've travelled a lot, I've had the chance to see a lot of beautiful places, eat the best food, and buy beautiful clothes. When you have discerning clients, they want to talk about the amazing things in life, so I'm able to discuss my own experiences with them. With my male clients, I talk about Rolex watches and hand-made suits from Italy. I can recommend places in Amsterdam and around the world they should go that suit their own personality and style. With my female clients, they like the perspective and advice I give them about issues in their lives. Even though I may be younger than them, sometimes it's good to have advice from someone who is younger, because they look at the world differently. We don't always talk about beautiful things, but also serious matters and world affairs. They pay a lot of money, but they get a lot in return. They look and feel stunning when they leave.

Is there an Amsterdam style?

Amsterdam is a small village in comparison to London or New York, but it has as much international allure. Internationalism is what the Amsterdam style is about. This is how I see my world and I think that comes across in KENVO too. People can come to me with any kind of hair, from anywhere in the world, and I can do it. Amsterdam has many international residents, but I also have people visiting me from across the Netherlands and the world, from Greece and England to the USA. Some of my clients are people who visit Amsterdam every year, who phone me and say: "Kenrick, I'm back in Amsterdam and my hair badly needs you." As well as internationalism, creativity is big in Amsterdam, and again you see that reflected in people's hair, from green hair to balayage. For my own creativity, it's nice to have those kinds of things around me, but I won't do everything a client asks. If someone comes in, sits in my chair and tells me they want to have green hair, I'll tell them that I don't think it will suit their skin and eyes because it's not natural. If they really want it, I'll tell them they need to look for another hairdresser! I want to get the best out of people and I won't do unnatural styles or colours.

What are your future plans?
At the moment I'm renting a chair in a salon on Willemsparkweg, but I want to have a whole salon of my own for KENVO Hair and Make-up in Amsterdam Oud Zuid. That's where I live and where most of my clients come from. Eventually I want to have my own chain of KENVO Hair and Make-up salons. I want to bring my identity and change the whole hairdressing world. I also want to give all my hairdressing colleagues and peers a new status. Your parents will always tell you they want you to be a doctor or the president of a country, so when you tell them you want to be a hairdresser, they think you'll only gain so much status in that kind of career. I want to change this perception and show people you can build your own company, you can have people working for you, and those people can help you build a better salon than others. As well as earning money, I want to make sure I treat my colleagues and employees well. This is important; you're working with people, not robots. Ultimately, my future is about building a hair and make-up business that's better than all the other businesses that are out there now.

Describe the Amsterdam neighbourhood you live in.
Oud Zuid is very chic. I also love the centre of Amsterdam, but for me it's better to live in Oud Zuid because it's more quiet, greener and is home to more people who love the beautiful things in life. It's one of the more expensive places in Amsterdam to live, but the people living there love things like beautiful watches, amazing food and tailored suits. Especially when it comes to eating food, it's not only about eating it, it's about tasting every ingredient in the food and thinking about where it comes from and how it's made. That's Oud Zuid.

Are there any other neighbourhoods in Amsterdam where you enjoy spending time?
We have a saying in Oud Zuid that when you live there, you'll only leave the neighbourhood by plane. It's because it has everything you could possibly

need. Even if you need to buy clothes, you have places like PC Hooftstraat or Pauw Mannen for luxury brands on Van Baerlestraat. Since I'm still young, I also spend quite a lot of time in the city centre and I have quite a few friends who live there. I really like de Negen Straatjes (Nine Streets) as there are a lot of good places to eat, drink and shop. One place I like doesn't really have a name, although people call it Wolfje. It's where a lot of creative young people go, especially models and others who are active in the fashion industry. There are a lot of people doing business in de Negen Straatjes too because it's got a good vibe.

Where are your favourite places to go for food and drinks?

One of my favourite places is the Conservatorium Hotel. I really like to go there for a gin and tonic, and the food is amazing too. It's a little expensive, but sometimes it's worth paying more to know they're doing their best to give you the best. It's one of my favourite places to be. To go out for a meal with a few friends in the evening, I'd recommend Le Garage in Oud Zuid. Everything about it is amazing and it's a place I really like to go to with my partner to eat good food, enjoy the surroundings and explore the wine list. The owner is a great sommelier and can always recommend the perfect wine to match each dish. Everything about Le Garage is very high quality.

What else do you like to do in your spare time?

There's a spa in Amsterdamse Bos that I really like, called Spa Zuiver. At the moment I'm really into fitness. I go to a health and fitness club in Oud Zuid called Great Club. It's really chic, and quite new so the facilities are amazing. I like to work out there because I think it's an important aspect of making my life better. It even helps with my work, because I stand a lot and do a lot of work with my hands. Through fitness, I'm not only getting healthier, but it gives me more energy and strength to hold a blow dryer!

What inspires you?

My inspiration comes from people. Inspiration for me is the people in Oud Zuid, the people on the streets across Amsterdam, and the people I meet when I'm travelling. My business is all about people. When someone first comes into the salon, I already have a sense of the kind of person they are, from the way they move, to the way they dress. Then when I speak to a person I get an even greater understanding. For example, a client once told me they like to go truffle hunting, but that they only like the white ones because they're more special than black truffles. That told me they like the exceptional things in life and are attuned to details, so I tailored my approach accordingly. It's the details that clients tell me that I find inspiring, and by learning about them and concentrating on the specifics, they come back again. When they come back, you've got yourself a business.

What is Amsterdam's best quality?

Amsterdam's best quality is the fact it's like a village, but gives you a feeling of being in an internationally oriented city too. Even though Amsterdam is so small, it has the ability to be international and big in its own way. Its village feeling also makes it feel warmer and more inviting than bigger cities. I love that about Amsterdam. There's really no other city like it in the world. The canals, the water, the small buildings and the old buildings all give Amsterdam its unique style and feeling.

What would you change about Amsterdam if you could?

I'd have a KENVO salon on every corner!

What is the trend in Amsterdam at the moment?

There's no single trend. The strength of Amsterdam is that there are lots of different people with every kind of style, who are also experimenting with every kind of trend. We have a lot of young people in Amsterdam who want their own businesses or who are developing creative concepts. You notice different styles and trends in Amsterdam neighbourhoods too. Amsterdam Zuid has a very classy feeling, while Oud West is where a lot of young people live. Some of these young people are studying to become lawyers and others are trying to break into the fashion world, so you notice an interesting combination of people following the mainstream world of fashion in their clothes, while others are making their own styles and pulling together a lot of different fashion concepts.

What advice would you give visitors to Amsterdam to blend in and live like locals during their stay?

It's very easy to live in or visit Amsterdam when you're from another country. Everyone in Amsterdam can speak English, so language is not often a barrier. Having the ability to talk to the locals makes a big difference when visiting a new place. To feel like a local, talk to the locals and just do what everybody else does: go out, have fun and try to live the big life. Welcome to Amsterdam!

Where do you go to have fun?

Anywhere and everywhere! My friends are aged between 20 and 50, so I probably do a wider range of things than most people. With older friends I really like to go to restaurants, to make the most of the great food we have in Amsterdam. Some of my favourite restaurants are Guts and Glory, Daalder and Mr Porter. With friends of my age, I like to go to de Negen Straatjes (Nine Streets) for some drinks where we can have long talks about our lives and future plans. I especially like Brix Cosy on Wolvenstraat. It's a bar that's a bit hipster-ish, but in a good way, and they also serve really tasty Asian-style snacks. I also like to go to festivals with my friends during the summer. Amsterdam is well known for its festivals and there are a lot to choose from.

Which are Amsterdam's best festivals?

In Amsterdam we have a really big gay community and supporting the community is a great festival called Milkshake. It's at the Westerpark in the Westergasfabriek, a former gasworks that's now a cultural venue. It's really nice because it's so open-minded; the organisers have managed to create an atmosphere where bisexual, transgender, gay people and straight people can all party together. It's an amazing open air party for everyone and happens every summer, around the time of Gay Pride, which is another great celebration. The other open air party I really like is King's Day. It used to be Queen's Day, but now we have a King, it's King's Day! It's so big and amazing. Even the trams don't work in Amsterdam on that day because everyone is partying. Everything is decorated in orange and the canals are alive, with all these amazing orange-themed boats going around with music playing. The whole city transforms into a party zone.

How can visitors to Amsterdam 'get lost' in in the city and discover it for themselves?

You can't really get lost in Amsterdam because it's not that big! But you can go to some of the amazing places in Amsterdam and lose yourself. Areas such as Museumplein and Dam Square, where the palace is, are famous and really beautiful sides of Amsterdam. I would really recommend the Rijksmuseum. Although lots of people go there and to the other museums, getting lost in a museum is a great thing to do in Amsterdam.

Is there a sound that reminds you of Amsterdam?

The sound of people peddling on their bicycles and ringing their bells. Cycling is such a way of life in Amsterdam, and when I visit somewhere else, bicycles always remind me of home. The difference is that in most places, it's not possible to cycle from one side of the city to the other, like it is in Amsterdam!

When you're not in Amsterdam, where are your favourite places to visit?

I work for myself so when I don't work, there is no money coming in and I'm not able to help my clients. Although I love to travel, that's always something I have to take into consideration. My partner needs to work in the US a lot, and he has lived in New York and San Francisco, which is his second home. The first time I went I fell in love with San Francisco, and my partner showed me the best places to eat and visit; it was amazing. Now we visit the US once or twice a year. I also love Palm Springs, and we stay at the Ace Hotel, which is one of the coolest hotels I've been to, with a kind of hippie-desert style in terms of decor. In Los Angeles I love The Standard

Hotel, a hip hotel in the downtown area. The pools outside really give you the feeling you're living the life. Every month or two I go somewhere closer to home to have good food and wine; I love Paris, Barcelona and Florence. We also go to Italy to get hand-made suits.

<u>What's the best thing about your life?</u>
I really enjoy the life my partner and I have together. He does something totally different; he's a tax lawyer and a partner in a large law firm. He's really into books and such, while I'm really into creativity. We're like the North and South Pole, and it works perfectly. Together we live life to the fullest.

Kenrick's Amsterdam

Places to visit

Dam Square
Dam, 1012 NP
Bus/tram: Dam

De Negen Straatjes
In between Prinsengracht and
Singel, 1016 EP
Bus/tram: Westermarkt

Gay Pride
www.amsterdamgaypride.nl
See page 82.

**Great: Health and
Performance Club**
Ruysdaelstraat 88 – 90, 1071 XH
+31 (0)20 763 0655
info@greatclub.nl
www.greatclub.nl
Bus/tram: Roelof Hartplein

KENVO Hair and Make-up
+31 (0)68 190 0288
www.kenvo.eu

King's Day
See page 78.

Milkshake Festival
www.milkshakefestival.com
See page 82.

Museumplein
Museumplein, 1071 DJ
Bus/tram: Van Baerlestraat or
Museumplein

P.C. Hooftstraat
Pieter Cornelisz Hooftstraat,
1071 CC
Bus/tram: Rijksmuseum

**Pauw Mannen Luxury
Denim**
Van Baerlestraat 66, 1071 BA
+31 (0)20 662 6253
www.pauw.com
Bus/tram: Museumplein (Van
Baerlestraat)

Pierot Coiffures & Beauté
Van Baerlestraat 148, 1071 BG
+31 (0)20 679 4120
www.pierot.nl
Bus/tram: Roelof Hartplein

Rijksmuseum
Museumstraat 1, 1071 XX
+31 (0)900 0745
www.rijksmuseum.nl
Tram: Rijksmuseum

Rob Peetoom salon
5th floor de Bijenkorf, Dam 1,
1012 JS
+31 (0)20 422 3902
amsterdam-beauty@
robpeetoom.nl
www.robpeetoom.nl
Bus/tram: Dam

Spa Sport Hotel Zuiver
Koenenkade 8, 1081 KH
+31 (0)20 301 0700
www.zuiveramsterdam.nl/spa
Bus: Koenenkade

Westergasfabriek
Haarlemmerweg 8E, 1014 BE
+31 (0)20 586 07 10
info@westergasfabriek.nl
www.westergasfabriek.nl
Bus: Van Hallstraat
(Haarlemmerweg)

Eating and drinking

Café Brix
Wolvenstraat 16, 1016 EP
+31 (0)20 639 0351
info@cafebrix.nl
www.cafebrix.nl
Tram: Spui (Niewezijds
Voorburgwal)

Conservatorium Hotel
Van Baerlestraat 27, 1071 AN
+31 (0)20 570 0000
reservations@
conservatoriumhotel.com
www.conservatoriumhotel.com
Tram: Van Baerlestraat

Guts and Glory
Utrechtsestraat 6, 1017 VN
+31 (0)20 362 0030
info@gutsglory.nl
www.gutsglory.nl
Bus/tram: Rembrandtplein

Mr Porter
Spuistraat 175, 1012 VN
+31 (0)20 811 3399
www.mrportersteakhouse.com
Tram: Dam (Raadhuisstraat) or
Dam (Paleisstraat)

Restaurant Daalder
Lindengracht 90, 1015 KK
+31 (0)20 624 8864
info@daalderamsterdam.nl
www.daalderamsterdam.nl
Bus: Buiten Oranjestraat

Restaurant Le Garage
Ruysdaelstraat 54/56, 1071 XE
+31 (0)20 679 7176
info@restaurantlegarage.nl
www.restaurantlegarage.nl
Bus/tram: Roelof Hartplein

Wolfje
Wolvenstraat 23, 1016 EM
+31 (0)20 320 0843
www.facebook.com/Wolvenstra
at-23-1451239075117871
Tram: Spui (Niewezijds
Voorburgwal)

See also

Ace Hotel Palm Springs
www.acehotel.com/palmsprings
Mari van de Ven
www.marivandeven.nl
**The Standard Hotel Los
Angeles**
www.standardhotels.com

Find out more about
Kenrick Vrolijk at
www.KENVO.eu or
www.facebook.com/
KenrickVrolijk

City map

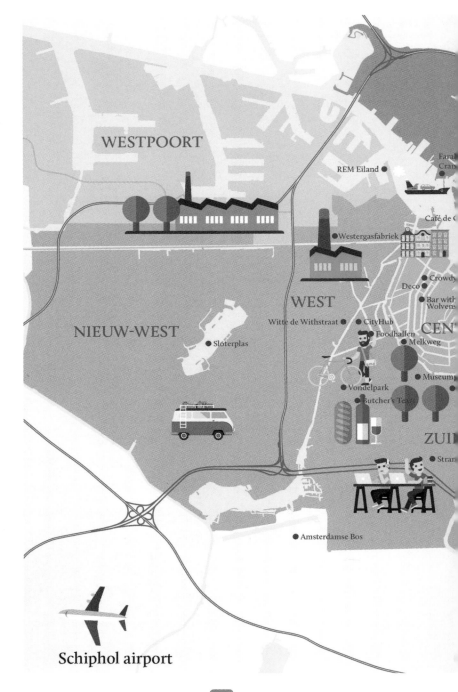

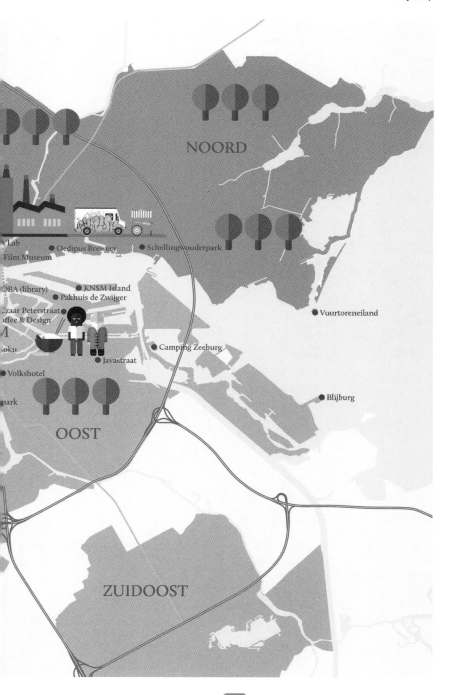

NOORD

A Lab
Film Museum

● Oedipus Brewery   ● Schellingwouderpark

OBA (library)
● KNSM Island
● Pakhuis de Zwijger

Czaar Peterstraat
offee & Design

● Vuurtoreneiland

oku

● Javastraat   ● Camping Zeeburg

● Volkshotel

● Blijburg

park

OOST

ZUIDOOST

Centre (Centrum)

The central area of Amsterdam is characterised by the famous canal ring lined with historic houses. The city centre's winding streets make it an ideal place for urban explorers, while an increasingly international and creative population give it a bohemian and trendy vibe. Nowhere in Amsterdam is very far away from the centre, and it's a place where pastimes such as socialising with a beer or coffee, or perusing concept stores, reign supreme.

Photo: Cyril Wermers

A work day in Central Amsterdam:

Morning

Crowdy Office
Spend some time at this co-working space full of people launching creative start-up projects. Page 121. Bus: Buiten Oranjestraat

Bruill & Brandsma
This antiques shop in Spiegelkwartier is ideal for inspiration-inducing browsing. Page 57. Tram: Prinsengracht (Leidsestraat)

Latei
Stop for a coffee in this atmospheric concept store and café. Page 168. Metro: Nieuwmarkt

Afternoon

De Vegetarische Traiteur
Pick up lunch at this deli that sells vegetarian food that even meat lovers enjoy. Page 54. Bus/tram: Marnixstraat

Ultra de la Rue
Stop in at this creative space to discuss counter cultures and trends. Page 56. Bus/tram: Dam

Openbare Bibliotheek Amsterdam (OBA)
Check your emails at Amsterdam's public library and enjoy stunning views over the city. Page 57. Tram: Muziekgebouw Bimhuis

Evening

Pianola Museum
Take in a musical performance at this quirky museum. Page 55. Bus/tram: Nieuwe Willemsstraat

Nam Kee
Treat your business associates to a meal in Chinatown's most popular family-run restaurant. Page 56. Metro: Nieuwmarkt

In 't Aepjen
Stop for a nightcap at this traditional Dutch pub, where sailors used to pay in monkeys instead of cash. Page 56. Bus/train/tram: Amsterdam Centraal

A day of play in Central Amsterdam:

Morning

The Cat Boat (De Poezenboot)
Visit this canal boat that is now home to previously homeless cats. Page 56. Bus/tram: Nieuwezijds Kolk

Six and Sons
Enjoy coffee and breakfast while casting your eye over the wares of this trendy concept store. Page 54. Bus: Buiten Oranjestraat

Noordermarkt
Get a feeling for local life at this market that sells organic food, vintage ware and textiles. Page 54. Bus: Buiten Brouwersstraat

Afternoon

The Cold Pressed Juicery
Stop for a juice and raw food fix alongside health-conscious Amsterdammers. Page 55. Tram: Van Baerlestraat

Museumplein
Wander around the Museum Quarter to take in an open air event or visit a museum. Page 55. Bus/tram: Museumplein

The Movies
Stop off at the oldest arthouse cinema in the Netherlands to watch a movie, or simply enjoy the architecture. Page 54. Bus/tram: Haarlemmerplein

Evening

Ibericus
Have an early evening glass of wine with a plate of delectable tapas. Page 54. Bus: Buiten Brouwersstraat

Moeders ('Mothers')
Enjoy dinner at this quirky restaurant with pictures of mothers lining the walls. Page 55. Bus/tram: Rozengracht or Marnixstraat

Café Nol
Sing along to Dutch schlager music while people-watching at this kitsch Jordaan spot. Page 54. Bus/tram: Marnixplein

Central Amsterdam neighbourhoods:

Haarlemmerbuurt

This neighbourhood well-known for its boutiques and concept stores centres on two streets: Haarlemmerdijk and Haarlemmerstraat. The area has even won awards for being the best shopping spot in the Netherlands. This is the locality of Amsterdam for casual socialising, in the many pavement and waterside cafés by day, and in the low-key bars by night.

Where the locals recommend:

The Movies

This cinema is the oldest arthouse cinema in Amsterdam that is still in operation. The cool art deco style makes you feel a part of history, while the food in the restaurant is pretty good too. Many locals go along for a combined food and film experience.
Haarlemmerdijk 161, 1013 KH
+31 (0)20 638 6016
info@themovies.nl
www.themovies.nl
Bus/tram: Haarlemmerplein

Small World

The Dutch love their sandwiches, and this catering company and deli just around the corner from Haarlemmerstraat is a favourite place for the locals to indulge. There's a huge selection of mostly Mediterranean fillings available with breads such as ciabatta and rosemary focaccia.
Binnen Oranjestraat 14, 1013 JA
+31 (0)20 420 2774
info@smallworldcatering.nl
www.smallworldcatering.nl
Bus: Buiten Oranjestraat

Six and Sons

This trendy concept store/café attracts Amsterdammers looking for design-conscious clothes and homeware. Casual browsers like to sit with a coffee and breakfast while casting an eye over the store.
Haarlemmerdijk 31, 1013 KA
+31 (0)20 233 0092
www.sixandsons.com
Bus: Buiten Oranjestraat

Ibericus

This neighbourhood deli and tapas spot is a local favourite, ideal for a post-shopping pit-stop for a glass of wine and a plate of the delectable slivers of ham. It's open throughout the day until early evening.
Haarlemmerstraat 93, 1013 JA
+31 (0)20 223 6573
www.facebook.com/
IbericusAmsterdam
Bus: Buiten Brouwersstraat

Two For Joy

This café roasts its own beans and has a huge selection for coffee lovers to try. The laid-back and cosy interior makes it a popular spot for locals to hang out.
Haarlemmerdijk 182, 1013 JK
+31 (0)20 221 9552
www.twoforjoy.nl
Bus/tram: Haarlemmerstraat

Jordaan

One of the most famous neighbourhoods of Amsterdam, Jordaan has a big community spirit and an eclectic mix of free-thinking residents known for speaking their minds. It's the neighbourhood where Rembrandt spent the last years of his life, and the location where Anne Frank went into hiding during World War II. While some families have lived in Jordaan for decades, it's also a favourite locality for artists, entrepreneurs and young families. The area is defined by a bohemian vibe, winding streets and hidden courtyards ripe for urban exploration, with a mix of long-established and chichi cafés, bars, restaurants and art galleries.

Where the locals recommend:

Café Nol

This café perfectly embodies the traditional side of Jordaan's personality. It's a kitsch spot where locals drink the night away while singing along to Dutch schlager music. It's perfect for people-watching and getting some insight into the cross-section of the locals who call Jordaan home.
Westerstraat 109, 1015 LX
+31 (0)20 624 5380
www.cafenol-amsterdam.nl
Bus/tram: Marnixplein

Noordermarkt

This Monday morning flea market is a place to find antiques and household bric-a-brac. Local creative residents particularly enjoy the neighbouring textiles market, while an organic farmers' market on Saturdays is the place to get great quality food.
Noordermarkt, 1015 MV
+31 (0)20 552 4074
info@noordermarkt-amsterdam.nl
www.noordermarkt-amsterdam.nl
Bus: Buiten Brouwersstraat

De Vegetarische Traiteur

This deli is for vegetarians who love the taste of meat. Offering an array of products consisting of soya and various vegetables, it's as close to meat as you'll get without actually consuming any.
Rozengracht 217H, 1016 NA
www.vegetarischetraiteur.nl
Bus/tram: Marnixstraat

Moeders
This quirky restaurant called 'Mothers' has pictures of people's mums lining every wall. When the restaurant first opened, everyone who donated a photo of their mother received a free meal. The restaurant still uses the mish mash of crockery locals donated too, while the menu offers traditional Dutch fare.
Rozengracht 251, 1016 SX
+31 (0)20 626 7957
info@moeders.com
www.moeders.com
Bus/tram: Rozengracht or Marnixstraat

Pianola Museum
Jordaan locals love a good dose of quirk, making it the ideal location for the century-old Pianola Museum. The small museum consists entirely of a lovingly kept collection of automatic pianos and thousands of music rolls that can be played on the museum's different instruments. There's also a regular schedule of daytime and evening concerts.
Westerstraat 106, 1015 MN
+31 (0)20 627 9624
info@pianola.nl
www.pianola.nl
Bus/tram: Nieuwe Willemsstraat

Museum Quarter
The area around Museumplein is one of the most well-known in Amsterdam. This isn't just for the museums of huge global and cultural importance, but also for some of the city's most exclusive shopping along P.C. Hooftstraat and the much photographed, larger-than-life I amsterdam sign. This part of the city is all about indulging yourself culturally and enjoying the buzz of the streets.

Where the locals recommend:

Museums
Clearly this is the neighbourhood to be in to visit the most celebrated museums in the city: the Rijksmuseum, the Van Gogh Museum and the Stedelijk Museum. Although these museums follow the well-trodden path of tourists, Amsterdam's community of creatives also love to delve in and out of the museums to gain inspiration and stop for a coffee in the museum cafés.

Museumstraat 1, 1071 XX
+31 (0)20 674 7000
info@rijksmuseum.nl
www.rijksmuseum.nl
Tram: Rijksmuseum

Museumplein 6, 1071 DJ
+31 (0)20 570 5200
info@vangoghmuseum.nl
www.vangoghmuseum.nl
Bus/tram: Van Baerlestraat or Museumplein

Museumplein 10, 1071 DJ
+31 (0)20 573 2911
reserveringen@stedelijk.nl
www.stedelijk.nl
Bus/tram: Van Baerlestraat or Museumplein

Open air events
Museumplein plays hosts to a regular cacophony of open air events, from music festivals to screenings of big sports matches. There's also an ice rink during the winter.
Museumplein, 1071 CX
Bus/tram: Museumplein or Van Baerlestraat

Home is...
The Amsterdam love affair with the concept store continues in Home is Amsterdam. The city's fashion lovers and design fans hang out here for new innovations and for a coffee at the back of the store.

Van Baerlestraat 89, 1071 AT
+31 (0)20 370 7315
info@homeis.nl
www.homeis.nl
Bus/tram: Roelof Hartplein

The Cold Pressed Juicery
Juice, salad and raw food bars are all the rage in Amsterdam at the moment, and this one combines all three. Health conscious Amsterdammers flock here for their health fix.
Willemsparkweg 8, 1071 HD
+31 (0)20 753 0919
info@thecoldpressedjuicery.com
www.thecoldpressedjuicery.com
Tram: Van Baerlestraat

Conservatorium
The building this hotel stands in has been part of the Museum Quarter's landscape for centuries. As well as well-heeled travellers, the Conservatorium attracts Amsterdammers looking for a classy, intimate meal or a gin cocktail in Tunes Bar.
Van Baerlestraat 27, 1071 AN
+31 (0)20 570 0000
info@conservatoriumhotel.com
www.conservatoriumhotel.com
Tram: Van Baerlestraat

Nieuwmarkt
This old Amsterdam district centres on the market square, which has been running a regular market since the 1600s. The square is dominated by the stately de Waag building, a key entry point into the city before the walls were taken down. This is also the area where Amsterdam's Chinatown can be found, where the city's first Chinese settlers laid down their roots. Nowadays, this is the place to find some of the best Chinese food in the city, as well as other Eastern cuisines, from Thai to Tibetan. The feeling on the streets is energetic, with Amsterdammers eager to discover the best deals from

the market and get involved with the vitality of Chinatown.

Where the locals recommend:

Markets
Nieuwmarkt square itself plays host to a daily market, an organic food market on Saturdays and a summertime antiques market on Sundays. It's the ideal place to get involved in Amsterdam life, or people-watch from one of the many cafés surrounding the square.
Nieuwmarkt 1012 CR
Metro: Nieuwmarkt

Nam Kee
One of the most popular family-run Chinese restaurants in Amsterdam, Nam Kee offers a selection of delectably prepared Chinese flavours. Locals love to go there for a quiet meal or for celebratory occasions with large groups. Nam Kee also has a cookery book if you can't get enough of the deliciousness.
Geldersekade 117, 1011 EN
+31 (0)20 639 2848
www.namkee.nl
Metro: Nieuwmarkt

Betty Blue
This bakery is just a stone's throw from Nieuwmarkt and serves locally loved breakfast pastries and coffees. The large interior is filled with mismatched furniture and industrial decor: giving it everything the local trendies love, and more.
Snoekjessteeg 1-3, 1011 HA
+31 (0)20 810 0924
info@bettyblueamsterdam.nl
www.bettyblueamsterdam.nl
Metro: Nieuwmarkt

In 't Aepjen
In 't Aepjen, meaning 'In the Monkeys', is found in a building dating back to the

15th century. It's named after the sailors returning from faraway lands, who paid in monkeys instead of money. Nowadays, it's a cosy place to have a beer, and still feels steeped in history.
Zeedijk 1, 1012 AN
Bus/train/tram: Amsterdam Centraal

Cine Qua Non
Just a short walk from Nieuwmarkt square is this shop specialising in arthouse films, movie posters, stills and postcards. The shop attracts film buffs from the across the city, and the world.
Staalstraat 14, 1011 JL
+31 (0)20 625 5588
cine.qua.nonsense@gmail.com
www.cinequanonline.com
Bus/metro/tram: Waterlooplein

Red light district (De Wallen)
This area is known for sex workers in windows, sex shops, peep shows, a sex museum, a 'Condomerie' shop, and plenty more. It's seedy, but perhaps not as much as it sounds: prostitution has long been tolerated in the city and sex workers have much better rights than elsewhere in the world, with a union and good police protection. Remember to be respectful: taking photographs of sex workers is forbidden. The area also has a lot more going on than sex, full of vibrant bars, eateries and shops. It's also the oldest part of the city, so expect to see plenty of gabled merchants' houses, often leaning at odd angles since they were built on stilts over the water so many years ago.

Where the locals recommend:

Ultra de la Rue
This multi-functional creative space is an exhibition, design

shop, event space and café. Regular 'creative sessions' are also held here, where counter cultures and trends are discussed over food.
Oudekerksplein 30, 1012 GZ
info@ultradelarue.com
www.ultradelarue.com
Bus/tram: Dam

The Cat Boat (De Poezenboot)
The red light district is just a five minute walk away from Central Station, where a boat full of stray cats can be found on a canal just west of the station. There's nothing else quite like it in the world; it's run by volunteers to give cats a safe refuge.
Singel 38.G, 1015 AB
+31 (0)20 625 8794
depoezenboot@gmail.com
www.depoezenboot.nl
Bus/tram: Nieuwezijds Kolk

Photo: De Poezenboot

Photo: De Poezenboot

In de Wildeman
Found inside a former distillery, this is a popular place to taste a whole host of different and original beers. With more than a dozen beers on tap and more than 200 bottled varieties, this is a serious place for beer lovers, with not even the distraction of background music.
Kolksteeg 3, 1012 PT
+31 (0)20 638 2348
info@indewildeman.nl
www.indewildeman.nl
Bus/tram: Nieuwezijds Kolk

Oude Kerk
Amsterdam's oldest building and parish church doubles as an art gallery, with a regular calendar of exhibitions and artist talks throughout the year.
Oudekerksplein 23, 1012 GX
+31 (0)20 625 8284
info@oudekerk.nl
www.oudekerk.nl
Metro: Nieuwmarkt

Public Library Amsterdam (Openbare Bibliotheek Amsterdam, OBA)
Just a stone's throw from Central Station, the OBA is a popular spot for locals to hang out. Offering more than just books, the top floor has a terrace, café and amazing views over the city.
Oosterdokskade 143, 1011 DL
+31 (0)20 523 0900
klantenservice@oba.nl
www.oba.nl
Tram: Muziekgebouw Bimhuis

Spiegelkwartier
Amsterdam's hub of antiques, art and trinkets, Spiegelkwartier ('Mirror Quarter') is a neighbourhood characterised by cute streets and quirky collectibles. It's been attracting antiques traders and art lovers for decades, and while it's the place to be if you fit into one of those categories, it's also a fabulous neighbourhood to wander and enjoy the traditional houses, stopping for a coffee or snack on street corners.

Where the locals recommend:

Bruill & Brandsma
You can take your pick of antiques shops to duck into along Nieuwe Spiegelstraat. This one is also a gallery and restoration studio, working with museums and collectors from far and wide. It's a fascinating insight into the world of antiques, and provides great inspiration to Amsterdam's creative community.
Nieuwe Spiegelstraat 68, 1017 DH
+31 (0)20 420 7359
bbc@chello.nl
www.bb-art.com
Bus/tram: Leidseplein or Prinsengracht (stop Leidsestraat)

De Appel
This contemporary arts centre hosts various installations and gives artists space to develop their projects.
Nieuwe Spiegelstraat 10, 1017 DE
+31 (0)20 625 5651
info@deappel.nl
www.deappel.nl
Tram: Keizersgracht (stops Leidsestraat or Vijzelstraat)

Soupenzo
Soup is a staple lunch item for Amsterdammers, meaning the menu options at Soupenzo are vast and varied, from spicy spinach to celeriac with salmon.
Nieuwe Spiegelstraat 54, 1017 DG
+31 (0)20 330 7781
soup@soupenzo.nl
www.soupenzo.nl
Bus/metro/tram: Waterlooplein

Dekker Antiquairs
This antiques store specialises in jewellery and watches in particular. It's a top spot to gain creative inspiration, or a vintage accessory.
Spiegelgracht 9, 1017 JP
+31 (0)20 623 8992
dekkerfa@xs4all.nl
www.dekkerantiquairs.com
Tram: Spiegelgracht

Four Leaves
There tends to be a big focus on coffee in Amsterdam, so this 'tea palace' is a welcome spot for the city's tea lovers to congregate. Sit and enjoy the aromas from the wide variation of teas; you can also take some home to brew yourself.
Spiegelgracht 21, 1017 JP
+31 (0)20 810 0539
info@fourleaves.nl
www.fourleaves.nl
Tram: Spiegelgracht

Photo: OBA

North (Noord)

A forgotten part of Amsterdam for a number of decades, Amsterdam Noord has seen a recent resurgence in popularity, with a number of new hotspots opening up against an industrial backdrop. Previously cut off from the rest of the city by the River IJ, the north is now connected to central Amsterdam by free ferries and car tunnels. It's a place where young families and trend-setters live in modern housing or shipping container apartments. These locals enjoy more space compared to other parts of the city, an emerging cultural scene, green open space and outdoor markets. New and established creative businesses are also locating their headquarters in Amsterdam Noord, including MTV Europe and Red Bull.

Photo: Cyril Wermers

A work day in north Amsterdam

Morning

A Lab
Have some laptop time at this huge co-working space loved by creatives. Page 116. Boat or bus: Buiksloterwegveer

The Coffee Virus
Enjoy a pit stop at this café full of local entrepreneurs. Page 126. Boat or bus: Buiksloterwegveer

Afternoon

Neef Louis
Get some creative inspiration from this vintage and design furniture shop. Page 185. Bus: Distelweg or Klaprozenweg

De Ceuvel
Wander around this creative community where entrepreneurs have converted houseboats into office space. Page 60. Bus: Mosplein

Evening

EYE Film Museum
Be inspired by the films and installations in this museum, or watch an arthouse film screening. Page 60. Boat or bus: Buiksloterweg

Tolhuistuin
Impress your business associates with a theatre performance or food event at this cultural venue. Page 60. Boat or bus: Buiksloterweg

A day of play in north Amsterdam

Morning

Vlooienmarkt IJ Hallen
Pick up a bargain at the biggest flea market in the Netherlands. Page 60. Boat: Veer NDSM Werf. Bus: Klaprozenweg

Noorderparkbar
Grab a coffee in this park café made from reclaimed materials. Page 60. Bus: Sneeuwbalstraat, Merelstraat or Mosplein

Afternoon

Schellingwouderpark
Visit this little known park via a pull ferry over the River IJ. Page 60. Bus: Wognumerplantsoen or Schellingwouderdijk

Oedipus Brewery
Enjoy tasting some of the brews at this quirky brewery and exhibition space. Page 60. Bus: Hamerstraat or Havikslaan

Evening

NDSM wharf
Visit this previous ship-building wharf for bars, restaurants and a summertime beach. Page 60. Boat: Veer NDSM Werf

Faralda Crane Hotel
Stay the night in design-conscious suites on top of this industrial crane. Page 190. Boat: Veer NDSM Werf

EYE Film Museum photo: Cyril Wermers

North Amsterdam

Where the locals recommend:

NDSM wharf
This former ship-building wharf is now a popular hangout full of bars, restaurants and outdoor seating overlooking the water. It's also a place where artists love to set up their studios, and a regular calendar of festivals and cultural events keeps people coming all year round. During the summer, Pllek becomes one of Amsterdam's most popular city beaches.
Neveritaweg 15, 1033 WB
+31 (0)68 168 6312
www.ndsmloods.nl
www.pllek.nl
Boat: Veer NDSM Werf

EYE Film Museum
Film and architecture buffs will love this eye-catching museum on the northern banks of the River IJ. Check out the exhibitions, film screenings and cinema concerts, or simply soak up the atmosphere in the bar, restaurant or library.
IJpromenade 1, 1031 KT
+31 (0)20 589 1400
info@eyefilm.nl
www.eyefilm.nl
Boat or bus: Buiksloterweg

Oedipus Brewery
Pop along to this quirky brewery on Fridays and Saturdays to taste the brews and enjoy the local art on display in the exhibition space. The brewery also organises occasional events, such as Burger Beer Battles.
Gedempt Hamerkanaal 85, 1021 KP
info@oedipus.com
www.oedipus.com
Bus: Hamerstraat or Haviksslaan

Schellingwouderpark
This former industrial waste site is now a park designed to preserve the local ecosystem. It's quieter than Amsterdam's other parks, making it a peaceful place for a walk, picnic or swim. The 25 acre park is accessed by pull ferries, adding a little adventure to the experience.
Schellingwouderdijk 95, 1023 NA
Bus: Wognumerplantsoen or Schellingwouderdijk

Café de Ceuvel
This eco-friendly café has become a popular hangout for creative people. This is thanks to De Ceuvel itself next door, a living laboratory where creative businesses have transformed old houseboats into sustainable workspaces. It's a great place to chill out and be inspired.
Korte Papaverweg 4, 1032 KB
+31 (0)20 229 6210
info@cafedeceuvel.nl
www.cafedeceuvel.nl
Bus: Mosplein

Vlooienmarkt IJ Hallen
The largest flea market in the Netherlands is found inside two massive old industrial halls, where a huge variety of quirky and practical goods can always be found.
Postbus 15, 1657 ZG
+31 (0)22 958 1598
info@ij-hallen.nl
www.ij-hallen.nl
Boat: Veer NDSM Werf
Bus: Klaprozenweg

Noorderparkbar
This peaceful café and bar in a park is made entirely of second hand materials found nearby. Sit with a coffee in the design conscious interior, or on deck chairs outside with a beer.
Floraparkweg 1, 1032 BZ
info@noorderparkbar.nl
www.noorderparkbar.nl
Bus: Sneeuwbalstraat, Merelstraat or Mosplein

Tolhuistuin
This cultural hotspot on the former site of Shell's offices hosts evening food, film and music events in its gardens during the summer. Inside there are also theatre and concert halls and a cosy café, making it a popular destination year-round.
IJpromenade 2, 1031 KT
+31 (0)20 763 0650
info@tolhuistuin.nl
www.tolhuistuin.nl
Boat or bus: Buiksloterweg

Cycling tour
A popular way to properly explore and enjoy northern Amsterdam is to hop on the ferry with your bicycle across the River IJ, then cycle along the historic dykes offering fabulous waterside views and an overview of some of the old mansion houses located here. Locals particularly recommend Nieuwendammerdijk, Schellingwouderdijk, Durgerdammerdijk and Buiksloterdijk.
Amsterdam Noord, 1023 BV

Pekmarkt
This trendy market sells organic goods on Fridays, which health conscious locals visit to do their weekly grocery shopping. On Saturdays the market sells vintage goods and curiosities. If you've got time to explore nearby, visit the Fashion&Tea concept store for coffee and fashion finds, and the nearby restaurant SmaaQt, loved by locals for its industrial chic interior and fresh menu.
Van der Pekstraat, 1031 EE
+31 (0)20 737 1412
info@pekmarkt.nl
www.pekmarkt.nl
Bus: Gentiaanstraat, Hagedoornplein or Meidoornplein

Photo: Pllek

South (Zuid)

Amsterdam's southern neighbourhoods are filled with hipsters and trendsetters, who enjoy living on leafy residential streets alongside fine examples of Amsterdam School architecture. The south is a distinctly foodie neck of the woods, with organic cafés and markets, health food shops, and an abundance of sought-after restaurants. This area is also home to Vondelpark, Amsterdam's most well-known outdoor space, while towards the southern outskirts are much-loved forested areas and glistening corporate centres filled with the city's suited and booted.

A work day in south Amsterdam

Morning

Mixtup
Rent a desk at this co-working space with a thriving artsy community. Page 115. Bus/tram: Ferdinand Bolstraat

Oma Ietje
Grab a coffee from this Swedish style café created from a crowdfunding campaign. Page 66. Bus: Hakfort. Metro: Bullewijk

Albert Cuyp Market
Feel inspired by wandering through one of the most vibrant and well-known markets in Amsterdam. Page 64. Tram: Albert Cuypstraat

Afternoon

Reuring
Treat your business associates to lunch in this restaurant serving fresh and seasonal food. Page 64. Bus/tram: Tweede van der Helststraat

Sarphatipark
Digest your lunch with a bracing walk around this park, named after philanthropist Samuel Sarphati. Page 64. Bus/tram: Tweede van der Helststraat

Strandzuid
Have a drink at this summertime beer garden and cosy winter retreat, in one of the more corporate parts of town. Page 65. Bus/tram: Europaplein. Bus/metro/train/tram: Station RAI

Evening

Amstelveenseweg
Pick a restaurant from this foodie hub for dinner. Page 64. Bus/tram: Olympisch Stadion

Café Gruter
Enjoy a nightcap at this traditional brown café, decorated with faded polaroid pictures. Page 65. Tram: Cornelis Schuytstraat, Van Baerlestraat or Jacob Obrechtstraat

citizenM
Stay over at this hip and convenient hotel for business travellers. Page 187. Bus/metro/train/tram: Station Amsterdam Zuid

A day of play in south Amsterdam

Morning

Amsterdamse Bos
Take a morning stroll in this 2,500 acre forest on the Amsterdam outskirts, home to a biodynamic goat farm and climbing park. Page 65. Bus: Kalfjeslaan

Corso Como
Enjoy a coffee at this airy Italian eatery. Page 65. Bus/metro/train/tram: Amsterdam Zuid

ZuiderMRKT
Whet your appetite by strolling through this biological market on Saturdays. Page 65. Bus/tram: Jacob Obrechtstraat

Afternoon

Tjin's Toko
Check out the speciality foods here and get some take-away Indonesian and Surinamese food for lunch. Page 64. Tram: Albert Cuypstraat

Vondelpark
Wander around Amsterdam's most famous park, and seek out the Vondelbunker for art and counter-culture events. Page 64. Tram: J.P. Heijestraat or Rhijnvis Feithstraat

Mumu Vitamin Chocolates
Stop off at this shop selling 'healthy' chocolate treats. Page 168. Tram: Stadhouderskade

Evening

Butcher's Tears
Enjoy some beers at this hipster brewery and tasting room. Page 64. Bus: Cornelis Krusemanstraat. Tram: Haarlemmermeer

The Fat Dog
Have a dinner of champagne and hotdogs at this à la mode restaurant. Page 164. Bus/tram: Cornelis Troostplein

Amsterdam Open Air
Join the revellers at this summertime festival in Gaasperpark, or check out a performance at the nearby Ziggo Dome. Page 66. Bus/metro (Gaasperpark): Gaasperplas Bus/metro/train (Ziggo Dome): Amsterdam Bijlmer ArenA

Southern Amsterdam neighbourhoods:

De Pijp

This old multicultural neighbourhood is a favourite of Amsterdam hipsters and trendsetters, who keep the cool boutiques, health food shops and organic cafés in business. It gets even livelier at the weekends, with bars spilling with revellers. Architecture buffs also love this part of the city, as plenty of examples of the Amsterdam School movement can be spotted here.

Where the locals recommend:

Albert Cuyp Market

This market is one of the most famous in Amsterdam and makes for a truly vibrant city experience six days per week (it's only closed on Sundays). A whopping 260 stands line the street, with everything for sale from seafood, street food and fresh bread, to flowers, clothes and fabric.

Albert Cuypstraat, 1073 BL
albertcuyp-markt.amsterdam
Tram: Albert Cuypstraat

Tjin's Toko

De Pijp is a neighbourhood of foodies, so there's no shortage of speciality food and cookery stores. This unassuming looking grocery store is tiny, but is stacked high with the otherwise hardest-to-find international ingredients. The store also sells delicious Indonesian and Surinamese food to take away.

Eerste van der Helststraat 64, 1072 NZ
+31 (0)20 671 7708
tjinstoko@gmail.com
www.tjinstoko.eu
Tram: Albert Cuypstraat

Sarphatipark

Amsterdammers love to be outside as soon as the weather's good enough, and this De Pijp park is named after physician and philanthropist Samuel Sarphati. De Pijp was the stomping ground of Sarphati, so it's apt that this verdant park is a favourite location for locals to picnic and socialise.

Sarphatipark, 1072 PB
Bus/tram: Tweede van der Helststraat

Pilsvogel

This traditional pub has a terrace ideal for people-watching with a beer in hand.

Gerard Douplein 14, 1072 VE
+31 (0)20 664 6483
info@pilsvogel.nl
www.pilsvogel.nl
Tram: Albert Cuypstraat

Reuring

This neighbourhood restaurant has a regularly changing menu revolving strictly around fresh produce. It's a laid-back hang-out for locals who love great food.

Lutmastraat 99, 1073 GR
+31 (0)20 777 0996
info@cafereuring.nl
www.cafereuring.nl
Bus/tram: Tweede van der Helststraat

Oud Zuid

This chic 'old south' neighbourhood is full of leafy residential streets, inhabited by discerning residents intent on enjoying the many cultural and foodie pastimes going on in the area. The neighbourhood is also the boastful home to Vondelpark, the huge outdoor space close to every Amsterdammer's heart. On the outskirts of Oud Zuid is the site of the Olympic Stadium, built for the 1928 Summer Olympic

Games, and now the location of a sport museum and a lot of surrounding housing developments attracting young Amsterdam families. Where the locals recommend:

Vondelpark

Famous during the 70s as a 'hippie' park, Vondelpark is now said to be the most densely populated part of the city when the sun is out. During sunny times, the 120 acre Vondelpark is where Amsterdammers flock to for picnics, al fresco drinks and open-air performances. Seek out the Vondelbunker for counter-culture concerts, cinema nights and art exhibitions.

Vondelpark, 1071 AA
Tram: J.P. Heijestraat or Rhijnvis Feithstraat

Amstelveenseweg

The Amstelveenseweg has quickly become the hub of often elegant foodie life in this distinctly food-loving neighbourhood. You can't go far wrong with restaurants along this strip. Try Supermercado for Spanish tapas in retro surroundings, Chi Amsterdam for classy Chinese, sushi and cocktails, or Ron Gastrobar for an anti-stylised food experience.

Amstelveenseweg, 1075 XR
Bus/tram: Olympisch Stadion

Butcher's Tears

This brewery and tasting room is open from 16:00 to 21:00 Wednesday to Sunday, attracting beer pilgrims from across the city. Hipsters and traditionalists interact at the long beer tables, bonding over their love of amber nectar.

Karperweg 45, 1075LB
+31 (0)65 390 9777
info@butchers-tears.com
www.butchers-tears.com
Bus: Cornelis Krusemanstraat
Tram: Haarlemmermeer

ZuiderMRKT
This biological outdoor market takes place on Saturdays and helps feed the fastidious foodie locals.
Jacob Obrechtstraat 44, 1071 KN
www.zuidermrkt.nl
Bus/tram: Jacob Obrechtstraat

Café Gruter
Peppered among the shiny facades of many Oud Zuid shops and restaurants are a number of traditional brown cafés: wood clad and slightly unkempt drinking holes that are a traditional part of Amsterdam drinking culture. Café Gruter is one of them, decked out with faded polaroid pictures, spilling out onto a terrace ideal for people-watching.
Willemsparkweg 73-75, 1071 GT
+31 (0)20 679 6252
info@cafegruter.com
www.cafegruter.com

Zuideramstel
This neighbourhood incorporates the most important business district of Amsterdam, De Zuidas or the 'Financial Mile'. Aside from the high rises and clear business focus, the area also has plenty of quiet residential areas and outdoor space. This creates an unusual blend of the corporate and the clean living, with lots of sports facilities and families enjoying the best of both worlds.

Where the locals recommend:

Tap Zuid
This neighbourhood beer café offers a global selection of beers from around the world in laid-back surroundings, with pavement seating for the warmer months.
Maasstraat 70, 1078 HL
+31 (0)20 205 2002
www.tapzuid.amsterdam
Bus/tram: Maasstraat

Kenko
This locally loved Japanese restaurant and sushi bar sates the corporate appetite for fresh and wholesome food. Kenko also does take-out sushi boxes, perfect for al fresco lunches and dinners.
Gustav Mahlerlaan 50
+31 (0)20 642 4600
info@kenkokitchen.nl
www.kenkokitchen.nl
Bus/metro/train/tram: Station Amsterdam Zuid

Amsterdamse Bos
Adjoining Zuideramstel is Amsterdam's very own forest. At more than 2,500 acres, it's three times the size of New York's Central Park. As well as plenty of outdoor space for brisk walks, there's a vast mixture of activity going on, including an open-air theatre, a biodynamic goat farm with produce for sale and a fun forest climbing park.
Amsterdamse Bos, 1182 DB
+31 (0)20 545 6100
www.amsterdamsebos.nl
Bus: Kalfjeslaan

Strandzuid
This bar is the Dutch interpretation of the German beer garden, and as well as abundant beers available on tap and by the bottle, there's also a city beach to relax at during the summer. In the colder months, this transforms into 'Zuidpool' ('South Pole') for a cosy, wintry backdrop to your eating and drinking. The surroundings are pristine on the edge of Beatrixpark.
Europaplein 22, 1078 GZ
+31 20 639 2589
info@unlimitedlabel.com
www.strand-zuid.nl
Bus/tram: Europaplein
Bus/metro/train/tram: Station RAI

Corso Como
This sleek and airy Italian

restaurant is flooded with natural light, and is ideal for an Italian meal or just a coffee and a catch-up with business colleagues or friends. Patrons tend to be the suited and booted local workers, but even the more casually dressed are not out of place here.
Strawinskylaan 77, 1077 XW
+31 (0)20 881 3131
info@triple-ace.nl
www.corsocomo.nl
Bus/metro/train/tram: Amsterdam Zuid

Zuidoost
This borough on the outskirts of the city, sometimes referred to as the Bijlmer, is a distinctly residential and green part of Amsterdam. Having been the focus of urban renewal projects over previous decades, Zuidoost is now characterised by apartment blocks, public parks and lakes. It's also the neighbourhood where the Ajax ArenA football stadium and entertainment spots such as the Heineken Music Hall can be found.

Where the locals recommend:

Gaasperpark
This park and nature reserve surrounds a huge lake with a 5km circumference. Outdoorsy types are kept entertained by the watersports centre offering canoeing, rowing, sailing and surfing lessons. It's also possible to explore the park on horseback, and stay overnight in the campsite.
Gaasperpark, 1108 AZ
Bus/metro: Gaasperplas

Ziggo Dome
Since the neighbourhood is the home of large entertainment venues in Amsterdam, check out the events listings at the Ziggo

Dome as well as the Heineken Music Hall. Plenty of big international musicians have played there, making it a great night out for visitors and Amsterdammers alike.

Arena Boulevard 61, 1101 DL
+31 (0)900 235 3663
info@ziggodome.nl
www.ziggodome.nl
Bus/metro/train: Amsterdam Bijlmer ArenA

Amsterdam Open Air

This annual open-air festival takes place in Gaasperpark every summer. It's all about music, camping and enjoying the nature in one of Amsterdam's much-loved parks.

Gaasperpark, 1108 AZ
info@amsterdamopenair.nl
www.amsterdamopenair.nl
Bus/metro: Gaasperplas

Kam Yin

Zuidoost has a high Surinamese population who moved to the area following Suriname's independence in 1975. As a result, this locally loved restaurant is a great spot to try both Surinamese and Indonesian cuisine.

Bijlmerplein 525, 1102 DP
+31 (0)20 409 5888
www.kamyin.nl
Bus: Anton de Komplein

Oma Ietje

Zuidoost is starting to become inhabited by hipsters and artists, as becomes clear from this Swedish style coffee house that emerged as a result of a crowdfunding campaign. It's all about coffee, sandwiches and "scandalously good cakes and cookies", while local artists showcase their work on the walls.

Heesterveld 3, 1102 SB
+31 (0)20 233 8150
info@omaietje.nl
www.omaietje.nl
Bus: Hakfort
Metro: Bullewijk

Photos: Oma Ietje

Photos: Amsterdam Open Air

East (Oost)

The eastern neighbourhoods of Amsterdam are being rapidly transformed by gentrification and renewal projects; many liken eastern neighbourhoods to De Pijp ten to 20 years ago. This multicultural area of Amsterdam is defined by vibrant streets, delicious ethnic cuisines and dozens of different languages permeating the air. It's also a region of particularly low lying land, meaning there's an abundance of man-made islands pocked with modern architecture, vast green spaces and a general beachy feeling. The dynamism, space and outdoor living make the area popular with young families and professionals.

Photo: Camping Zeeburg

A work day in east Amsterdam

Morning

Zoku
Stay and work at this innovative hotel-workspace concept. Page 188. Metro: Waterlooplein or Weesperplein Tram: Weesperplein

Home by Biggles
Stop for a coffee and slice of organic cake in this inspiring interiors store. Page 71. Bus/tram: Hogeweg

Frankendael Park
Enjoy a pre-lunch stroll through the previous estate of a wealthy Amsterdammer. Page 70. Bus/tram: Hogeweg or Hugo de Vrieslaan

Afternoon

De Kas
Treat your business associates to a lunch in this famous restaurant in a former greenhouse. Page 71. Bus/tram: Hogeweg

Studio/K
Do some work on your laptop in the hip café of this cultural venue. Page 70. Bus/tram: Javaplein

KNSM Island
Clear your mind with a stroll on this good-looking man-made island full of boutiques and cafés. Page 72. Bus: Levantplein or Azartplein. Tram: Azartplein

Evening

Volkshotel
This hub of entrepreneurial life is ideal for people-watching, a little work on the laptop or a creative business meeting. Page 193. Bus/metro: Wibautstraat

Girassol
Enjoy a Portuguese dinner overlooking the River Amstel. Page 71. Bus: Prins Bernhardplein

Canvas
Have a cocktail for a nightcap on the seventh floor of the Volkshotel. Page 71. Bus/metro: Wibautstraat

A day of play in east Amsterdam

Morning

De Ruyschkamer
Enjoy breakfast at this all-day neighbourhood café, lounge and dive bar. Page 71. Tram: Wibautstraat

The Netherlands Funeral Museum
Fans of oddball museums will enjoy this contemplative corner of eastern Amsterdam. Page 71. Bus/tram: Maxwellstraat or Kruislaan

Blijburg aan Zee
Take a pre-lunch visit to this artificial city beach. Page 72. Bus: Pieter Oosterhuisstraat

Afternoon

Vijfnulvijf
Enjoy an Asian lunch in this vintage-styled eatery. Page 70. Bus/tram: Molukkenstraat

Javastraat
Get a feeling of local life in Indische Buurt on this vibrant street. Page 70. Bus/tram: Javaplein

't Nieuwe Diep Distillery
Buy spirits made on-site in this magical pumping station. Page 70. Bus/tram: Soembawastraat or Insulindeweg

Evening

Hannekes Boom
Go for food and drinks at this waterside retreat with a beachy vibe. Page 72. Tram: Muziekgebouw Bimhuis

easylaughs
Enjoy an evening of laughs by this uber-talented improvised comedy group. Page 71. Tram: Korte 's-Gravesandestraat

Camping Zeeburg
Experience alternative city accommodation at this campsite with a countryside-island feeling. Page 191. Tram: Flevopark

Indische Buurt ('Indies neighbourhood')

This vibrant neighbourhood is a melting pot of cultures from Moroccan to Turkish, with an estimated 100 languages spoken in the area, and street names such as Timorplein and Borneostraat reflecting the multiculturalism. This diversity makes it a great place to find delicious cuisines and explore colourful residential streets. As well as the buzz of the neighbourhood, locals love to spend time in the wide open space of Flevopark, looking out over the lake, Nieuwe Diep.

Where the locals recommend:

Javastraat
This street is the centre of the neighbourhood, making it a great place to wander to soak up local life, and indulge in the produce of the many bakeries and pastry shops.
Javastraat, 1094 HB
Bus/tram: Javaplein

't Nieuwe Diep Distillery
Found inside a magical old pumping station in Flevopark, this distillery produces around 100 of its own spirits. Enjoy samples in the tasting room during the week, buy bottles to take home, or enjoy a tour at 16:00 every Friday.
Flevopark 13, 1095 KE
+31 (0)62 537 8104
info@nwedlep.nl
www.nwedlep.nl
Bus/tram: Soembawastraat or Insulindeweg

Studio/K
One of the hubs of gentrification in Indische Buurt, Studio/K is a café, bar, cinema and club, making it a daytime or evening venue, however chilled out or hectic you like it.
Timorplein 62, 1094 CC
+31 (0)20 692 0422
info@studio-k.nu
www.studio-k.nu
Bus/tram: Javaplein

Bedford Stuyvesant
This Javastraat café is a trendy spot along a buzzing street to stop for a coffee and a chat. Locals love to stop off here while window shopping during lazy weekends.
Javastraat 55, 1094 HA
+31 (0)20 334 2175
info@bedfordstuyvesant.nl
www.bedfordstuyvesant.nl
Bus/tram: Javaplein

Vijfnulvijf
This foodie hotspot offers top notch Asian fare in vintage-style surroundings with mismatched tables and chairs. It paves the way for a laid-back meal of bright flavours.
Insulindeweg 505, 1094 MK
+31 (0)20 358 5388
info@vijfnulvijf.nl
www.vijfnulvijf.nl
Bus/tram: Molukkenstraat

Watergraafsmeer
This largely residential eastern neighbourhood is a favourite with the city's professional workers and young families who enjoy a little space, but great access to the city centre. This neighbourhood is on the lowest lying land in the whole of Amsterdam, and the reclaimed land (polder) was first pumped dry in the 1600s. Nowadays residents enjoy the area for its abundant green spaces, from garden allotments to larger parks, and great access to the water, on the Amstel River on one side or the Amsterdam Rijnkanaal on the other.

Where the locals recommend:

Frankendael Park
This park is the only real reminder of the estates of wealthy Amsterdammers common in this neighbourhood in the 17th and 18th centuries. It's still possible to visit the original landowner's house on the seven acre plot, as well as the ornamental gate and restored gardens, all of which offer a slice of Amsterdam history.
Middenweg 72, 1097 BS
+31 20 423 39 30
info@park-frankendael.nl
www.park-frankendael.nl
Bus/tram: Hogeweg or Hugo de Vrieslaan

Javastraat photo: Cyril Wermers

The Netherlands Funeral Museum

Fans of obscure museums find another one to add to their list at this museum looking at funeral culture in the Netherlands over the centuries. The collection includes funeral coaches from throughout the ages and historical accounts of burial customs. It may be a little morbid for some visitors' liking, although others find it a magnificently peaceful spot to reflect in.

Kruislaan 124, 1097 GA
+31 (0)20 694 0482
info@totzover.nl
www.totzover.nl
Bus/tram: Maxwellstraat or Kruislaan

De Kas

This famous Amsterdam restaurant is found inside a former greenhouse, meaning it's flooded with natural light and graced with the grandeur of unusual architecture. Staying true to its roots, the restaurant grows much of its ingredients in its own greenhouses and herb garden, and during the warmer months diners also have the option to sit among the fragrant herbs outside.

Kamerlingh Onneslaan 3, 1097 DE
+31 (0)20 462 4562
info@restaurantdekas.nl
www.restaurantdekas.nl
Bus/tram: Hogeweg

Home by Biggles

This popular home decor store carries distinctive pieces of interior design ideal for finishing the look of any room. It's also a popular spot for locals to stop off to indulge in coffee and organic cake.

Middenweg 46hs, 1097BR
+31 (0)20 752 6555
info@mylemonade.nl
www.homebybiggles.com
Bus/tram: Hogeweg

easylaughs

Just a stone's throw from Watergraafsmeer is the home of this much-loved improvised comedy group. Audiences love the off-the-cuff nature of the performances that are wildly different every time.

Nieuwe Achtergracht 170, 1018 WV
+31 (0)61 902 6015
www.easylaughs.nl
Tram: Korte 's-Gravesandestraat

Wibautstraat

This street in Watergraafsmeer is often considered to be a separate neighbourhood or locality, due to the fact it's such a hub of life in eastern Amsterdam. The wide road is one block from the River Amstel and runs parallel to it. Although it's not the prettiest stretch of Amsterdam, it's practical due to its major transport hub, and is favoured by locals for the many sources of entertainment nearby.

Where the locals recommend:

Werkplaats

An east Amsterdam hub of entrepreneurial life attached to the trendy Volkshotel, this is a great place to people-watch the eclectic mix of co-workers based here. Alternatively, grab your laptop and a coffee and get your head down in the café for a while.

Wibautstraat 150, 1091 GR
+31 (0)20 261 2100
info@volkshotel.nl
www.volkshotel.nl
Bus/metro: Wibautstraat

Stek

This breakfast and lunch spot with hip industrial style offers an indulgent menu of all day breakfasts, steak dishes from tartare to steak mezzes, and hearty seasonal dishes. One of the newer additions to the Wibautstraat, it's already a firm favourite with the locals.

Wibautstraat 95, 1091 GK
+31 (0)6 365 77000
info@stek-amsterdam.com
www.stek-amsterdam.com
Bus/metro: Wibautstraat

De Ruyschkamer

Just around the corner from Wibautstraat is this neighbourhood café, lounge and dive bar, which is open all day for breakfast, bites and beers. There's also a regular calendar of events including live music, making it an ideal spot to soak up the feeling of local life for a few hours.

Ruyschstraat 34, 1091 CC
+31 (0)20 670 36 22
thuis@deruyschkamer.nl
www.deruyschkamer.nl
Tram: Wibautstraat

Girassol

In between Wibautstraat and the River Amstel is one of the oldest Portuguese restaurants in Amsterdam. With tables spilling out onto the riverside path, it's the perfect spot to enjoy fresh Portuguese flavours on mild Amsterdam days.

Weesperzijde 135, 1091 ES
+31 (0)20 692 3471
info@girassol.nl
www.girassol.nl
Bus: Prins Bernhardplein

Canvas

Also part of the Volkshotel complex, Canvas is on the seventh floor of the building. Although it's a restaurant and cocktail bar too, the locals really love to come here for the lively clubbing experience it offers.

Wibautstraat 150, 1091 GR
+31 (0)20 2612 110
info@volkshotel.nl
www.volkshotel.nl
Bus/metro: Wibautstraat

Zeeburg

This neighbourhood in the Eastern Docklands area is one of the more modern parts of the city, characterised by its network of man-made islands, peninsulas and connecting bridges. Known for its contemporary architecture, Zeeburg is a popular neighbourhood for young professionals and the city's international community, who love the easy access to Amsterdam Central Station, a little more accommodation space for their money, and views across the water of Amsterdam's traditional streets. During sunnier months, the abundance of man-made islands and waterside spots make it an especially popular locality.

Where the locals recommend:

KNSM Island

This man-made island is the perfect size for an afternoon walk while browsing a smattering of artsy homeware shops and boutiques. Unusual architecture and chichi cafés complete the clean-cut picture on this island haven.
KNSM Island, 1019
Bus: Levantplein or Azartplein
Tram: Azartplein

Hannekes Boom

One of the city's favourite places during summertime, Hannekes Boom is a place locals love for food, drinks and chilling out on the quayside. There's a laid-back beachy vibe by day and mid-week, while at the weekends, there's a DJ and dancing all night.
Dijksgracht 4, 1019 BS
+31 (0)20 419 9820
www.hannekesboom.nl
Tram: Muziekgebouw Bimhuis

Blijburg aan Zee

This artificial city beach attracts Amsterdammers in droves when the sun cracks a ray. It's perfect for swimming, sunbathing and chilling out at the beach bar, with beach parties going on into the night.
Pampuslaan 501, 1087 LA
+31 (0)20 416 0330
blij@blijburg.nl
www.blijburg.nl
Bus: Pieter Oosterhuisstraat

Espressofabriek

This IJburg café is a favourite spot of local residents, who enjoy the new varieties of coffee beans and the work of the skilled baristas. It's definitely the place in Zeeburg for coffee fanatics.
IJburglaan 1489, 1087 KM
+31 (0)20 774 7965
www.espressofabriek.nl
Bus/tram: Van Limburg Stirumstraat

Diemerpark

Lesser known but double the size of Vondelpark, Diemerpark offers a true slice of nature in Amsterdam. Wildlife abounds, with deer, grass snakes, kingfishers and 200 bird species. Cyclists, skaters and canoeists enjoy outdoor adventures here, while the quiet beach is a popular spot with families. The warmer months see the park play host to festivals and outdoor performances.
Diemerpark, 1095
Bus/tram: Diemerparklaan

Werkplaats - Photo: Mark Groeneveld

West

The western neighbourhoods of Amsterdam are found on the city's former agricultural land, which has been turned into post-war 'garden towns'. Many of these family oriented and multicultural neighbourhoods are undergoing ongoing redevelopment and improvements. Artists and other creative communities are starting to move in, while new cultural and artistic spaces are springing up all the time. With open space, plenty of cultural pastimes and trendy eateries, residents of western neighbourhoods enjoy a good quality of life with short commuting times into the city centre.

Foodhallen photo: Cyril Wermers

A work day in west Amsterdam

Morning

CityHub
Stay and work at this workspace-hotel ideal for travelling entrepreneurs. Page 188. Bus/tram: Ten Katemarkt

Street Art Museum Amsterdam
Gain creative inspiration from this street art tour of murals commissioned to improve the Geuzenveld-Slotermeer neighbourhood. Page 77.

OT301
Take a look inside this centre for alternative culture and the arts. Page 78. Tram: Jan Pieter Heijestraat (Overtoom)

Afternoon

De Foodhallen
Enjoy a business lunch using great quality produce in these eateries found inside an old tram station. Page 162. Bus/tram: Ten Katemarkt

Het Sieraad
Spend some time on your laptop in this renovated space for creative entrepreneurs. Page 76. Bus: Witte de Withstraat Tram: Postjesweg or Witte de Withstraat

Witte de Withstraat
Take a wander along this street brimming with art galleries and creative projects. Page 77. Bus: Witte de Withstraat Tram: Postjesweg or Witte de Withstraat

Evening

REM Eiland
Enjoy dinner with an entrepreneurial flavour in this restaurant suspended over the River IJ. Page 79. Bus: Koivistokade

Podium Mozaïek
Check out a performance at this cultural venue found inside a former church. Page 76. Bus/tram: Bos en Lommerweg

VLLA
Have a nightcap at this creative venue with a rolling schedule of artistic events. Page 77. Bus: Jan Tooropstraat

A day of play in west Amsterdam

Morning

Western Islands walk
Start the day with a walk around these interconnected islands, home to a cool, creative community. Page 79.

World Fashion Centre
Visit this centre for new and established fashion labels and eclectic events. Page 79. Bus: Delflandlaan or Koningin Wilhelminaplein. Tram: Delflandlaan

Şerifoğlu Café & Patisserie
Indulge in Turkish coffee and baklava at this renowned café. Page 77. Bus/tram: Plein '40-'45

Afternoon

Hartje Bos
Get some picnic lunch ingredients from this quirky deli, which also sells local arts and crafts. Page 76. Bus/tram: Karel Doormanstraat

Sloterplas
Have a picnic lunch overlooking this huge ecologically protected lake. Page 77. Tram: Sloterpark

Het Massagehuys
Treat yourself to a massage in this authentic massage house and tea parlour. Page 76. Bus/tram: Mercatorplein or Marco Polostraat

Evening

Frits
Have a burger and beer at this hip neighbourhood hangout. Page 76. Bus/metro: Mercatorplein

Westergasfabriek
Visit this venue inside a former gasworks for evening performances, cool bars and arthouse cinema screenings. Page 79. Bus: Van Hallstraat

Hotel Not Hotel
Stay over at this original hotel where every room is an immersive piece of artwork. Page 190. Bus: Witte de Withstraat Tram: Postjesweg or Witte de Withstraat

Western Amsterdam neighbourhoods:

Bos en Lommer

This family orientated and multicultural neighbourhood has residents enjoying the best of both worlds, with easy access to both the city centre and open green spaces. Trendier locals have started calling the area BoLo, increasing its cultural kudos even more. The locality is said to be home to residents speaking more than 120 different languages, making it one of the most eclectic of Amsterdam's neighbourhoods. It's had a mini redevelopment drive in recent years, meaning the area is now peppered with some cooler eating and drinking spots. Bos en Lommer is also becoming home to more points of architectural interest than previously, with some of the newer residential redevelopments winning major architecture prizes.

Where the locals recommend:

Erasmuspark

Amsterdammers love nothing more than sharing food over a picnic or barbecue in an open space, and Erasmuspark is the focus of this pastime in Bos en Lommer. Named after the famous Dutch theologian and philosopher Desiderius Erasmus, the park is particularly unique as it's surrounded entirely by canals.
Jan van Galenstraat, 1056 BW
Bus/tram: Jan van Galenstraat

Hartje Bos

This small neighbourhood deli sells gorgeous ingredients, ready to cook meals and an eclectic mixture of products made locally, from bow ties to jam. There are also occasional evening events with themed food and live music.
Admiraal de Ruijterweg 275, 1055
Bus/tram: Karel Doormanstraat

Bos en Lommerplein market

This relatively recently renovated outdoor market runs all day Tuesday to Saturday and sells an eclectic array of goods. It's a great way to capture a slice of local life.
Bos en Lommerweg, 1055 RW
Bus/tram: Erasmusgracht

Podium Mozaïek

This cultural venue is found inside a former church and plays host to world music, theatre and dance reflective of the many different nationalities living in the area. At the weekends, Theatercafé Mozaïek serves a Turkish brunch from 11:00 to 15:00, with a feast of small plates that have attracted a loyal following.
Bos en Lommerweg 191, 1055 EE
+31 (0)20 580 0381
info@podiummozaiek.nl
www.podiummozaiek.nl
Bus/tram: Bos en Lommerweg

Van de Buurt

This café is all about a simpler and local way of life. Food is locally sourced, including crayfish from the canals, and entertainment comes in the form of a piano and board games. Locals just love whiling away afternoons here.
Gerard Callenburgstraat 1, 1055 TV
+31 (0)20 370 1661
info@vandebuurt.nl
www.vandebuurt.nl
Bus/tram: De Rijpstraat

De Baarsjes

This trendy neighbourhood has a mixture of young professionals and artists, who love the fact they live just a 15 minute bicycle ride from the city centre. The locals also have plenty to keep them entertained closer to home. De Baarsjes has been the focus of investment in many cultural projects, resulting in the emergence of a number of multifunctional art spaces. This is another western neighbourhood with a strong multicultural flavour, with dozens of different international residents bringing a vibrant mixture of cultures to the locality.

Where the locals recommend:

Het Sieraad

Previously a technical school that opened in the 1920s, this impressive building was renovated in 2005 to become a space for creative entrepreneurs. Spaces are hired out on a regular basis for art exhibitions and performances, while Lokaal Edel is the on-site restaurant and bar. Styled like a vintage living room, it's a popular place for socialising and laptop working.
Postjesweg 1, 1057 DT
+31 (0)20 820 0928
info@edelevents.nl
www.edelevents.nl
Bus: Witte de Withstraat
Tram: Postjesweg or Witte de Withstraat

Het Massagehuys

This 'massage house' of minimalistic design has walls lined with massage oils and cast iron teapots ready and waiting for your post-massage tea or infusion. Locals love the authentic and invigorating environment.
Jan Evertsenstraat 110, 1056
+31 (0)20 612 3251
info@massagehuys.nl
www.massagehuys.nl
Bus/tram: Mercatorplein or Marco Polostraat

Frits

This neighbourhood bar is all about burgers and beers in a hip but cosy interior. A beer and a burger is a steal at less than €10. It's a place to spend the whole evening, with plenty

of craft beers to try, and open until 1:00 or later every day.
Jan Evertsenstraat 135, 1057 BV
+31 (0)20 233 9796
www.frits-amsterdam.nl
Bus/metro: Mercatorplein

Witte de Withstraat
This street has emerged as a well-known area filled with galleries and spaces running artistic projects. It's the ideal place in De Baarsjes to wander idly and gain creative inspiration.
Witte de Withstraat 127, 1057
Bus: Witte de Withstraat
Tram: Postjesweg or Witte de Withstraat

Café Cook
This traditional Amsterdam brown café has an interior that feels like a cosy living room, and a huge terrace for afternoons in the sun.
James Cookstraat 2, 1056 RZ
+31 (0)20 612 0547
www.cafecook.nl
Bus/tram: Mercatorplein or Marco Polostraat

Geuzenveld-Slotermeer
This area was previously full of farmland, but after World War II was redeveloped as one of the popular post-war 'garden towns'. Since the early 2000s, the area has been subject to an ongoing urban renewal project — one of the largest in Europe — that has seen the neighbourhood become a more popular residential area for families, couples and those who don't mind a short commute into Amsterdam. This is a particularly diverse neighbourhood, with an estimated 65% of local residents originating from outside the Netherlands.

Where the locals recommend:

VLLA
Along with the redevelopment of this neighbourhood have come new projects and spaces promoting creativity and culture. VLLA is one of them, found inside an old funeral home, and now a bar, club and stage rolled into one. Private rooms where families used to mourn are now artist studios, while an eclectic schedule of events involves performances, art installations, dinner and movie nights, and Friday night club nights with a DJ.
Willem Roelofsstraat 9, 1062 JX
+31 (0)64 610 8272
info@vlla.nl
www.vlla.nl
Bus: Jan Tooropstraat

Sloterplas
This lake was dried out in the 1600s and then dug out again in the 1950s as part of the garden city model. The huge lake is ecologically protected since it's home to some rare wildlife. Watersports lovers feel at home here, with everything from canoeing to sailing available. Quieter corners of the surrounding Sloterpark are home to private allotments and small gardens.
Christoffel Plantijngracht 4, 1065 DA
+31 (0)20 617 5839
sloterplas@topsail.nl
watersportcentrumsloterplas.nl
Tram: Sloterpark

Street Art Museum Amsterdam
This museum is actually a street art tour where a local Geuzenveld-Slotermeer resident takes curious visitors on a tour of hidden street art and murals that have been especially commissioned in the neighbourhood.
streetartmuseumamsterdam.com

Plein '40-'45
This market is a hub of local life, perfect for trinket shopping and people-watching. It's open daily from 9:00 to 16:00.
Plein '40-'45, 1063 KP
winkelcentrum-plein4045.nl
Bus/tram: Plein '40-'45

Şerifoğlu Café & Patisserie
This traditional Turkish café does the best desserts in Amsterdam. It's the ideal spot for a pit stop for Turkish coffee and baklava.
Slotermeerlaan 115, 1063 JN
www.serifoglu.nl
Bus/tram: Plein '40-'45

Osdorp
Another of Amsterdam's post-World War II 'garden towns' that has undergone significant renewal in recent years, Osdorp is known as a family-focused residential neighbourhood. With large tracts of greenery and increasingly striking new architecture, Osdorp is steadily becoming a popular suburb for Amsterdammers to raise their families.

Where the locals recommend:

Theater De Meervaart
This theatre and cultural venue plays host to hundreds of performances every year, and has hosted big name comedy talent such as Bill Bailey and Alan Davies.
Meer en Vaart 300, 1068 LE
+31 (0)900 410 7777
www.meervaart.nl
Bus/tram: Ruimzicht

WoZoCo
Architecture fans should visit the WoZoCo, or Oklahoma apartments, for an example of the innovative architecture the neighbourhood has become known for. The apartments have blocks protruding from them at odd and unexpected angles, giving the impression they are hanging at apparently perilous proportions. The

apartments were designed by architects MVRDV to meet the needs of the increasingly populous locality.
Corner of Ookmeerweg and Reimerswaalstraat, 1069 AH
Bus: Baden Powellweg or Reimerswaalstraat

Markt Tussenmeer
This outdoor market running only on Tuesdays has been previously shortlisted for the 'best market in the Netherlands' accolade.
Tussen Meer, 1068 GA
+31 (0)20 518 0800
Bus/tram: Osdorpplein

Dierenweide Osdorp
This petting zoo in a random location in the middle of a residential area is home to sheep, donkeys, pigs and more. It's a great place for families and to experience a countryside-in-the-city feeling. The zoo has a social conscience too, providing employment to people with disabilities.
Botteskerksingel 30b, 1069 XT
+31 (0)20 610 1808
www.cordaan.nl
Bus: Osdorper Ban or Saaftingestraat
Metro: Baden Powellweg

Restaurant Syriana
This restaurant has a Middle Eastern grotto-style interior and a glass conservatory with views of Amsterdam's only windmill open to the public, the Sloten Windmill. The food on offer is delicious Syrian and Lebanese cuisine, with the option to smoke hookah water pipes.
Akersluis 8, 1066 EZ
+31 (0)20 669 0933
info@syriana.nl
www.syriana.nl
Bus: Langsom

Oud West
Bordering Vondelpark and Amsterdam's famous canal ring, this neighbourhood is home to the city's movers and shakers who love the proximity to the city's best-loved social spots. It's a family-friendly residential area with a distinct hint of cool, with plenty of bars, cafés and foodie spots to meet the needs of the professional, multicultural residents. There are some interesting places of historical interest in this neighbourhood too, such as the Hollandsche Manege, the oldest horse riding school in the Netherlands, whose current building is also a national monument (rijksmonument).

Where the locals recommend:

OT301
In the past, this location has been squatted in by a group of artists and then a film academy. Nowadays it's a centre celebrating alternative culture, and plays host to concerts, art workshops and music studios. There's also a non-profit print shop and a vegan restaurant, De Peper, on-site.
Overtoom 301, 1054 HW
ehbk@ot301.nl
www.ot301.nl
Tram: Jan Pieter Heijestraat (Overtoom)

Du Cap
This café, bar and restaurant is locally famed for its huge outdoor terrace that becomes one of the liveliest places in western Amsterdam during the summer.
Kwakersplein 2H, 1053 TZ
+31 (0)20 612 4455
etendrinken@ducap.nl
www.du-cap.nl
Bus: Kinkerstraat
Tram: Clercqstraat or Kinkerstraat

Bellamystraat
For those interested in experiencing a slice of Amsterdam's industrial history, taking a stroll down the village-like Bellamystraat is just the ticket. The Olympiagebouw at number 49 used to be a cinema, and subsequently a mosque, then a Turkish cultural centre. It's now a dance school. Number 74 is a forge that has been in operation for more than 100 years, number 80 was previously a country house retreat, and the pretty courtyard at number 91 used to be a diamond cutting company, and subsequently a cocoa factory.
Bellamystraat, 1053 BP
Bus/tram: Ten Katemarkt or J.P. Heijestraat

Lalibela
This locally loved, buzzing restaurant serves traditional Ethiopian food at great prices. A little off the beaten track, it's a neighbourhood gem with a loyal following.
Eerste Helmersstraat 249, 1054 DX
+31 (0)20 683 8332
www.lalibela.nl
Tram: J.P. Heijestraat (Overtoom)

LAB111
Found inside a former pathology lab, this cinema for film buffs shows everything from arthouse to cinematic documentaries. Filmgoers can enjoy a food and film package, while the generally curious will enjoy exploring the vegetable garden peppered with beehives.
Arie Biemondstraat 111, 1054 PD
+31 (0)20 616 9994
info@lab111.nl
www.lab111.nl
Tram: J.P. Heijestraat (Overtoom)

Slotervaart
Another of Amsterdam's post-war 'garden towns', this previous agricultural land is now a predominantly residential area. Characterised by apartment blocks pocked with garden squares, Slotervaart is a multicultural neighbourhood where residents enjoy a quieter pace of life, with barbeques and

picnics during the warmer months a popular pastime.

Where the locals recommend:

World Fashion Centre
The place for fashionistas to visit, both established and emerging fashion labels showcase their designs here. As well as fashion label showrooms, it's also a popular spot for fashion related events. Opposite is the stylish WestCord Fashion Hotel.
Koningin Wilhelminaplein 13, 1062 HH
+31 (0)20 511 0173
info@worldfashioncentre.nl
www.worldfashioncentre.nl
Bus: Delflandlaan or Koningin Wilhelminaplein
Tram: Delflandlaan

Coffeemania
This trendy café — a small chain — takes its coffee seriously, with infinite options of coffee beans and froths, milks and syrups.
Ottho Heldringstraat 3, 1066 AZ
+31 (0)20 760 0361
www.coffeemania.nl
Tram: Jacques Veltmanstraat or Heemstedestraat

Old West
This second hand shop for children's clothes and toys is a local favourite. With a cute and quirky interior and a great choice of clothes, it's a place to get acquainted with local life and Amsterdam's sharing economy while picking up some bargains for the kids.
De Clercqstraat 63, 1053 AD
+31 (0)20 750 8165
oldwestamsterdam@gmail.com
www.oldwestamsterdam.nl
Tram: De Clercqstraat

Du Maroc
With a large local Moroccan population, Slotervaart is the place to try some Moroccan food, and this simple eatery is the place to do it. With a wide range of Moroccan and international

foods on offer at great prices, you'll feel like you've stumbled on a local secret.
Comeniusstraat 513, 1065 BX
+31 (0)20 617 3408
www.restaurantdumaroc.nl
Bus/tram: Cornelis Lelylaan

SodaSoda
Embracing Amsterdam's clean-living ideals, this store is focused on hand-made, eco-friendly and health conscious products, such as beeswax cloths to replace cling film and dishwashing powder made of salts instead of chemicals and plastic. Although it's predominantly an online store, customers are able to visit the office to pick up their products by prior arrangement.
Winkler Prinshof 9II, 1065 XL
www.sodasoda.nl
Tram: Robert Fruinlaan

Westpoort
This neighbourhood incorporates Westerpark and the Western Islands. Westerpark is a spirited, gentrified neighbourhood, full of independent shops, trendy cafés and a healthy smattering of cultural pursuits. Modern architecture blends in with the famous Amsterdam School style, while wide waterways and green spaces mean spending time outdoors is a way of life.

Where the locals recommend:

Western Islands walk
Previously the home of ship-works and the West India Trading Company's warehouses, the interconnected islands of Bickers Island, Prinsen Island and Realen Island are now home to artists in quirky canal boat studios and the city's creative workforce.
Western Islands, 1013

Westergasfabriek
This former gasworks building is now a destination for food, coffee and culture, with pavement cafés, food and design markets, special club nights and an arthouse cinema. It's also a favourite location for creative businesses to locate.
Polonceaukade 27, 1014 DA
+31 (0)20 586 0710
info@westergasfabriek.nl
www.westergasfabriek.nl
Bus: Van Hallstraat

REM Eiland
This totally unique restaurant is found suspended above the River IJ inside an old pirate TV tower. It's the location from which opportunists broadcast an alternative progamme, offering another choice to the single channel available in the Netherlands before the 1960s.
Haparandadam 45-2, 1013 AK
+31 (0)20 688 5501
www.remeiland.com
Bus: Koivistokade

Westerpark
As well as its huge tract of green space, Westerpark itself is also home to restaurants, a jazz café, a zoo, bars, a cinema, TV studios and a monthly market on Sundays. This cultural and creative hub has also made a name for itself for being the first park in the Netherlands with free Wi-Fi.
Haarlemmerweg, 1014 BE
Bus: Van L. Stirumstraat

Buurtboerderij
This multi-purpose 'neighbourhood farm' is a quirky and down-to-earth place to spend some time. Listen to live music most Wednesdays and Sundays, eat a cheap and tasty three course menu, or pick blackberries outside.
Spaarndammerdijk 319, 1014 AA
+31 (0)20 337 6820
info@buurtboerderij.nl
www.buurtboerderij.nl
Bus: Spaarndammerdijk

Events and key dates

An outline of national holidays and popular events, as well as quirky and vibrant annual festivals in Amsterdam.

January

New Year's Day: National holiday

National Tulip Day
Head over to Dam Square for this annual mid-January event organised by Dutch tulip growers, where anyone can come to pick free tulips.

Fashion Week
This bi-annual fashion show with a focus on Dutch fashion attracts fashion fans from across the Netherlands and Europe.
www.fashionweek.nl

Grauzone Festival
The new-wave music, art and film festival has impressive line-ups and an avid following of those who love the arts.
www.grauzonefestival.nl

Whisky Weekend
Take part in nosings and tastings while smoking cigars and listening to Scottish music.
www.whiskyamsterdam.nl

Jumping Amsterdam
This dressage and showjumping event attracts horse-lovers and thrill-seekers to Amsterdam every year.
www.jumpingamsterdam.nl

Flamenco Biennale
Dance lovers are wowed by sultry performances by world renowned and up-and-coming flamenco talent.
www.flamencobiennale.nl

February

24H Oost
A series of 24H Amsterdam events take place across the city during the year. This edition involves workshops, parties and performances in the east of the city.
www.iamsterdam.com

Pop Arts Festival
This festival for all things puppet and object theatre, dance, mime and visual artistry, offers a varied and quirky programme every year.
www.popartsfestival.nl

Wonderland Festival
This indoor house and techno festival is for those who want to party all day and all night.
www.verknipt.org

Cross-linx Festival
This travelling indie and classical music festival visits different cities in the Netherlands throughout the month, stopping off for a cacophony of events in Amsterdam.
www.cross-linx.nl

March

24H West
A series of 24H Amsterdam events take place across the city during the year. This edition involves workshops, parties and performances in the west of the city.
www.iamsterdam.com

5 Days Off
This five day electronic music festival hosts events across the city and attracts clubbers and media art lovers.
www.5daysoff.nl

Pink Film Days (Roze Filmdagen)
This Amsterdam event is much-loved, particularly in the city's LGBTQ community, and has been running since 1996. Films from across LGBTQ cinema are screened at locations throughout the city.
www.rozefilmdagen.nl

Amsterdam Coffee Festival
This event celebrates one of Amsterdam's great loves: coffee. With dozens of artisan roasters, barista-run workshops, coffee tastings and live music, this is the place to get a caffeine fix in March.
amsterdamcoffeefestival.com

Cinedans
This festival for international dance films, documentaries and interactive installations attracts an artsy crowd every year. There are also lectures, debates and workshops about film and dance.
www.cinedans.nl

National Restaurant Week
This bi-annual event gives foodies cut price meals at top restaurants.
www.restaurantweek.nl

Chocoa Festival
This chocolate festival comes complete with plenty of tastings and chocolate workshops.
www.chocoa.nl

HISWA Amsterdam Boat Show
Celebrate the city's affinity with the water at this annual show for boating and watersports.
www.hiswarai.nl

April

Easter Sunday and Easter Monday: National holidays

King's Day (Koningsdag)
This national holiday on 27 April is to celebrate King

Willem-Alexander's birthday. The city turns orange on this day as a show of Dutch national pride, and everything from parties and parades to a giant flea market take place on Amsterdam's streets.

Tulip Festival
Celebrating the famous symbol of the Netherlands, this festival sees more than 400,000 tulips adorning participating locations across Amsterdam.
www.tulipfestival.com

Imagine Film Festival
This film festival celebrates everything horror, sci-fi, cult, anime and fantasy, attracting filmmakers and fans from across the globe.
www.imaginefilmfestival.nl

Sounds of the Underground (SOTU)
This alternative and indie music event takes places in cool venues in and around Amsterdam's famous Vondelpark.
www.sotufestival.com

Meibock Festival
The spring version of the Bokbierfestival in autumn, the Meibock Festival is all about sampling bottled and draught 'bok' beers.
www.pint.nl

Springsnow Festival
Celebrate the annual blanket of blossom that falls from the trees in what has become known as the Springsnow Festival. During this time, people are encouraged to explore the Elm Route, an 8km long walking and cycling path, as well as various art installations celebrating nature's confetti.
www.springsnow.nl

May

Dodenherdenking
4th: Remembrance of the Dead (Dodenherdenking), commemorating members of the armed forces of the Kingdom of the Netherlands who died in wars or peacekeeping missions since World War II

Bevrijdingsdag
5th: Liberation Day, celebrating the end of the occupation by Nazi Germany during World War II. Expect many parties across the Netherlands.

Ascension Day, Pentecost Sunday (Whitsunday), Pentecost Monday: National holidays

Hemeltjelief Festival
This Ascension Day family festival involves Amsterdam bands and DJs playing on stages lining the River IJ, with plenty of theatre and crafts going on too.
www.hemeltjelieffestival.nl

Vondelpark Open Air Theatre
This al fresco theatre starts in May each year in Amsterdam's famed Vondelpark, and continues throughout the summer.
www.openluchttheater.nl

World Press Photo
This annual travelling exhibition of the world's best news photos from the year before kicks off in Amsterdam.
www.worldpressphoto.org

Pacha Festival
This annual festival for clubbers kicks off the summer season of dance.
www.pachafestival.com

Rolling Kitchens
A haven for foodies, this annual food truck festival happens in Westergasfabriek, where people eat an amazing array of food.
rollendekeukens.amsterdam

ArtZuid
This four month event comes to Amsterdam every two years, and involves outdoor installations of stunning sculptures in southern Amsterdam.
www.artzuid.nl

909 Festival
This techno festival has a good helping of the Amsterdam quirk, situated in the forest in Amsterdamse Bos.
www.909.nl

June

Taste of Amsterdam
This Amstelpark food festival offers visitors culinary delights, workshops and live cook-offs.
www.tasteofamsterdam.com

Holland Festival
This festival has been running since 1947, giving Amsterdammers the best theatre, dance and opera productions from around the world.
www.hollandfestival.nl

UNESCO World Heritage Weekend
During this weekend each summer, all nine Dutch UNESCO World Heritage Sites run a series of events highlighting their importance to Dutch culture. In Amsterdam, this revolves around Amsterdam's Canal Ring, which is one of the heritage sites.
whc.unesco.org

ZOOmeravonden
Saturday evenings in the summer are all about visiting Amsterdam's Artis Royal Zoo for late openings, live music and workshops for children.
www.artis.nl

International Theatre School Festival (ITs)
This long-running festival gives Dutch and international theatre performers the opportunity to show off their talents to the public.
www.itsfestivalamsterdam.com

Open Garden Days
Private gardens of the impressive homes lining Amsterdam's canals open to the public for a weekend in June, for a usually unseen perspective on the city.
www.opentuinendagen.nl

dOeK
This unusual festival involves a collective of improv jazz musicians jamming together with amazing skill.
www.doekfestival.org

Architecture Day
This annual event has tours and a series of special events exploring Amsterdam's new architecture and new ideas.
www.dagvande-architectuuramsterdam.nl

July

Amsterdam Gay Pride
This celebration of the commitment to equality of the LGBTQ community involves a weekend full of festivities. It attracts hundreds of thousands of revellers every year to a vibrant array of events.
www.pride.amsterdam

Fashion Week
This bi-annual fashion show with a focus on Dutch fashion attracts fashion fans from across the Netherlands and Europe.
www.fashionweek.nl

Over het IJ Festival
This outdoor festival on the banks of the River IJ brings together theatre, DJs and food. This trendy summertime festival also has improv and poetry readings inside shipping containers.
www.overhetij.nl

Milkshake Festival
This vibrant and free-spirited summer festival is filled with music, performance art and a chilled-out vibe.
www.facebook.com/milkshakefestival

Julidans
This modern dance festival consists of two weeks packed full of dance performances.
www.julidans.nl

Comedytrain International Summer Festival
Amsterdam's Toomler comedy club hosts well-known stand-up comedians from across the world for six weeks over the summer.
www.toomler.nl

Amsterdam Roots Festival
This celebration of roots music involves vibrant indoor and outdoor events and a whole host of international stars.
www.amsterdamroots.nl

Hortus Festival
Listen to classical music amid the peaceful surroundings of Amsterdam's botanical gardens. Evening events run throughout the summer.
www.hortusfestival.nl

Kwaku Festival
This month-long series of events celebrates cultural diversity, originating from the abolition of slavery in Suriname and the Dutch Antilles in the mid-1800s. The festivities centre on Nelson Mandelapark and include music events, a Caribbean market, street food vendors selling international flavours, and the Kwaku Cup football tournament.
www.kwakufestival.nl

August

Grachtenfestival (Canal Festival)
This famous festival centres on Amsterdam's historic canal belt, with classical concerts permeating the stunning surroundings. The pièce de résistance is the Prinsengracht Concert, which takes place on a pontoon and is broadcast live on Dutch TV.
www.grachtenfestival.nl

Uitmarkt
This popular event officially opens the cultural season, attracting hundreds of thousands of international visitors to the huge range of musical performances.
www.uitmarkt.nl

World Cinema Amsterdam
This event sees two weeks of indoor and open air screenings of the best of international cinema.
www.worldcinemaamsterdam.nl

Mysteryland
This dance festival is all about bright costumes, themed stages and electronic music.
www.mysteryland.nl

De Parade Theatre Festival
Every year a travelling theatre tours the Netherlands and arrives in Amsterdam's Martin Luther King Park in August. There's everything

from outdoor performances to productions in secret locations.
www.deparade.nl

Pluk de Nacht
This free open-air film festival is all about watching films by the waterside from deck chairs.
www.plukdenacht.nl

September

Dam Tot Damloop (Dam to Dam Run)
This 10 mile (16.1km) race takes runners all the way from central Amsterdam to Zaandam. There's also a shorter four mile course for those who want to build up their stamina slowly, and a shorter course for children.
www.damloop.nl

24H Zuid/Zuidoost
A series of 24H Amsterdam events take place across the city during the year. This edition involves workshops, parties and performances in the south east of the city.
www.iamsterdam.com

Amsterdam Jazz Festival
Dutch and international jazz artists come together to create lively shows for jazz fans.
www.amsterdamjazzfestival.info

Amsterdam City Swim
This public event sees thousands of swimmers powering along a 2,000 metre course through the city's canal routes.
www.amsterdamcityswim.nl

Valtifest
This uber-quirky annual festival has a different theme every year, with an accompanying dress code that is strictly adhered to by most festival-goers. Accompanying

the unofficial fashion show is music by a host of DJs and artsy pastimes.
www.valtifest.nl

Amsterdam Fringe Festival
Theatre, art, comedy and dance performances take over the city during this ten day festival.
www.amsterdamfringefestival.nl

Fotoweek
Photography exhibitions and workshops invade Amsterdam for a week, compelling everyone to become amateur photographers.
www.defotoweek.nl

Discovery Festival
This interactive science festival encourages discovery and features scientific experiments and installations, as well as music and cocktails.
www.discoveryfestival.nl

Amsterdam Heritage Days
Famous buildings, key monuments and private residences open their doors to the public free of charge for one weekend a year only.
www.iamsterdam.com

October

Amsterdam Marathon
This marathon has been going since the 1970s, attracting avid runners and their supporters in droves.
www.tcsamsterdammarathon.nl

24H Noord
A series of 24H Amsterdam events take place across the city during the year. This edition involves workshops, parties and performances in the north of the city.
www.iamsterdam.com

Bokbierfestival Festival
The autumn version of the Meibock Festival in spring,

the Bokbierfestival is all about sampling bottled and draught 'bok' beers, and there are dozens of varieties to choose from.
www.pint.nl

Amsterdam Music Festival
The most famous DJs flock to this dance festival for a weekend of partying.
amsterdammusicfestival.com

Amsterdam Halloween Festival
Think gruesome costumes, horror movie marathons and themed food during this much loved annual tradition.
www.halloweenamsterdam.com

KLIK! Amsterdam Animation Festival
Perfect for lovers of animated films, this festival looks at the latest innovations and the best animated films.
www.klik.amsterdam

Afrovibes
Some of the most talented African performers put on stunning shows over the course of a long weekend.
www.afrovibes.nl

November

Amsterdam Light Festival
The city is illuminated by lights and installations by artists and designers during this festival that runs until January. Plenty of events run during the festival, including a Christmas light parade, canal cruises and special menus in restaurants.
www.amsterdamlightfestival.com

Museum Night
More than 50 museums in Amsterdam stay open late on the first Saturday of every November. Expect special tours, workshops, food, drink and entertainment.
www.museumnacht.amsterdam

International Documentary Film Festival (IDFA)
The newest and best documentary films from around the world are shown in Amsterdam to captive audiences.
www.idfa.nl

Amsterdam Art Weekend
Galleries across Amsterdam put on special exhibitions showcasing the most talented up-and-coming artists.
www.amsterdamart.com

International Storytelling Festival
Storytellers from around the world are gathered for a series of special events to celebrate the art of storytelling.
www.facebook.com/
Storytellingfestivalamsterdam

Meesterlijk
This independent design fair celebrates artisans and craftsmanship, covering everything from jewellery and fashion to food design and furniture.
www.meesterlijk.nu

December

5th: Sinterklaas
when presents are exchanged for Saint Nicholas (Sinterklaas) Day

Christmas Day and Boxing Day: National holidays

Lovedance Festival
A series of mostly clubbing events and parties mark World Aids Day on 1 December every year.
www.lovedance.nl

Merry Jazzmas
This annual event sees the performance of festive songs with a jazzy twist in the Royal Concertbouw.
www.concertgebouw.nl

Winterparade
Live acts and performances (mostly in Dutch) take place around a 500-seater table adorned with festive food and hungry revellers.
www.tafelvandeidee.nl/
winterparade

Winter ice rinks
A few locations in Amsterdam have festive rinks for ice skating:, including Leidseplein, Museumplein and Jaap Eden.
www.kermisplaza.nl
www.iceamsterdam.nl
www.jaapeden.nl

Winter markets
Amsterdam and the surrounding area is filled with winter markets during the Christmas period. Some of the best and most popular are in Rembrandt Square, Haarlem and slightly further afield in the picturesque Keukenhof estate in Lisse.

See also: business events and key dates (p144)

Photo: Ruud Jonkers - IDFA

Performance by Tanja Ritterbex at Ornis A. Gallery, during Amsterdam Art Weekend 2015. Photo: Fabian Landewee

Cycling around is the best way to gain inspiration.

Martien Mellema
Creative Director for Vogue Netherlands

Tell us about your background and how this led to you becoming the Creative Director for *Vogue Netherlands*.

After finishing fashion school, I started working at a weekly magazine, which was the best way to learn the ropes of working in an editorial environment. I got a lot of chances there. After that, I was asked to be the fashion director for a magazine that was a bit more underground, where I worked for a while. It was good for me to learn more about the different aspects of fashion, including the commercial, non-mainstream and experimental sides of things. I went on to freelance for *Mexx, Vogue Bambini* and various other magazines and fashion brands. In the late 1980s, *Elle* was launched in the Netherlands and I became the first fashion editor for the publication. It was great to start working on a more international scale. We went on to launch *Elle Junior* and *Elle Girl*. When Condé Nast launched *Glamour* in the Netherlands, I became the fashion and style director there. And from there, we launched *Vogue Netherlands*.

Which project are you most proud of?

I really enjoy the challenge of any new project and working hard with the team to make things happen. Every edition of the magazine is so different and there's always a great sense of achievement when the magazine is published and you see the fruits of your labour. If I had to choose one achievement I'm particularly proud of, it was always my dream to launch *Vogue Man Netherlands*, and I was finally able to do this in 2015. There's so much going on in menswear with denim, sneakers and youth culture, so I'm grateful I'm now able to have my own input into this area of the fashion scene.

What does a typical day at *Vogue Netherlands* involve for you?

A typical day involves me juggling a lot of different things. I'll go around to visit all our different teams who are shooting various features for us. Since I love my bicycle, I will usually cycle between the different locations, in true Amsterdammer style! I also spend quite a lot of time in the art department's office, discussing the look and feel of each feature we're working on. My job involves a lot of talking and generally keeping up with what the team are doing.

Describe the fashion aesthetic of Amsterdam.

The Amsterdam style has a down-to-earth and free-spirited feeling. It's a city that looks great in denim; Amsterdam is actually the denim centre of the world. It started in the 1990s when Pepe Jeans moved its headquarters from London to Amsterdam. Around the same time, the Dutch denim brand G-Star started to become popular on an international scale. Employees of these brands eventually branched out and developed their own denim brands and styles, meaning the number of denim brands in Amsterdam grew and grew. That attracted more brands such as Hilfiger Denim and Levi's Vintage Clothing, and suddenly, Amsterdam was the denim capital of the world. Now we even have a House of Denim Jean School in the city. When it comes to denim to wear myself, I'm personally a big fan of Levi's Vintage and Japanese brands such as 45rpm.

What are your future plans?

Vogue Man Netherlands is still in its infancy, so I'm really focused on making that a huge success. I'm really inspired by following all the interesting changes happening in the fashion world and crafting innovative ways to integrate these changes into magazines. That is a never-ending task that gives me a real buzz, so I'll be doing that for a long time yet. And finally, it's been my dream for quite some time now to make documentaries for children, showcasing nice simple stories about how people across the world live and how we share a lot of the same ideas and values.

Where is your favourite place to work in Amsterdam?

I really like working from the *Vogue Netherlands* office, which is located a little bit outside of the city centre in the Zuidoost neighbourhood. I like it because it feels a bit anonymous, which gives me a feeling of freedom. It's close to a neighbourhood which I think is interesting, called the Bijlmermeer, or 'the Bijlmer' as a lot of Amsterdammers say. It's really vibrant, it's multi-cultural and there's so much going on, meaning there's a lot to explore and discover. I really believe this is becoming a new hub for creative people in Amsterdam because it's more affordable than other parts of the city.

Where are the best places to eat near where you work?

The Bijlmermeer is a great neighbourhood to visit for world cuisine. Since it's a neighbourhood with a traditionally high immigrant population, it's one of the best parts of the city to go to try food from Suriname and Java. My favourite is Padjak de Smeltkroes. It's quite a casual, canteen-style restaurant and the flavours are amazing. World of Food is a food market inside a converted parking garage, where there are lots of different stands where you can try delicious food from around the world.

Have you got any favourite cafés that are good for business meetings?

I really like planning my meetings in various different cafés all over the city and I have two particular favourites. Café-restaurant De Ysbreeker is a café and brasserie in a really old building. I love the Art Deco style and the terrace that overlooks the River Amstel. My other favourite is Bakery Gebroeders Niemeijer, really near Amsterdam Central Station. It's an artisanal French bakery that has a really nice feeling inside.

Tell us about the Amsterdam neighbourhood you live in.
I've lived in Amsterdam for my whole life and I feel most at home in the east of the city. It's where I grew up and where my husband and I are bringing up our son and daughter, who are now teenagers. The east is also a part of the city where there are a lot of changes, particularly with the construction of more man-made islands for people to live and work on. I live in IJburg, which is a newer part of the city; I love the mix of people and cultures there. The city centre is a 30 minute bicycle ride away, and I love the combination of having access to Amsterdam's busy city centre, but also being surrounded by a very chilled-out locality at home. Since IJburg is made up of islands, you get a real sense of freedom just from the fact you are over the water. With all the water surrounding us, it also means we can swim in the summer and ice-skate in winter.

Where are your favourite places for food and drink in your neighbourhood?
I really like Mchi, which has a great mix of Asian food. They have sushi, Asian tapas and Chinese dishes like Peking duck. The food is fresh and great quality, while the ambience is very mellow. Pizza Heart is our favourite for a take away pizza, which we have for a treat every once in a while! Nearby, Blijburg beach is a great place to have a drink in the evening. My family and I consider Blijburg to be 'our beach'!

Where's good for a cocktail in the city?
I like Canvas on the top floor of the Volkshotel. It's got a very creative feeling and a lot of people from the creative industries like to go there. Some people go for a cocktail or two, others go to dance the night away. I personally love to go for a caipirinha. I also like the Twenty Third Bar at the Okura Hotel in De Pijp. It's one of only two Okura Hotels in Europe and has transported a genuinely Japanese feeling to its location in Amsterdam. The bar is very high-end, popular for champagne or cocktails, and has views that give a great overview of the city.

Where do you eat out in different Amsterdam neighbourhoods?
In the west of the city, I love eating at the relatively new Restaurant DS in De School, which is an old technical school. It's also a nightclub, concert venue, exhibition space and gym, but I love the restaurant for its fresh tasting menus. The south of Amsterdam is the best place to discover secret Japanese restaurants — every time I go I discover a new favourite. In the east of the city, Café Kadijk is the best place to go for Indonesian food; they

serve very simple but tasty small plates. Wilde Zwijnen in Indische Buurt is excellent for modern Dutch food. The interior has a bit of a rustic feel making it really cosy. Toko Ramee, near the famous Albert Cuyp Market, sells ingredients for Indonesian cooking and has some amazing and cheap take-away dishes. It's one of the oldest stores in the city.

How do you get creative inspiration in Amsterdam?
Cycling around is the best way to gain inspiration. I look at the people and the architecture of the city, but even just the feeling of being on a bike makes me feel inspired. Luckily I spend a lot of time cycling, so I gain inspiration easily!

What music would be on your ideal soundtrack to Amsterdam?
Herman Brood was a Dutch musician and is considered by many to be the only Dutch rock 'n' roll star. Any music by him should be on everyone's soundtrack to the city. I've seen him perform and he was amazing. Herman Brood also had a good working relationship with the photographer, Anton Corbijn, who has given us some great inspiration for Vogue Man Netherlands.

Where do you go to get away from it all?
The Hortus Botanicus is an old botanical garden found unexpectedly in the centre of Amsterdam. It's an inspiring place to pop into for some peace and reflection. Sauna Deco is one of my favourite places to relax in Amsterdam. It's a spa on the Herengracht in the midst of the canal district. It has a decadent feeling because the interior was previously part of a 1920s Parisian department store that was shipped over to Amsterdam. You can go in to use the huge sauna, where you can lay down on comfortable beds. There are lots of places to sit and relax, or you can get a massage too for an extra treat. Being active is a form of relaxation for me too, and one activity I love doing is boxing at the Conservatorium Hotel. It's an excellent workout and I feel reinvigorated by the end.

Where are your favourite places for enjoying Amsterdam's cultural pursuits?
Huis Marseille is a photography museum that has very good exhibitions of mostly Dutch, Japanese and South African work. Tropenmuseum is an ethnographic museum and one of the largest museums in the city inside a really grand building; it's also a great place to take children.

What is Amsterdam's best quality?
I'm always impressed by the fact that Amsterdam is like a small town, yet there's so much going on. Particularly for people in creative industries, there's this amazing feeling of people creating so many new things

together, and the city has a real atmosphere of freedom for us creative people. And you can't talk about the best things in Amsterdam without mentioning the canals: they are iconic and make the city like nowhere else in the world.

What's the current trend in Amsterdam?
The current trend is definitely for people to get back to their roots, and start something that belongs to them. You see this in the entrepreneurial spirit in the city, with people setting up their own and often very creative businesses. And you see this in fashion and style too. People are looking for authentic brands and local craftsmanship. The Amsterdam sneaker label Filling Pieces by the designer Guillaume Chin embraces this trend, as does Zoe Karssen.

How can visitors to Amsterdam live like locals during their stay?
The best way to live like a local is to get a bike and cycle everywhere. Cycling is also a great way to explore and discover the city. Even if you decide to walk instead of cycle, just wander around without using your phone's navigation system for the most interesting and authentic experiences.

Which part of Amsterdam should be given more kudos?
The north of Amsterdam (Amsterdam Noord) is really up-and-coming. It used to be very industrial and boring, but there's so much going on there now and it's a great part of the city to explore. One of my top recommendations for Amsterdam Noord is the EYE Film Museum. It's in a really modern building by the water and is an interesting place to explore everything about film. Hotel de Goudfazant is a great place to eat in Amsterdam Noord. It's a large dining room in this huge, previously industrial space and they serve really creative Dutch and French cuisine.

How would your friends describe you?
Energetic, curious and sociable.

What's the best thing about your life?
Working in fashion has been my life for more than 30 years now and I love it, particularly working with a team to create a story.

Martien's Amsterdam

Places to visit

Amsterdam Oost (east)
Train: Station Amstel or
Muiderpoort

Bijlmermeer
1102 - 1104
Bus/metro/tram: Bijlmer ArenA

Blijburg Aan Zee
Pampuslaan 501, 1087 LA
+31 (0)20 416 0330
blij@blijburg.nl
www.blijburg.nl
Bus: Pieter Oosterhuisstraat

Conservatorium Hotel
Van Baerlestraat 27, 1071 AN
+31 (0)20 570 0000
info@conservatoriumhotel.com
www.conservatoriumhotel.com
Tram: Van Baerlestraat

EYE Film Museum
IJpromenade 1, 1031 KT
+31 (0)20 589 1400
info@eyefilm.nl
www.eyefilm.nl
Boat/bus: Veer Buiksloterweg

Hortus Botanicus
Plantage Middenlaan 2a, 1018 DD
+31 (0)20 625 9021
www.dehortus.nl
Bus/tram: Artis

Huis Marseille
Keizersgracht 401, 1016 EK
+31 (0)20 531 8989
info@huismarseille.nl
www.huismarseille.nl
Tram: Keizersgracht
(Leidsestraat)

IJburg
1087 GJ
Bus:, Diemerparklaan,
Lumierestraat, Pieter
Oosterhuisstraat or
Vennepluimstraat
Tram: Diemerparklaan,
IJburg, Lumierestraat or
Vennepluimstraat

Sauna Deco
Herengracht 115, 1015 BE
+31 (0)20 623 8215
info@saunadeco.nl
www.saunadeco.nl
Bus/tram: Nieuwezijds Kolk

Tropenmuseum
Linnaeusstraat 2, 1092 CK
+31 (0)88 004 2800
info@tropenmuseum.nl
www.tropenmuseum.nl
Bus/tram: Eerste van
Swindenstraat

Eating and drinking

**Bakery Gebroeders
Niemeijer**
Nieuwendijk 35, 1012 MA
+31 (0)20 707 6752
info@gebroedersniemeijer.nl
www.gebroedersniemeijer.nl
Bus: CS Prins Hendrikplantsoen
Bus/metro/train/tram: Amsterdam
Centraal

Café Kadijk
Kadijksplein 5, 1018 AB
+31 (0)6 1774 4411
info@cafekadijk.nl
www.cafekadijk.nl
Bus: Kadijksplein

**Café-restaurant De
Ysbreeker**
Weesperzijde 23, 1091 EC
+31 (0)20 468 1808
info@deysbreeker.nl
www.deysbreeker.nl
Tram: Wibautstraat/Ruyschstraat

Canvas
Wibautstraat 150, 1091 GR
+31 (0)20 261 2110
hello@volkshotel.nl
www.volkshotel.nl/canvas
Bus/metro: Wibautstraat

De Goudfazant
Aambeeldstraat 10H, 1021 KB
+31 (0)20 636 5170
www.hoteldegoudfazant.nl
Bus: Hamerstraat or Johan van
Hasseltweg
Boat: Veer Zamenhofstraat

Mchi
IJburglaan 1295, 1087 JJ
+31 (0)20 776 6004
info@mchi.nl
www.mchi.nl
Bus/tram: Lumierestraat

Padjak de Smeltkroes
Bijlmerdreef 1289, 1103 TV
+31 (0)20 495 2076
info@smeltkroeszo.nl
www.smeltkroeszo.nl
Bus: Station Ganzenhoef or
Grubbehoeve

Pizza Heart
Pampuslaan 34, 1087 LA
+31 (0)20 416 5225
www.pizzaheart.nl
Bus: Pieter Oosterhuisstraat

Restaurant DS
De School, Doctor Jan van
Breemenstraat 3, 1056 AB
+31 (0)20 737 3197
info@deschoolamsterdam.nl
www.deschoolamsterdam.nl
Bus/tram: Scheldestraat

Toko Ramee
Ferdinand Bolstraat 74, 1072 LM
+31 (0)20 662 2025
info@tokoramee.com
www.tokoramee.com
Tram: Albert Cuypstraat

Twenty Third Bar
Ferdinand Bolstraat 333, 1072 LH
+31 (0)20 678 7111
www.okura.nl/culinary/twenty-
third-bar
Bus/tram: Scheldestraat

Wilde Zwijnen
Javaplein 23, 1095 CJ
+31 (0)20 463 3034
info@wildezwijnen.com
www.wildezwijnen.com
Bus/tram: Javaplein

World of Food
Develstein 100, 1102 AK
info@worldoffoodamsterdam.nl
www.worldoffoodamsterdam.nl
Bus: Develstein

See also

Find out more about Martien Mellema at www.vogue.nl and on Instagram @martienvoguenl

Photo: Raymond van Mil

chapter 2

Work

Find out where to rent office space or plug into one of Amstrerdam's many co-working offices.

Working in Amsterdam
Emerging creative start-up hub

Amsterdam has been quietly working its way up the ranks to become one of the most attractive cities to live, work and be an entrepreneur. The city is now one of the best places in Europe to be creative, free-spirited and successful in business.

Amsterdam enjoys a unique set of circumstances that have fostered this environment: a history of innovation for its central role in global maritime trade, the well-known liberal mind-set of the Dutch that sparks creativity, and a large English-speaking community.

With these factors combined, it's no wonder the city has utterly embraced the concept of co-working, and has developed a thriving start-up mentality, particularly since the Amsterdam Startup initiative launched in 2014 to help make the city even more attractive to start-up founders. More benefits are being launched all the time, from start-up visas to additional investment funds. Start-up founders are rightly given a lot of kudos in Amsterdam, hailed as being sources of innovation with the potential for positive societal change.

Dutch start-ups are now said to generate at least €500 million a year, and 60% of job growth comes from companies that were formed in the last five years. There are more than 1,000 start-up companies in Amsterdam and dozens of investors looking out for the next innovation to back. Furthermore, consumers in Amsterdam are tech-savvy, making it the perfect spot to launch new tech products. Non-tech products do extremely well too, and industries such as fashion are booming: Amsterdam is now widely considered to be the denim capital of Europe. Added to the noticeable success of businesses, an estimated 50,000 foreign nationals live and work in Amsterdam, and with 178 nationalities making up the fabric of the city, English is as prevalent on the streets as Dutch is.

The informal culture and commonplace flexible working in Amsterdam makes the city a popular choice for those looking for a great work-life balance. The unemployment rate in the Netherlands is one of the lowest in the EU, but many people choose to work part-time or flexible hours to enjoy the other areas of their lives too. Amsterdam is the ideal city to do this in, with a buzzing arts community, a flourishing restaurant and bar scene, and picturesque waterways everywhere. With most places just a walk, cycle or boat journey away, life couldn't be much better for Amsterdam's spirited workforce.

Essentials

Find out a little bit more about the practicalities of moving to Amsterdam to work or to set up a business.

Bank accounts

It's possible to open a Dutch bank account by visiting any branch of your bank of choice. Check with the bank in advance which documents they need to see in order to open the account. Usually, you'll need to bring some ID (passport or identity card), an official document proving your Dutch address e.g. a tenancy agreement if you're renting an apartment, and your personal public service number (burgerservicenummer), which you get when you register with the local municipality to where you're living. If you are originally from a country outside the EU, you must also bring your residence permit.

Most Dutch banks charge an annual fee for their bank accounts, and taking out a credit card incurs an additional charge.

If you want to open a business bank account, you will need to bring additional documents to your bank of choice. These documents include the deed of incorporation of your business, names of your legal representatives, a notary document stating the addresses of the company directors in their country of origin, copies of the company license and business registration certificate. Some banks may require more documentation, so check in advance of visiting the bank. It can take up to three weeks

to set up a business bank account.

Some of the major banks in Amsterdam include:
ABN AMRO:
www.abnamro.nl
ING:
www.ing.nl
Rabobank:
www.rabobank.nl
SNS-bank:
www.snsbank.nl
Triodos:
www.triodos.nl

Business insurance

In the Netherlands, you are not obliged to take out business insurance specifically for risks you may run into as a company owner. There are a number of voluntary insurance schemes to cover various elements of business life, such as company liability, professional indemnity and buildings insurance. It's always best to gain advice from a financial advisor to discuss the particular requirements and risks of your business.

There are various financial advice organisations specialising in the needs of expats in Amsterdam, including:
Expats Amsterdam:
www.expatsamsterdam.com
Expat Finance:
www.expatfinance.nl
Horlings:
www.horlings.nl
Trifium:
www.trifium.nl

Business registration

Setting up a business in the Netherlands is widely known as setting up a B.V. — a private limited liability company. You can even do this from your home country if this is more convenient. To set up a B.V., you first need to set up a bank account and then check

your proposed company name is available with the Chamber of Commerce (Kamer van Koophandel). Then you'll need to have a notarial deed of incorporation drawn up in Dutch, which allows the company's data to be registered with the Trade Register at a local Chamber of Commerce. The Chamber of Commerce automatically forwards all business registration details to the tax authorities, who will then contact you. The whole process takes up to two weeks.
Chamber of Commerce:
www.kvk.nl

Directory enquiries

There are various Dutch services available to search for the contact information of businesses and individuals.

These include:
De Telefoongids:
www.detelefoongids.nl
Telefoonboek:
www.telefoonboek.nl
Yellow Directory:
www.searchyellowdirectory.com
Zoekenbel:
www.zoekenbel.nl

Healthcare

Anyone living in the Netherlands must register with a Dutch health insurer. You will then pay a monthly contribution towards your healthcare, part of which will be deducted from your wages if you have an employer, and you pay the rest directly to the insurer. This gives you access to healthcare in the Netherlands. The basic package costs around €100 per month and includes GP appointments, hospital stays, medical prescriptions and outpatient services such as physiotherapy.

Some of the main health insurers in the Netherlands are:

Aegon:
www.aegon.nl
DSW Zorgverzekeraar:
www.dsw.nl
ONVZ:
www.onvz.nl
Univé Verzekeringen:
www.unive.nl
Zilverenkruis:
www.zilverenkruis.nl

You can also use a price comparison website such as Zorgwijzer: www.zorgwijzer.nl

Municipal taxes

Individuals and businesses have to pay taxes to the local municipality. The value of the tax is calculated by the local municipality each year, and is called the WOZ-waarde. Additional municipal taxes include a waste collection levy, a sewage levy and a water purification levy for properties connected to the sewage network. New residents and business owners should contact their local municipality when they move in to find out the rates payable for the specific property.

Sim cards

While most international sim cards can operate on Dutch mobile phone networks, you're likely to get better call and data rates by getting a Dutch sim card. Lebara stands can often be found in the city centre and at Schiphol airport, where free sim cards are handed out. Alternatively, you can buy a sim card from any mobile network's shop.

These are some of the most commonly used mobile providers in Amsterdam:

Hi:
www.hi.nl
KPN:
www.kpn.com
Lebara:
www.lebara.nl
Telfort:
www.telfort.nl
T-Mobile:
www.t-mobile.nl
Vodafone:
www.vodafone.nl

Social security

Those residing and working in the Netherlands have to pay a contribution to the Dutch social security system, Sociale Verzekeringsbank (SVB). The exact contribution required is calculated alongside your tax contributions.

Tax

Foreign nationals living and working in the Netherlands pay different types of taxes depending on their tax residency status. If you receive income solely from within the Netherlands, you will be considered a non-Dutch tax resident. If you work for an employer, the employer will automatically pay your taxes to the tax authority (Belastingdienst). Everyone living in the Netherlands has to complete an income tax return by 1 April every year, declaring income from work, home, shares, savings and investments. Foreign nationals working in the Netherlands receive a 30% tax exemption for the first 96 months of living in the country.

Owners of businesses in the Netherlands have to pay Corporation Income Tax (CIT) and Value Added Tax (VAT). CIT is charged at 20% on the first €200,000 of taxable profits, and 25% on taxable profits over €200,000. A VAT rate of 21% is applied to most goods and services, while a 6% rate of VAT is applied to goods and services such as food, newspaper advertisements and hotel accommodation.

Belastingdienst:
www.belastingdienst.nl

Utilities and service connections

Gas and electricity

Gas and electricity is often included in the monthly rent for residential and business properties. If this isn't the case, it's usually possible to transfer the previous tenant's connection over to your name. If you want to change provider or look for a better deal, and you're allowed to in the terms of your rental agreement, contact one of the major energy suppliers or use a price comparison website.

The major gas and electricity providers in the Netherlands are:

Eneco energie:
www.eneco.nl
EnergieDirect:
www.energiedirect.nl
Eon:
www.eon.nl
Essent:
www.essent.nl
Oxxio:
www.oxxio.nl
Nederlandse Energie Maatschappij:
www.nle.nl
Nuon:
www.nuon.nl

Price comparison websites include:

Energievergelijker:
www.energievergelijken.nl
Price Wise:
www.pricewise.nl
Utility Provider:
www.utility-provider.nl

Internet connection

There are many internet packages available in Amsterdam, many of which include TV and phone connection too. Approach one of the main internet providers or use a price comparison website to see which package and provider best meets your needs. Remember to research this early on if you want internet connectivity as soon as possible after moving into a premises.

Main internet providers in the Netherlands include:
KPN:
www.kpn.com
T-Mobile:
www.t-mobile.nl
Tele2:
www.tele2.nl
Vodafone:
www.vodafone.nl
Ziggo:
www.ziggo.nl

Price comparison websites include:
Internetten:
www.internetten.nl
Utility Provider:
www.utility-provider.nl

Telephone lines
Phone lines are often included in internet packages. See the main internet providers section and price comparison websites listed above.

Television packages
TV packages can often be included with internet and telephone lines, but there are also plenty of standalone packages. Contact one of the main providers directly, or use a price comparison website to help you find the best deal for you.

The main television providers are:
CanalDigitaal:
www.canaldigitaal.nl
KPN:
www.kpn.com
Ziggo:
www.ziggo.nl

Price comparison websites include:
Digitalevisie:
www.digitelevisie.nl
Internet Bestellen:
www.internetbestellen.nl

Water
The Amsterdam area is served by the water provider, Waternet. Water meters installed in residential and business properties measure water consumption, calculating how much you owe as a result. As soon as you move into a property, note the meter reading and then register with Waternet.

Waternet:
www.waternet.nl

Visas, work and residence permits
Residents originating from within the EU and EEA can live and work in Amsterdam without a work permit, visa or residence permit. EU and EEA nationals are, however, advised to register with the Immigration and Naturalisation Service (IND). Ask for a registration certificate when you do this, since the tax authorities and banks may ask to see this certificate. You must also register with the local Municipality Administration (GBA) where you live. When you register as living in the Netherlands, you will be given a unique Burgerservicenummer (BSN) or Sofi number, which is needed by employers to register you for tax.

Foreign nationals from outside the EU and EEA can apply to the IND for a combined residence and employment permit (GVVA), on the basis of being a highly skilled migrant, or working as a self-employed person.

Immigration and Naturalisation Service (IND):
www.ind.nl

Useful resources

City of Amsterdam course
The City of Amsterdam runs free five day courses for those who have recently arrived in the city, introducing them to different practical aspects of life in Amsterdam. The course lasts for about three hours every day and involves excursions while discussing the practicalities of work, taxes, healthcare and more.
www.amsterdam.nl/immigratie/inburgering

Other resources
DutchStartupDatabase:
www.dutchstartupdatabase.com
Expatcenter:
www.iamsterdam.com/expatcenter
Expatica:
www.expatica.com
I Am Expat:
www.iamexpat.nl
Just Landed Netherlands:
www.justlanded.com/netherlands
StartupJuncture:
www.startupjuncture.com

Find a job in Amsterdam

Although it's advisable to come to Amsterdam with a job lined up and with some savings to help you find your feet, there are plenty of resources and an abundance of recruitment agencies in the city to help you find employment. If you're not from the Netherlands but have the right to work there, make this explicitly clear on your job applications. The Dutch prefer CVs that get to the point succinctly, so keep your CV to a maximum length of two pages. Include factual information about your work history and education, and add a bit of personality with what you like to do in your leisure time. Although employers and recruitment agencies say it's preferable for applicants to learn Dutch, many also accept English-speaking candidates. Social media is widely used in the Netherlands, especially LinkedIn and Twitter, so keep your online profiles as current as your offline ones.

General job boards

I amsterdam job search
The I amsterdam website has a job search specifically for jobs in the city for non-Dutch speakers. There are typically thousands of jobs being advertised at any one time in a broad range of different fields. There's also an interactive jobs map of companies in Amsterdam recruiting English speakers. http://goo.gl/56WlDf

Monsterboard
The search function for this jobs portal is in Dutch only, but vacancies in English-speaking companies are written in English. They tend to advertise hundreds of vacancies daily across all sectors.
www.monsterboard.nl

Together Abroad
This jobs board is aimed specifically at non-Dutch people looking for a job in the Netherlands. There's a vast selection of jobs across all industries in Amsterdam, as well as practical information for newcomers to the country seeking employment.
www.togetherabroad.nl

Other general job boards:
Expatica:
jobs.expatica.com/netherlands
I Am Expat:
iamexpat.nl/career/jobs-netherlands
Jobs in Amsterdam:
www.jobinamsterdam.com
Careers in Holland:
www.careersinholland.com

Start-up jobs

Dutch Startup Jobs
This is the main online hub for start-up jobs available across the Netherlands, many of which are in Amsterdam. The website also features a handy list of hundreds of start-ups based in the Netherlands if you'd prefer to approach a company proactively instead.
www.dutchstartupjobs.com

AngelList
This start-up jobs portal advertises many start-up jobs in the Amsterdam area, most of which have a technical or developer focus. The website also lists start-up companies and investors in Amsterdam, as well as a few hundred jobs at any one time.
www.angel.co/amsterdam

StartUs
This international jobs board typically has a few hundred opportunities advertised for Amsterdam start-ups at any one time.
www.startus.cc/jobs/amsterdam

Other start-up job boards
F6S:
www.f6s.com
JobFluent:
www.jobfluent.com
Startupbootcamp:
www.startupbootcamp.org/jobs
Tech.eu:
www.techstartupjobs.com
Tech Startup Jobs:
www.techstartupjobs.com

Creative jobs

Most jobs in creative sectors in Amsterdam are advertised via the general or start-up job boards. There are a few specialist agencies listed below, or contact creative advertising and media agencies directly to find out about available opportunities.

Aquent
This agency specialises in jobs in design and creative fields, with a handful of Amsterdam jobs available at any one time.
www.aquent.nl

The Creative Movement
This jobs website lists creative jobs in the UK and Amsterdam. The site only advertises a few jobs at a time, but specialises in both freelance and permanent jobs for people working in graphic design, PR, marketing and digital.
www.thecreativemovement.com

Other creative job boards
Amsterdam Ad Blog:
www.amsterdamadblog.com/jobs
Intermediair:
www.intermediair.nl

Services

UWV WERKbedrijf
The Dutch public employment service has branches across Amsterdam, where staff can provide advice to jobseekers as well as information about job vacancies.
www.uwv.nl

Hiring staff

There's a huge amount of talent in Amsterdam, but it can be tricky to find exactly the right person for the job you need done. Be as specific as you can in job adverts and if you're a start-up company, advertise on start-up specific job websites to target people who are already engaged in the start-up world. Most of the websites listed on page 101 ('Find a job') are also good places to look for staff.

If you're looking for English-speaking staff, advertise the job in English and look for agencies and websites that specialise in recruitment for non-Dutch speakers. Educate yourself about Dutch employment laws and practices before you hire staff. For example, the working day is no longer than nine hours and the working week around 40 to 45 hours.

Some agencies and resources to help you hire staff in Amsterdam include:

Undutchables
This recruitment agency specialises in matching an international workforce with English-speaking opportunities in the Netherlands. Candidates of all levels of experience are represented here, and there are other perks for those trying to recruit staff, such as breakfast meetings with talks on relevant subjects and a searchable portal.
www.undutchables.nl

Unique
This Dutch agency specialises in finding candidates for multilingual jobs in the Netherlands. Candidates are especially strong in the fields of account management, brand development and marketing.
www.unique.nl

Blue Lynx
This agency specialises in recruiting international staff for businesses in the Netherlands, with candidates skilled in a number of professions, from marketing to technical leads.
www.bluelynx.com

Other agencies and resources for hiring staff:
Adams Multilingual Recruitment:
www.adamsrecruitment.com
Kelly:
www.kellyservices.nl
Michael Page:
www.michaelpage.nl
thegiglab:
www.thegiglab.com
Uitzendbureaus (recruitment agencies):
www.uitzendbureau.nl/uitzendbureaus/amsterdam

Office space

Many start-up companies may start their business in their home to try to save costs. If you wish to do this and are renting an apartment in Amsterdam, check the terms of your rental agreement to make sure you're allowed to. Others prefer the flexibility and sense of community co-working spaces bring (see p112). However, if you think hiring an office space would better suit your needs, Amsterdam has an abundance of options to match different criteria. Choose a neighbourhood that makes sense to you, whether it's about the location, the size of premises you can get for your money, transport links or the related businesses already in the area. Then start your hunt using one of the many commercial property portals and real estate agencies, which are a combination of international portals and local Amsterdam specialists. Before signing a contract, it's prudent to gain advice from a commercial property advisor or legal representative.

Office space portals

Launchdesk
Support an Amsterdam start-up while finding an office for your own start-up! Launchdesk was founded in Amsterdam, and now helps hundreds of businesses find work space. There are always dozens of office spaces being advertised on the website, as well as desks at co-working spaces.
www.launchdesk.nl

WehaveAnyspace
This website lists different types of working spaces available in Amsterdam, including co-working spaces, serviced offices and office spaces. It's particularly useful for users who need to be located in a specific neighbourhood in the city, but are flexible about the type of space they take on.
www.wehaveanyspace.com/en/office-space-amsterdam

Funda in Business
This straightforward website lists dozens of commercial properties available to rent at any one time, with easy to scan costs and office sizes. If you want a broader idea of what's out there, there's also a tab for browsing commercial properties that were recently rented.
www.fundainbusiness.nl/winkel/amsterdam

Other office space portals and agents:
Search Office Space:
www.searchofficespace.com
Colliers International:
www.colliers.com/en-gb/netherlands
The Office Operators:
www.theofficeoperators.com

Commercial property agents

Office Time
This agency has a great track record of sourcing office space and is used to working with start-ups as well as established businesses.
www.officetime.nl

DRS Real Estate
This easy-to-search commercial real estate agency has dozens of listings in the Amsterdam area at any one time.
offices.drs.eu

Savills
This global real estate brand has a specialist branch for sourcing commercial property in the Netherlands, with many properties in the Amsterdam area.
www.savills.nl

Other commercial real estate agencies:
Flexas:
www.flexas.nl
Amsterdam Beautiful:
www.amsterdambeautiful.nl
Kantoorruimtevinden:
www.kantoorruimtevinden.nl

Commercial property advisors

HG
This portal makes it easy to search for lawyers of different specialisms in Amsterdam.
www.hg.org

Russell
This law firm has commercial property law specialists who can advise on commercial property contracts and other legalities involved in renting an office.
www.russell.nl

AMS
This Dutch law firm has specialists in real estate and tenancy law who can advise on aspects of commercial property leasing.
www.amsadvocaten.com

For me, being an entrepreneur in Amsterdam is great because I think it's one of the best cities in the world to live in.

Photo: Julia de Boer - juliadeboer.com @TheNextWeb.com

Boris Veldhuijzen van Zanten

Entrepreneur, CEO and
co-founder of The Next Web

Tell us about your background. We hear you started out in circus school...
That's correct. I dropped out of school when I was 14 and applied to the circus school. I graduated after three years and then applied to art school. I graduated cum laude five years later and was accepted into a very exclusive art school in Amsterdam that comes with a stipend, a studio and access to the best artists in the world. It was during those two years that I really got involved with the World Wide Web and saw an opportunity to use my creativity to participate in this growing phenomena.

You're described as a 'serial entrepreneur'. Tell us about where your entrepreneurial journey has led you to so far.
A few years ago I was introduced to someone as "Boris, a serial entrepreneur". The person I met introduced himself as "Marc, a successful serial entrepreneur". I was amused and shocked at the same time, and he could tell. He explained to me that there are lots of serial entrepreneurs in the world, but usually those are just people who keep on failing at whatever they do, so end up calling themselves a "serial entrepreneur". I too have failed more often than I have succeeded, but I did sell my first company in 1999 and my second company in 2003, and I founded The Next Web (TNW) which is a successful company as well.

The Next Web is considered to be one of the most popular tech blogs in the world. Tell us how it started and how you made it so successful?
I wish I knew the answer to that so I could do it again! But seriously; we started off with a conference, which seemed like a cheaper option than sponsoring one. We wanted to get attention for a start-up we were about to launch, and this seemed like a good plan. We figured that even if we ran the event only to break even, it would still be cheaper than sponsoring someone else's event. Of course, we lost money on the first event and it was a lot harder than we thought, but we also enjoyed it and our audience loved it and pleaded with us to do more of these events. Then we launched a blog with a similar idea; we figured it would be better to have our own media channel to promote our events than having to negotiate with media

partners every year. We calculated that we would have to sell 60 extra tickets a year to be able to afford one full-time writer, so it made sense. Then the blog started growing faster than expected, and we started hiring more writers, and then we added adverts, and the whole thing got a lot bigger than we ever expected. One day I was complaining about the blog to someone and he said: "Well sure, that's a problem all media companies have." I went back to my co-founder and said: "You know, I just found out we are a media company!"

You were one of the members of the prestigious Startup Europe Leaders Club. What did this involve and which initiatives are you most proud of?
It involved travelling to Brussels once a quarter with a bunch of very successful European entrepreneurs and talking to politicians about the state of technology and innovation in Europe. It was always great to be able to share what we knew and see our informal tips being turned into formal questions or even policy. I also learned that being a politician is very different from being an entrepreneur. And as you can tell, I also learned how to answer questions more diplomatically too!

What is it like being an entrepreneur in Amsterdam?
The ecosystem for entrepreneurs is small and intimate. Most people know each other and are eager to help each other as well. Although the start-up scene is probably smaller than in London or Berlin, the quality of Dutch entrepreneurs seems high. We also have lots of Dutch people ending up at bigger foreign companies. There's a Dutch group of entrepreneurs who keep track of which Dutch people are active at C-level in companies around the world, and it's amazing to see how influential we are. For me, being an entrepreneur in Amsterdam is great because I think it's one of the best cities in the world to live in. I can travel by bicycle to the office, and then walk along the canals at lunchtime to get a sandwich. The kids can walk to the office after school and almost everything is at most a 20 minute bike ride away.

You also run TNW Labs, launching new start-ups. What innovation or start-up are you most excited about at the moment?
There's a company called Mila that I really like. I often joke that if TNW would disappear, I would apply to Mila and start doing helpdesk work for them. They analyse your inbox and show you which contacts are new this week. You can then invite them to LinkedIn, send them a welcome message or pass them on to your sales department, all with one click. It changes your inbox from being a to-do list filled by other people to a source of revenue. I love it and think they have a very bright future ahead of them.

Where's your favourite place to work in Amsterdam and what's the view out the window?
Our office is really amazing. It's across from the Dutch central bank, De Nederlandsche Bank, and our view is over a park. I don't have a desk at the office, so I'll work at a table or sitting on a couch. I also do most of my meetings walking around the park. If someone wants to discuss something, I'll buy them a coffee at our favourite coffee bar on the other side of the park, which is a place called Frederix. They serve great coffee, have free Wi-Fi and it's run by really kind people. It's amazing to me that we can walk around, watch the birds, discuss work and come back feeling refreshed instead of exhausted. I don't enjoy sitting in a small room around a table with fluorescent lighting. This is so much better.

What are your future plans?
My main focus is to build TNW into a worldwide tech media company. There's such a huge opportunity now because the whole world is turning digital. That's too exciting to pass up.

Tell us about the Amsterdam neighbourhood where you live. What's the vibe and what do you like about it?
I first moved to Amsterdam in 1996 and have been living there ever since. In 2001, I moved into the house we're currently living in, which is on a quiet side street in the city centre. We bought part of an old school, so our home is really just four school-rooms. It's big and light with high ceilings. We have several shops nearby and I really enjoy leaving the office between 17:00 and 18:00, taking one of the kids to the local supermarket to find something to eat, and then going home to prepare the meal. As we walk around the city, we always bump into people we know and chat with the many shop owners we're familiar with. It feels like living in a small city within a really big city.

What's your favourite place to eat out in your neighbourhood?
There are a few places I frequent. For those who have kids, there's a place called De Carrousel which serves pancakes. It's nothing fancy, but it has a nice view and children love it there. I also like Eetcafé De Fles which is situated in a basement. It's popular with students, with affordable but great food. You can also look into the kitchen and have a chat with the chef. He loves his work and is always working on something special. There's also a place called Restaurant Panini which is a family restaurant that's great for lunch. If the weather is nice, they have three small tables outside. It's located on a busy street and directly in front of the traffic lights, so if you pick a table around 18:00 you can see everybody on their bikes stop right in front of you. It's great for casual flirting, or just watching the locals.

Where is your favourite bar in the city?
There's a cute little bar in the Wolvenstraat that doesn't have a name.
People simply call it 'Wolfje' or the 'Wolvenstraat bar'. It is located at
number 23 and attracts some of the more hip Amsterdam locals. You'll
often see actors or models hanging out at the bar. I've been going there for
years and know the owners and most of the people who work there.

What do you like to do in your spare time in Amsterdam?
We have a very small boat that we enjoy taking on a tour of the canals
when the weather is nice. I also enjoy just walking into town on Saturdays,
buying WIRED magazine at The American Book Store and then reading it
at the Wolvenstraat bar. Sometimes we will go to the Klimmuur Centraal
indoor climbing wall next to Central Station and spend a few hours
climbing with the whole family.

Is there a certain smell you associate with Amsterdam?
The canals do create a very distinctive smell. You don't notice it much
when you're living there, but when you return to the city after being away
for a while you do notice it. We also have a beautiful zoo in Amsterdam,
and when the wind is blowing from that direction you can smell the
animals.

Where is your favourite chill-out place in the city?
I have a subscription to the health club at the Amstel Hotel, which is
an InterContinental hotel. I go there in the mornings to work out but
sometimes I'll also go at the weekend or evenings just to use the sauna or
hammam and relax in one of the deckchairs. When the weather is nice
you can sit outside and watch the boats go by. The Amstel Hotel is one of
the most luxurious hotels in Amsterdam and you really feel rich when you
hang out there.

Where's a good place to get a coffee in the city?
As well as Frederix which is close to the office, there's The Village Bagels,
which has great coffee and has a very nice informal terrace where you can
sit and look at the canal or the people walking by. A very special experience
is to go to the Amstel Hotel when the weather is nice and ask if you can
have your coffee on the terrace. You'll overlook the River Amstel and all the
little boats that pass by. You'll feel like the King of Amsterdam sitting there.
And if you stay long enough, you can go straight into an Aperol Spritz and
watch the sun go down over the city.

What is Amsterdam's best quality?
There's a certain atmosphere you could call laid-back or relaxed that I
really enjoy. People are kind and open, and they enjoy creative initiatives

and behaviour considered outside the norm. There's a lot of room for experimentation, including the dangerous kind, and people won't quickly judge or restrict you.

Is there anything you would change about Amsterdam if you could?
I wouldn't mind if it was bigger. If you compare Amsterdam with other well-known cities, you quickly see how tiny it is on the map. That's also one of the advantages of the city too, of course.

Where are good places to 'get lost' in Amsterdam?
I often go to the Albert Cuyp Market on Saturday to buy fish and fresh vegetables. It's a great experience to just start at one end and walk all the way to the other end of the market. Along the way you'll find a wide variety of products and many small food stands where you can get a quick snack. On Sunday, when you've got a hangover from enjoying everything Amsterdam has to offer, take a walk through the Vondelpark. You'll see a nice combination of healthy people jogging and people feeling awful because of their hangovers. There are many places where you can get a drink or breakfast, while enjoying a great view over the park and the people walking through it. There's also the Utrechtsestraat, which is packed with small shops selling clothing, design furniture, jewellery and other cool stuff. If you're looking for a gift for a friend, this is a great place to spend way too much money.

How would you advise visitors to Amsterdam to blend in and become citizens of the city for the duration of their stay?
Apart from doing all the regular stuff, I'd advise people to find a small bar and just stay there for a while in the morning. Then you can see how Amsterdam wakes up, what people's morning routines are, and how families travel to school together on bikes. In other big cities, those things tend to be more hidden. Dutch people enjoy meeting foreigners and practicing their English, so if you get a chance, try to have dinner at someone's house. We regularly have people over for dinner and we see that they really enjoy the experience.

What's the current trend in Amsterdam?
They say coffee is the new oil. There seem to be new coffee bars opening up around town every week. I enjoy coffee as well, so I don't mind.

Interview

Boris's Amsterdam

Places to visit

Albert Cuyp Market
Albert Cuypstraat, 1072 CN
albertcuyp-markt.amsterdam
Tram: Albert Cuypstraat

**InterContinental Amstel
Hotel (health club)**
Professor Tulpplein 1, 1018 GX
+31 (0)20 622 6060
amstel@ihg.com
amsterdam.intercontinental.com
Tram: Weesperplein

Klimmuur Centraal
Dijksgracht 2, 1019 BS
+31 (0)20 427 5777
amsterdam@deklimmuur.nl
www.deklimmuur.nl
Tram: Muziekgebouw Bimhuis

Natura Artis Magistra (zoo)
Plantage Kerklaan 38-40, 1018 CZ
+31 (0)900 278 4796
info@artis.nl
www.artis.nl
Bus/tram: Plantage Lepellaan

The American Book Center
Spui 12, 1012 XA
+31 (0)20 625 5537
info@abc.nl
www.abc.nl
Tram: Spui (Nieuwezijds
Voorburgwal)

Utrechtsestraat
Utrechtsestraat, 1017
www.utrechtsestraat.amsterdam
Bus/tram: Keizersgracht
(Utrechtsestraat) or Prinsengracht
(Utrechtsestraat)

Vondelpark
Vondelpark, 1017 AA
www.hetvondelpark.net
Tram: J.P. Heijesstraat or Rhijnvis
Feithstraat

Eating and drinking

Amstel Terraces
InterContinental Amstel Hotel,
Professor Tulpplein 1, 1018 GX
+31 (0)20 622 6060
amstel@ihg.com
amsterdam.intercontinental.com
Tram: Weesperplein

**De Carrousel
Pannenkoeken**
H.M. van Randwijkplantsoen 1,
1017 ZW
+31 (0)20 625 8002
info@decarrouselpannenkoeken.nl
www.decarrouselpannenkoeken.nl
Tram: Weteringcircuit/Weteringsch

Eetcafé De Fles
Prinsengracht 955, 1017 HJ
+31 (0)20 624 9644
info@defles.nl
www.defles.nl
Tram: Weteringcircuit/Weteringsch
or Keizersgracht (Vijzelstraat)

Frederix Micro Roasters
Frederiksplein 29, 1017 XL
+31 (0)20 223 1803
info@frederixcoffee.com
www.frederixcoffee.com
Bus/tram: Frederiksplein

Restaurant Panini
Vijzelgracht 3-5, 1017 HM
+31 (0)20 626 4939
info@restaurantpanini.nl
www.paniniamsterdam.nl
Tram: Weteringcircuit/
Weteringsch or Keizersgracht
(Vijzelstraat)

Village Bagels
Vijzelstraat 137, 1017 HJ
+31 (0)20 427 2213
www.villagebagels.nl
Tram: Keizersgracht (Vijzelstraat)

Wolfje
Wolvenstraat 23, 1016 EN
+31 (0)20 320 0843
www.facebook.com/Wolvenstra
at-23-1451239075117871
Tram: Spui (Nieuwezijds
Voorburgwal)

See also

Mila
www.mila.com
The Next Web
www.thenextweb.com
Wired Magazine
www.wired.com

**Find out more about
Boris Veldhuijzen van
Zanten at www.boris.to
and on Twitter @Boris**

Co-working

The concept of co-working suits the open-mindedness and self-motivation of the Dutch perfectly, so it's no wonder co-working spaces have really taken off in Amsterdam, particularly in recent years. In addition, the Netherlands has experienced a sharp increase in the proportion of self-employed workers, with more than 15% of the total workforce now working for themselves. So it makes sense the Dutch workforce is looking for thriving and inspiring places to work.

There are now dozens of co-working spaces across Amsterdam, some designed for those working in specific industries, and others with an 'anything goes' attitude. What all of them have in common is that they come with ready-made communities of like-minded people who are entrepreneurs, creators and innovators.

The provision of co-working spaces rarely ends at a desk and Wi-Fi connection thesedays, and co-working spaces in the emerging creative centre of Amsterdam are no different. As well as perks such as gourmet coffee and organic teas, co-working spaces often have a buzzing calendar of events, workshops and networking opportunities. Some Amsterdam spaces even provide a free communal lunch; others have gardens or rooftop terraces. Some offer business matchmaking and access to accelerator schemes; others have homely living rooms and coffee corners. And some come with on-site barbers and bicycle repair shops; others have photo studios and 'Nerd Yoga'.

As well as providing an atmosphere ripe for entrepreneurial activity and business success, the cheaper cost of co-working over renting an office space is a distinct pull for Amsterdam's nomadic workers. Day passes in the city's co-working spaces start from €20, part time flexible memberships start from €65 per month, and unlimited full time memberships start from €160 per month. And for those who are happy to exchange space for their skills and pay in 'social capital' instead, Amsterdam even has free co-working spaces peppered throughout the city.

The co-working scene in Amsterdam matches the city's personality down to a tee, combining quirk and creativity with an inherent drive to innovate. Whether co-workers are looking for a loft space or canal-side industrial building; whether they want to work alongside techies and developers or artists and designers; and whether they want flexible memberships so they can roam, or all-encompassing hubs helping every aspect of their working lives: there's most certainly a space for everyone in Amsterdam.

Photos: Impact Hub

Impact Hub

The vibrant international community of Impact Hub is an exciting place to be in Amsterdam's entrepreneurial scene. More than a co-working space, Impact Hub prides itself on bringing people together and sparking change for a better world through entrepreneurial ideas. As a result, Impact Hub members in Amsterdam range from those working on sustainability innovations to tech and creative change-makers. Subsequently, different levels of Impact Hub membership mean members can be involved as much or as little as they like in the community. As well as desk space, storage, fair trade coffee, organic fruit and tea, members have access to Friday afternoon networking events, hosted business matchmaking and access to acceleration programmes. Membership ranges from €75 per quarter for Friday afternoon access, to €240 per month for unlimited access.

Haarlemmerweg 10c, 1014BE
+31 (0)20 427 4283
amsterdam@impacthub.net
amsterdam.impacthub.net
Bus: Van Limburg Stirumstraat

Photos: The Startup Orgy

The Startup Orgy

This suggestively named co-working provider has two Amsterdam spaces, one in a canal-side loft and one in an industrial conversion. The inspired architecture of both paves the way for enlivening working locations for those wanting to get ahead with their business. Both spaces have a living room dedicated to the use of networking and hosting special events, while Ethiopian coffee and organic tea are available on tap. Part time membership starts from €99 per month and full time 'residency' starts from €225 per month.

www.thestartuporgy.com
Groenburgwal 24, 1011 HW
Reguliersdwarsstraat 73, 1017 BK
Tram: Muntplein

Photos: Mixtup

Mixtup

With a stark industrial interior and a calendar of events targeted at creative innovators, Mixtup is a visionary hub with an artsy community. Membership includes all the basics such as tea, coffee and internet connection, as well as shared facilities including a photo studio, lounge, 'coffee corner' and garden. Membership starts from €160 per month for full time, 24/7 access, from €65 per month part time, or €40 per day.

Eerste Jacob van Campenstraat 59, 1072 BD
+31 (0)68 151 3153
studio@mixtup.nl
www.mixtup.nl
Tram: Stadhouderskade (Ferdinand Bolstraat)

Photos: A Lab

A Lab

Coined as 'Amsterdam's ultimate living lab', this huge industrial space in the burgeoning north of Amsterdam prides itself on experimenting and creating, whether it's through technology, design, journalism, music, or any other of the 33 specially designed labs on-site. More than 300 creatives have already made A Lab their working home, making it a great place to hunker down alongside those at the forefront of Amsterdam's creative community.

Read an interview with A Lab's co-founder Árpád Gerecsey on p146

Overhoeksplein 2, 1031 KS
+31 (0)20 820 2363
info@a-lab.nl
www.a-lab.nl
Boat/bus: Buiksloterweg

Photos: Seats2Meet

Seats2Meet

The Dutch have a long tradition of autonomous working and openness, which has resulted in the idea that co-working doesn't always have to come at a financial cost. Seats2Meet has developed large open workspaces for people to drop into with their laptops free of charge; they even provide free tea, coffee and a buffet lunch. Since workers are not paying in cash, they're asked to contribute with 'social capital' instead, which means interacting with other users in the space and sharing expertise and ideas. The Seats2Meet website allows users to search and book an available space for a given day and time.

www.seats2meet.com

KantoorKaravaan

This quirky roving working space provider offers desks to work at in the middle of nature. The idea is that you can still work while enjoying holidays away from the city centre, but it's equally perfect for those who want some space for creative inspiration while they work. Kantoor-Karavaan usually has at least one space in operation in the Amsterdam area, and past spaces include a space floating on an island, and one inside a converted caravan. The spaces have Wi-Fi, coffee machines, small kitchens and compost toilets. Payment can be in cash or you can pay in alternative ways that benefit KantoorKaravaan and local surroundings.

+31 (0)64 905 8282
info@thetippingpoint.nu
www.kantoorkaravaan.nl

Photos: KantoorKaravaan

More co-working locations

Spaces

This globally recognised co-working provider has three impeccably designed spaces in Amsterdam. Comfortable chairs and book-adorned shelves give a homely feel, while booths and phone rooms offer a little privacy. Airy kitchens and in-house baristas provide creature comforts and a genuine home from home. Members also love the calendar of events and opportunities for networking with entrepreneurs and business owners from an eclectic array of industries. Membership includes access to other Spaces locations across the world during office hours.
spacesworks.com/amsterdam

Herengracht 124-128, 1015 BT
+31 (0)20 794 4700
amsterdam.hg@spacesworks.com
Bus/tram: Dam/Raadhuisstraat

Vijzelstraat 68-72, 1017 HL
+31 (0)20 240 4400
amsterdam.vs@spacesworks.com
Tram: Keizersgracht (Vijzelstraat)

Barbara Strozzilaan 101-201,
1083 HN
+31 (0)20 240 2400
amsterdam.za101@spacesworks.com
Bus/metro/tram: Station Rai

WeWork

With two canal-side locations in Amsterdam, WeWork brings its creative and community feeling to the city. Glass panelled corridors make the cosy spaces bright and inclusive, and the buzzy atmosphere is a real draw for members intent on realising their dreams. Weekly events, lounges and game rooms are ideal for networking and letting off steam, while micro-roasted coffee powers people through the day.
www.wework.com/amsterdam
joinus@wework.com

Weteringschans 165C, 1017XD
+31 (0)20 705 9565
Tram: Weteringcircuit /
Weteringschans

Weesperstraat 61-105, 1018 VN
+31 (0)20 705 9567
Bus/metro/tram: Waterlooplein

Het Nieuwe Kantoor

This Dutch co-working provider combines professionalism, simple design and creative passion. Applied to the two Amsterdam co-working spaces it runs, this results in a hard-working community of thinkers and creators. Different levels of membership means there is a package to suit all needs.
www.hnk.nl

Van Diemenstraat 20-200, 1013 CP
+31 (0)20 240 4430
receptie.amsterdamhouthavens
@hnk.nl
Bus: Barentszplein

Burg. Stramanweg 102-108, 1101 AA
+31 (0)20 240 4300
receptie.AmsterdamArena
@hnk.nl
Bus: Ventweg

Boven de Balie

This loft co-working space is found above Café De Balie and is the co-working home of an array of online entrepreneurs and freelancers. The sociable space offers a communal lunch every day and free tea, coffee and snacks, while there are plenty of rooms and breakout areas for meetings.
Kleine Gartmanplantsoen 10,
1017 RR
+31 (0)85 888 2211
info@bovendebalie.nl
www.bovendebalie.nl
Bus/tram: Leidseplein

The Thinking Hut

This co-working space in a former horse stable attracts a mixture of designers, marketing professionals, developers and start-up founders. Hosting regular events, workshops and opportunities for expert consultancy, membership of The Thinking Hut offers more than just a desk.
Mauritskade 55c, 1092 AD
+31 (0)62 735 7216
info@thethinkinghut.com
www.thethinkinghut.com
Tram: Korte 's-Gravesandestraat

Workspace Six

Attracting an array of tech, design, copywriting and start-up professionals, Workspace Six offers a design-conscious interior and a ready-made network of like-minded people. Workspace Six also runs a regular programme of courses to help members expand their skillset.
Tussen de Bogen 6, 1013 JB
+31 (0)61 528 7411
www.workspace6.com
Bus: Buiten Oranjestraat

Hackers & Founders

The people who run a monthly Meetup for technology entrepreneurs and developers also run this co-working space for technology start-ups and freelancers. Members have a fixed desk, lockable storage space, coffee by Lot Sixty One Coffee Roasters and 'Nerd Yoga' every Wednesday.
Herengracht 504, 1017 CB
building@hackersandfounders.nl
www.hackersandfounders.nl
Tram: Keizersgracht (Vijzelstraat)

B Amsterdam

This hub for creatives is found in an unassuming looking building that was previously IBM's HQ. It's been transformed into a place where creatives and entrepreneurs can flourish, with desk space, office space, photo studios and the home of Startupbootcamp. Renting a desk is just the tip of the iceberg in this thriving community.

Johan Huizingalaan 763a, 1066 VH
+31 (0)20 261 2518
www.b.amsterdam
Bus: Henk Sneevlietweg

Photo: Boven de Balie

BounceSpace

This self-styled rebellious and creative co-working space also has an espresso bar, barber shop and bicycle repair shop on-site, creating a multifunctional workspace members love. The 'un-office' space attracts creatives and entrepreneurs with innovative ideas, who love the grand industrial space as much as the proximity to Vondelpark.

Overtoom 141, 1054 HG
+31 (0)20 223 1624
contact@bouncespace.eu
www.bouncespace.eu
Tram: Eerste Constantijn Huygensstraat

Photo: The Thinking Hut

Crowdy Office

Found in an old canal-house in Haarlemmerbuurt, Crowdy Office is ideal for those who love the boutiques and thrumming cafés of the neighbourhood. It's part of the Crowdy House launch platform for designers and makers, so freelancers are mostly graphic designers and other creatives, who have a designated work area and access to a photo studio. Daily group lunches and Friday afternoon drinks are a popular part of the Crowdy Office routine.

Brouwersgracht 246, 1013 HE
hi@crowdyhouse.com
www.crowdyoffice.com
Bus: Buiten Oranjestraat

Photo: Rowena Dring

Co-working portals

Deskbookers:
www.deskbookers.com

Desk Near Me:
www.desksnear.me

Launchdesk:
www.launchdesk.nl/en/desk-amsterdam

See also: Work-stay spaces on page 188

Photo: Rowena Dring

1. Boven de Balie
2. The Thinking Hut
3. Hackers & Founders
4. Hackers & Founders

Free Wi-Fi

If you enjoy the buzz of cafés or public spaces to do your work, you'll be pleased to know that free Wi-Fi can be found in plenty of locations across Amsterdam.

Here are our top tips for connecting to Wi-Fi for free in Amsterdam:

Instabridge
The Instabridge app automatically connects you to Wi-Fi as soon as you're in range of participating providers. Hundreds of bars, cafés and public spaces provide free Wi-Fi in the Amsterdam area, meaning you can be online whenever you're in range.
www.instabridge.com

Free Wi-Fi cafés
For those who want to hunker down in a café with their laptop for a while, this online map of Amsterdam shows all the cafés that provide Wi-Fi free of charge.
www.wifi-amsterdam.nl

Museums
Many of Amsterdam's museums offer free Wi-Fi, making them ideal spots to sit with a coffee and a laptop in the often inspiring and airy adjoining cafés. The Rijksmuseum and the Van Gogh Museum are two particular favourites.
www.rijksmuseum.nl
www.vangoghmuseum.nl

Amsterdam Airport Schiphol
Travellers can connect to Wi-Fi free of charge at Amsterdam's airport, convenient for those who need a quick internet fix before they fly out.
www.schiphol.nl

See also: Seats2Meet on page 117

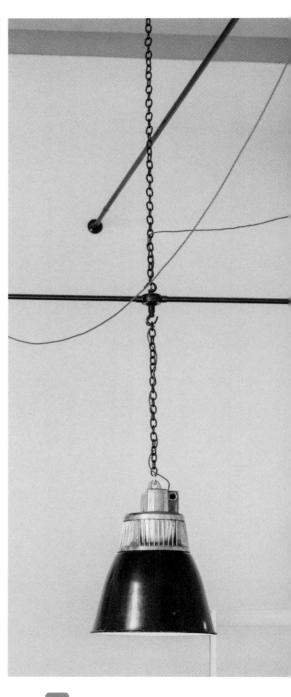

Working lunch
Business lunch etiquette

Business lunches occur frequently in Amsterdam, although they may be shorter and less formal than in the countries neighbouring the Netherlands. On the whole, the Dutch do not necessarily want to use a business lunch to develop a deep social connection, but they will use a business lunch as an opportunity to foster trust and find out more about who they're working with.

Professional/formal lunches
For those working in professional services and sectors such as finance, business consultancy and PR, business lunches are likely to take place in a local restaurant for the dagmenu (daily menu). The lunch may even take place in an on-site canteen or café in your business associate's offices. A business lunch is likely to be arranged one to two weeks in advance, and in most cases it will be organised directly with the person you're meeting. The Netherlands is a non-hierarchical society, so only on rare occasions will you deal with a person's secretary or personal assistant.

Business attire is generally quite conservative in professional sectors, so wear what is normal for the industry you're working in. If you don't wear a suit, it is advisable to wear a smart jacket over an open neck shirt or blouse. The Dutch love colour, so don't feel shy about wearing something bright unless it's a particularly formal meeting, or if it's an especially conservative sector you're working in.

Shake hands and introduce yourself to everyone at the beginning of the lunch. If you suggested the lunch meeting, be prepared to act as the host, by undertaking tasks such as selecting the wine. Make it clear whether or not you are paying for the meal if you're the host: it's not uncommon to 'go Dutch' and split the bill, but be clear in your language from the outset if you're 'inviting' your guests for a meal, or simply suggesting a catch-up over lunch. If you're the guest, follow your host's lead: order the same number of courses as everyone else, try to eat at the same pace and practice good table manners. A Dutch lunch is unlikely to consist of more than a main course and a coffee. Also ensure your mobile phone is on silent and demonstrate your good manners by treating the waiting staff politely. Service will be included in the bill, although if the waiting staff are particularly good, it's common to leave an additional 5% to 15% tip.

Conversation at a business lunch is likely to be a combination of business and social pleasantries. Take your host's lead if you're unsure, and don't ask any questions that are too personal. Treat everyone at the table as an equal, whatever their job title, and ensure everyone has a chance to have their say. Remember the Dutch value directness, so follow suit and don't be ambiguous, which could cause mistrust.

It's more common to go out for a longer, more upscale meal to mark a significant business occasion, such as signing a contract or closing a deal.

It's uncommon to be invited into a business associate's home for a business meal. In the unlikely occasion you are, dinner is likely to be served at around 19:00 and you should ensure you arrive punctually at the agreed time. Bring a bottle of wine or some flowers to show your appreciation, and follow-up with a thank you message the following day.

Creative

Generally speaking, the more creative the sector you work in, the less formal the business lunches will be. Those working in art, design, technology and the start-up world may also have lunches in local restaurants with a dagmenu, but the venue may equally be in a funky café or in a meeting room of a co-working space.

The same general rules of etiquette apply, although attire may be a little more casual and lunch meetings may be a little longer to build the stronger social rapport that is more common in creative industries. Although the Dutch value the distinction between the working day and social time, those working on creative and entrepreneurial ventures are more likely to blur the lines between work and play, with post-work drinks more common, sometimes followed by dinner.

Working lunch

Here are our top tips for business lunch options to suit different occasions:

Professional lunches

Café Nielsen

This comfortable café offers the ideal combination of class and cosiness for an unpretentious business lunch. The menu offers a wide choice of club and speciality sandwiches — a favourite of the Dutch at lunchtime — as well as freshly baked quiches and inventive salads.
Berenstraat 19, 1016 GG
mail@nielsen-ontbijt-lunch.nl
www.nielsen-ontbijt-lunch.nl
Bus/tram: Elandsgracht

De Stadskantine

This canteen style eatery perfectly typifies the preference of the Dutch for a quick, fuss-free and laid-back business lunch. Choose from the daily meat, fish or vegetarian option and eat at communal tables. The reasonable prices make it a popular option for start-up workers.
Van Woustraat 120, 1073 LT
+31 (0)20 774 1847
www.destadskantine.nl
Bus/tram: Ceintuurbaan/Van Woustraat

Café-Restaurant Dauphine

This classy French restaurant is ideal for business meetings that require a little more wow factor. The modern design gives an airy and elegant feel. You can be restrained on the lunch with a baguette, or go all out with steak, swordfish and seafood.
Prins Bernhardplein 175, 1097 BL
+31 (0)20 462 1646
info@caferestaurantdauphine.nl
www.caferestaurantdauphine.nl
Bus: Prins Bernhardplein

De Ysbreeker

This restaurant by the water has a brasserie feel and a menu with enough choice to suit all palates, from moules frites and burgers to toasted sandwiches and salads. The canal-side location and low-key ambience give it a comfortable backdrop to a business lunch.
Weesperzijde 23, 1091 EC
+31 (0)20 468 1808
info@deysbreeker.nl
www.deysbreeker.nl
Tram: Wibautstraat/Ruyschstraat

Creative lunches

Wink

This small, family run restaurant has a menu that changes twice a week, with a focus on local, fresh produce. Its understated and intimate interior make it the ideal spot for a mid-week, casual business lunch.
Govert Flinckstraat 326hs, 1073 CJ
+31 (0)20 752 6243
info@bijwink.nl
www.bijwink.nl
Bus/tram: Ceintuurbaan/Van Woustraat

Brix

This restaurant is popular for its twice weekly evening live music, but it's also an easy-going and cosy spot during the day. Exposed brick walls and distressed wood give it a sense of industrial chic, while the reasonably priced menu includes small sharing plates or filling steaks and pastas. It's ideal for a business tête-à-tête over food.
Wolvenstraat 16, 1016 EP
+31 (0)20 639 0351
info@cafebrix.nl
www.cafebrix.nl
Tram: Spui (Niewezijds Voorburgwal)

Scandinavian Embassy

This breezy café serves some of the most raved about coffee in the city, alongside a small selection of lunch plates, such as delectable smoked salmon with poached eggs. There are only a few tables, but if you can grab one, it makes the perfect location for inspiring business meetings discussing creative ideas.
Sarphatipark 34, 1072 PB
+31 (0)61 951 8199
www.scandinavianembassy.nl
Bus/tram: Tweede van der Helststraat

The Coffee Virus

Located just by the A Lab co-working space, this café is filled with the entrepreneurial spirit the local co-workers bring. At every table there's a conversation about the latest innovations and inventions, giving it the perfect buzz in the background for your own business meetings. The regularly changing menu is filled with fresh sandwiches, toasties, soups, salads, and of course, coffee. The Coffee Virus will also cater for meetings happening in A Lab's meeting rooms.
Overhoeksplein 2, 1031 KS
+31 (0)62 819 7012
info@thecoffeevirus.nl
www.thecoffeevirus.nl
Boat/bus: Veer Buiksloterweg

Order-in

Deliveroo

This company works with some of the best loved restaurants in Amsterdam to deliver to your door. Participating restaurants include popular chains and independently run eateries, meaning you can have a bespoke experience of Amsterdam's dining scene in your meeting room.
www.deliveroo.nl

Sumo Sushi Express
For a healthy sushi lunch, Sumo Sushi Express delivers across Amsterdam and orders can be made easily by phone or online. There are several platter packages ideal for business meetings.
+31 (0)20 420 7822
+31 (0)20 261 1861
www.sumosushiexpress.com

Pesto Presto
This sandwich shop delivers a choice of sandwich lunches to your business meeting. Order online using a simple form, with options including soups and salads as well as a mixture of sandwich lunchboxes.
www.pestopresto.nl

Ashoka
This Indian and Nepalese restaurant is totally raved about by diners. For an alternative business lunch idea for your office or meeting room, Ashoka also provides a series of business catering packages. It's a great way to impress business associates with alternative lunchtime flavours.
www.ashokarestaurant.nl

Photo: De Ysbreeker

Photo: The Coffee Virus

Photo: The Coffee Virus

Amsterdam is small, cosy and it's village-like, but there is such a lot of stuff going on.

Photo: Inga Powilleit

Ben Lambers and Tatjana Quax

Founders of Studio Aandacht

Introduce yourselves.

Tatjana: I'm the co-founder of Studio Aandacht and the styling director for the studio. Ben and I are a husband and wife team, and before we founded Studio Aandacht, I was the style editor for the Dutch edition of Elle Decoration magazine. After about five years in that role, Ben and I decided to start out on our own. It seemed like the right time because during the early 1990s there was a new trend emerging of companies wanting to show their brands with a focus on lifestyle. The advertising, campaigning, commercial television and print worlds all changed. They became focused on lifestyle, and they wanted to show people really 'living' brands.

Ben: I'm the other co-founder of Studio Aandacht; 'aandacht' is the Dutch word for 'attention'. That's an important aspect of our work, as every project we work on gets the same love and attention from us. I'm also the creative director, I do art direction and graphic design, as well as photography and exhibition design. In addition, I'm the head designer of the Stedelijk Museum in 's-Hertogenbosch, which is a museum of contemporary art and design. I do almost all their visual communications. One week I could be doing graphic design with the museum, and the next I could be doing a photoshoot with Brabantia. I'm lucky I'm able to have such a broad perspective and can bring so many creative aspects together.

What kind of projects do you work on?

Tatjana: I started out as an image maker for brands like Sony, Ligne Roset and IKEA, as well as designers such as Moooi by Marcel Wanders, and the Dutch artist and founder of Atelier Van Lieshout, Joep van Lieshout. I also worked with furniture design studios such as Piet Hein Eek, Ineke Hans and studio Job, all frontrunners of the so called 'Dutch Design'.

Ben: These frontrunners are people of around our age. In the beginning, we got a lot of small, incidental projects, but we slowly became more famous in the design world, as did the people we were working with. Gradually, more established brands became interested in our work, and that's how we have become bigger. So now we're working with Brabantia, for instance, and we do almost all their images for advertising, PR and packaging. We shoot hundreds of images each season.

Tatjana: We occasionally work for brands such as Philips, doing the styling for commercials. In those situations we're part of a big team, where people hire us. But an increasing amount of the work we do now is for our own clients, where we choose the teams we want to work with. For each project we team up with specialists. Since each piece of work is so different, we might need extra fashion stylists and models if it's a fashion project, or carpenters and set builders for magazine productions and museum exhibitions. For every project we take on, we work with people from our 'family', because we consider them to be family after working together for so long.

What are the characteristics of Studio Aandacht's work ethos?
Tatjana: It's really important for us to stay small. We like the fact we're partners in business and in love. We have a family, and the people we work for are our clients but also our friends. That's important in a long-term business. For me, it's also important that we have a connection with the younger generation, so I've been guest teacher at art academies for more than ten years now. Schools from places such as Denmark and as far away as South Korea visit our studio for workshops. As time goes on, some of the students team up with us at Studio Aandacht too. For example, our first intern, Mae Engelgeer, is now a famous textile designer. Over the years, we've been growing like a real family, with a lot of grown up children developing their own expertise.
Ben: It's also really important to us that we talk to clients using visuals. It makes things much easier for people who aren't necessarily creative. If we rely on words only, there is room for broad interpretations, whereas using visual examples is a quick way to steer people in the right direction.
Tatjana: If you see a picture which is right, you feel it. You remember it. It's something you take with you. People don't remember written marketing statements.

What kind of results do you see by remaining strictly creative rather than corporate?
Ben: I used to work for an advertising agency and we had a lot of corporate and government clients. It used to take months to write reports for them, and the whole process was about following strict rules and ticking boxes on a checklist. It's very 'un-creative'. Instead, Studio Aandacht is aiming for the final picture. We work quickly, easily and non-hierarchically, sitting around the table with decision-makers and CEOs who tend to really enjoy our process. We see how companies find it really inspiring. Since we've been working with Brabantia, we've seen the whole interior of their office change. It used to be a very technical company, like a factory. Now, three years later, it's very bubbly and creative and they use a lot more colour. This is not without success either; their sales went up 15% too. We like witnessing how we've influenced change.
Tatjana: We recently started working on a very big project for Ahrend,

a design-led office furniture company. They did the offices for the Rijksmuseum and they wanted to work with us on their HQ showroom. We invited the management board to our studio and made an 'inspiration presentation' for them. We showed them moods for every aspect of the office, from the lighting, flooring and room dividers, to the colours and signage. They quickly saw the different things we could do and we made very quick progress. That's how we like to work and corporate clients find this especially refreshing.

What changes in the creative landscape have you noticed since you first set up your studio?

Tatjana: I think the general public as a whole has changed. For example, when the slow food trend started 20 years ago, it was nice to buy your meat at the organic butcher; it was something special. Now, the generation below us do their shopping in the organic supermarket and it's become normal. When I was 18, there was more focus on climbing a career ladder. Now our children are reaching that age, there's much less focus on this rigid way of living. I think that Studio Aandacht's way of working is something the next generation understands a lot, because brands and people are looking to communicate and tell their story, and are searching for ways to be more human. That's something we've been doing since the beginning.

Ben: People used to pay advertising agencies a lot of money. But clients don't buy into the strategic hocus pocus and big marketing plans anymore. Most of the companies we work for pretty well know where they're heading. Through the internet, there's more transparency about what different agencies can or can't do. The whole facade is falling down. What you end up with is raw creativity really thriving. These are people who have a pure form of creativity; they have to do it. We recognise these people, but I'd describe it as a subconscious wavelength that we feel with other creatives. It's like tuning a radio and looking for the right station; you can do exactly the same with people.

You've written some design books too. What are they about?

Ben: Our first book, *How They Work*, was published in 2008 and is all about the Dutch 'rock star' designers, where we feature all the big names in the Dutch design world, such as Piet Hein Eek, Marcel Wanders, Studio Job and Hella Jongerius. Our second book, *How We Work*, was published in 2014 and is about the current generation of designers like Joris Laarman, Formafantasma and Scholten & Baijings. We were also given the chance to do an exhibition at the Stedelijk Museum in 's Hertogenbosch, based on this second book. It was 1,000m² and a big opportunity for us.

Photo: Inga Powilleit

What's the best discovery you made while doing your work?

Tatjana: A friend of ours owns an interiors store, Jan de Jong Interieur, with her husband in Leeuwarden, in the northern Netherlands. Their store is one of the oldest interiors stores in the country.

Ben: They found a local craftsman from a nearby village, who still made and sold his own hand-made furniture. He didn't sell much furniture anymore, but continued making it regardless. Our friends asked him to make side tables for them using their own designs, and it turned out to be a really big success. They were very keen on using environmentally-friendly material, and that's how I came up with the name 'slow wood' because the paint took days to dry!

Tatjana: This brand really flourished worldwide. Suddenly they were getting calls from Paris, but they couldn't handle it, because the tables took too long to make.

Ben: The whole picture was right. The designs, the name, the little worlds we created on these tables. It became a blogging hit! If you search for 'slow wood' you still find lots of blogs about it and many design magazines such as *MilK* loved the pictures.

What does creativity feel like in Amsterdam at the moment?

Tatjana: The Amsterdam creative scene is really international and there are lots of creative agencies and freelancers working for brands based in cities across Europe. In every part of Amsterdam there's something interesting and creative going on, whereas in cities like Berlin, Copenhagen, London or Paris, you have to travel to certain neighbourhoods to find a creative space or project. In Amsterdam we're spoiled. Even if you just go into a shop to get a salad, you notice the menu has been well designed, the brand is decent and the store and people are nice. You find sparks of creativity everywhere and you get the feeling that design details have been thought about.

Ben: You see that there's a lot of eagerness in the creative world in Amsterdam, but importantly there are also enough larger companies in the city to pay the creative people properly. In other cities, you see a situation where there is an abundance of creativity, but nobody is able to earn money with it, or people are prepared to work a lot for nothing. So in Amsterdam we are definitely very lucky that creativity can prosper, which is reflected in all the small shops and initiatives that have a brilliant identity, elaborate posters and innovative signage. Sometimes it's too much; everything is designed. It's still difficult to start out as a designer or creative person in Amsterdam because the rents are high. It's more of a place where artists come to in order to sell their work. They use the city like Amsterdam was originally intended, as a trading city, which it has been since the 17th century.

Where do you work?

Ben: Before we got our studio in IJburg in 2013, we worked from our home, which is also in IJburg. Whereas the centre of Amsterdam has a very historical style and feeling, these newer man-made islands like IJburg, the KNSM district and all the islands that are planned in the coming years, have a much more modern, almost Scandinavian feeling.

Tatjana: When our studio was in our home, we had a work area on the ground floor, but it was really homely too. So people we worked with would come in, and if we were making soup, they'd stay for lunch or dinner.

Ben: It was perfect for the designers we worked with because they were often in the same situation as us. Many designers also work with their partners and many base their businesses at home. That's why it was a very natural thing for us to do too. But when the larger clients started to come — the CEOs from the big companies — we thought we should have a separate studio. We also needed the space for photography. So this studio we've found facing the north by the water is perfect as a photography studio too. The light is very bright because IJburg is an island and the water around it functions as a big reflecting mirror.

What is life like as a husband and wife team?

Ben: We've became one person in a way; we're very symbiotic in work and life. Work and life is blurred for us anyway, so we just try to enjoy life and everything we're doing every day. I start very early and stop round 16:00 to do the grocery shopping and the cooking. I love to cook for my boys.

Tatjana: It's funny, but when we start a project we almost always start with a fight. It's a very quick way to come to the point. You can't do this in normal working situations, but it's very effective. Once we have finished the fight we know where we stand and what our responsibilities are.

Describe the area where you live.

Ben: IJburg is a neighbourhood of man-made islands that is more than 15 years old; everywhere we live and work now used to be water! When we moved in, there were just a few houses and a supermarket, so over time we have watched the islands evolve. People who initially moved to IJburg were typically younger couples taking advantage of the more affordable housing options. Then they all had families around the same time; our street was featured in the newspaper as being the street where most children live in the whole of the Netherlands. We live in a very nice villa street, and although we don't own a villa, we're overlooking the lucky bastards who do!

Tatjana: IJburg also has a lot of experimental housing, such as the water villas that we overlook from our studio. These villas were designed by the Dutch architect Marlies Rohmer, where individual houseboats are floating on the water. It's funny in the summer, because tourists and architecture students flock to the area to look at the floating neighbourhoods! Some of the first people to build homes in IJburg had a lot of freedom over design, so you can find all kinds of interesting buildings covered in wood or coloured tiles.

Where do you go to eat out?

Ben: IJburg is a really nice place to sleep and then go to work, and although there are a few restaurants that are ok, if we want to take people out for a really great meal, we'll go elsewhere. We like Café Modern, which is a really nice place in Amsterdam Noord. I'm friends with the chef and we are in the process of making a cookbook.

Tatjana: We also go to De Goudfazant, which is a hotel and restaurant in Amsterdam Noord. We go there at least once a month since it opened about ten years ago. It's situated in a former garage, and the big garage doors open during the summer so you can overlook the River IJ.

Ben: During the summer, there's a great pop-up restaurant called Lighthouse Island (Vuurtoreneiland) on a UNESCO-protected island that you have to reach by boat. You make a reservation and buy a boat ticket for a three-hour, four-course dinner in this amazing setting.

Where do you go shopping?

Tatjana: We buy a lot of our things directly from designers, since we know them and work with them regularly. For example, we'll have someone like Sjoerd Vroonland over for dinner, and he'll bring new designs along and show them to us. So for us it's a bit like old news when we see things in the shops. However, there's a part of Amsterdam we really like that is still up-and-coming, called Czaar Peterstraat. It started out with just a few nice cafés and restaurants, a good winery and a cheese store. Now there are more design elements coming in, with some little designer shops. There's one shop called Dreamboat that I would really recommend. It's owned by Stephanie Rammeloo, who is an Amsterdam designer, and she has made her own very special collection.

Ben: We want everything she sells.

Tatjana: There's also a shop across the street from our studio called Bloem en Zee. We worked with them when we did a project for the Holland Flower Council, for which they arranged all the flowers. They're really good with flowers and they use some really unusual varieties. Anytime I need to do something original with flowers, or need an unusual type of flower, they always have it.

What's the most curious shop you have come across?

Ben: Stuffed animals are quite trendy at the moment and there's a high-end taxidermy store called Luxury by Nature on the island that is really popular. You won't believe the things you see.

Tatjana: It's fascinating.

What do you think about the Amsterdam trend of concept stores?
Tatjana: The fact that loads of brands are playing 'concept store' is something to watch out for. You go in and you see the same stuff everywhere; it's all more or less alike. It's easy, something quite current and people like it; there's definitely a big market for it. But what I really like in Amsterdam are those small stores and brands from designers who are going their own way. Frozen Fountain is the founding father of good design stores in Amsterdam, and they're still one of the best.
Ben: Frozen Fountain is the best example of a design store in the city. It's run by Dick Dankers and Cok de Rooy; those guys are really top of the bill, and they help out young designers too.

Where is your favourite chill-out place?
Ben: We really like Blijburg. Blijburg started as a small semi-legal beach-house hang-out for hipsters overlooking the River IJ. It was built on empty land and it had to be moved a few times. It gradually grew and grew and became very popular with Amsterdammers. Now Blijburg has its own spot. You can go during the summer or winter; in the winter it's nice and quiet, and you can sit around the fire and eat a good meal. It's great for us, as it's right here on our doorstep, although you can also get a boat from Central Station. Our sons work there too.
Tatjana: During the summer, they turn Blijburg into a campsite and ask a handful of designers to make original sleeping pods for people to stay the night in. There's a restaurant and summertime pop-ups such as an organic snack bar. There are hammocks, fire pits and music performances on the beach. There's a lot of creativity in Blijburg, which we like. The beach house is used for meetings and functions too; the Mayor of Amsterdam was even there recently. It's a special place with a lot of interesting things happening.

What is the best thing about Amsterdam?
Tatjana: It's small, it's cosy and it's village-like, but there is such a lot of stuff going on. Every neighbourhood is really close to the centre, and you can walk through the centre in a single day. Most other cities are a lot bigger and you have to travel a lot to get from one part to another.

What would you change about Amsterdam if you could?
Ben: I don't understand why we still have the red light district. We've got this beautiful centre with these amazing buildings, and yet there are still prostitutes in the windows. People always say how the Dutch people are so open-minded when they talk about the red light district, but the reason I'm open-minded is not because of that neighbourhood!
Tatjana: I agree, I think we should be discouraging people from going there. I would rather advise visitors to Amsterdam to go the Vondelpark or visit the many museums and galleries.

Is there any advice you would give visitors to the city to blend in and live like Amsterdammers?

Ben: Grow a beard!

Tatjana: It's good to find a place where you can stay for a longer time, rather than just a hotel. A big advantage of Amsterdam is that everybody speaks English, so it's easy to blend in. It's not like going to Beijing or something; there's no culture shock for many people.

Ben: I would tell people to take it easy and not to try to do too much. Don't go to the coffeeshops to smoke weed too much. Go to the Vondelpark during the summer and drink a beer in a really nice local pub. Don't be afraid of the bar lady; Amsterdammers can be really direct but don't take it personally!

Tatjana: Even if people from Amsterdam are direct, it's not in a nasty way. In other cities you can feel really neglected in a café or restaurant, or be taken advantage of as a tourist. That will not happen in Amsterdam. My final piece of advice would be: don't be afraid of getting on a bike, although you might want to practice cycling before you come to the city if you're not used to it!

What is the current trend in Amsterdam?

Tatjana: Meetings in hotel lobbies or restaurants. There are a lot of new hotels where people like to go, especially the W Hotel in the city centre at the Dam. Mr Porter is the hotel's steakhouse restaurant, which is also a nice place where people like to meet. The Hoxton hotel and the Conservatorium Hotel are also popular.

Ben: Meeting in hotels is not something that Amsterdammers used to do, but it's definitely something which is new and trendy.

Where is the hippest place to hang out in Amsterdam?

Ben: Amsterdam Noord is where the real people are, but for how long?

Tatjana: Amsterdam Noord is how the Haarlemmerstraat used to be when we were starting out in the creative world. This is the part of Amsterdam where they used to make huge ships in the beginning of the last century, and most houses you'll find there are from that period. They were built for the workers from the shipyards that closed down years ago. Now new houses are being developed in the area that the original inhabitants unfortunately can't afford.

Have you discovered anywhere else in the world that has an 'Amsterdam feeling'?

Tatjana: We spent a lot of time in Copenhagen recently and it's a really nice city. I thought it was quite similar to Amsterdam in many ways, with a bit of a Dutch vibe.

Ben: It's a very young city and the people are very fashionable. I never saw so many beautiful young women on bicycles. Not even in Amsterdam…

Ben & Tatjana's Amsterdam

Places to visit

Amsterdam Noord
1020-1039
Boat: Veer Buiksloterweg, Veer IJplein

Blijburg Aan Zee
Pampuslaan 501, 1087 LA
+31 (0)20 416 0330
blij@blijburg.nl
www.blijburg.nl
Bus: Pieter Oosterhuisstraat

Bloem en Zee
IJburglaan 444, 1086 ZJ
contact@bloemenvoorijburg.nl
www.bloemenvoorijburg.nl
Bus/tram: Steigereiland

Czaar Peterstraat
1018 PR
Tram: Coehoornstraat or Eerste Leeghwaterstraat

Dreamboat Design Studio & Store
Czaar Peterstraat 145, 1018 PH
stephanie@dreamboat.nu
www.dreamboat.nu
Tram: Eerste Leeghwaterstraat

Floating houses by Marlies Rohmer
www.rohmer.nl
Bus/tram: Steigereiland

Frozen Fountain
Prinsengracht 645, 1016 HV
+31 (0)20 622 9375
enquiry@frozenfountain.nl
www.frozenfountain.nl
Tram: Prinsengracht (Leidsestraat)

IJburg
1087 GJ
Bus: Diemerparklaan, Lumierestraat, Pieter Oosterhuisstraat or Vennepluimstraat
Tram: Diemerparklaan, IJburg, Lumierestraat or Vennepluimstraat

Luxury by Nature
Diemerparklaan 52, 1087 GM
info@luxurybynature.nl
www.luxurybynature.nl
Bus/tram: Diemerparklaan

Vondelpark
1071 AA
Tram: J.P. Heijesstraat or Rhijnvis Feithstraat

Eating and drinking

Café Modern
Meidoornweg 2, 1031 GG
+31 (0)20 494 0684
www.modernamsterdam.nl
Bus: Meidoornplein

Conservatorium Hotel
Van Baerlestraat 27, 1071 AN
+31 (0)20 570 0000
info@conservatoriumhotel.com
reservations@conservatoriumhotel.com
www.conservatoriumhotel.com
Tram: Van Baerlestraat

The Hoxton
Herengracht 255, 1016 BJ
+31 (0)20 888 5555
www.thehoxton.com
Tram: Dam (Raadhuisstraat) or Dam (Paleisstraat)

De Goudfazant
Aambeeldstraat 10H, 1021 KB
+31 (0)20 636 5170
www.hoteldegoudfazant.nl
Bus: Hamerstraat or Johan van Hasseltweg
Boat: Veer Zamenhofstraat

Mr Porter
Spuistraat 175, 1012 VN
+31 (0)20 811 3399
www.mrportersteakhouse.com
Tram: Dam (Raadhuisstraat) or Dam (Paleisstraat)

Restaurant Vuurtoreneiland (Lighthouse Island)
Oostelijks handelskade 34, 1019BN (boat departures)
info@vuurtoreneiland.nl
www.vuurtoreneiland.nl
Bus/tram: C. van Eesterenlaan or tram: Rietlandpark

W Hotel
Spuistraat 175, 1012 VN
+31 (0)20 811 2500
www.wamsterdam.com
Tram: Dam (Raadhuisstraat) or Dam (Paleisstraat)

See also

Ahrend
www.ahrend.com
Atelier Van Lieshout
www.ateliervanlieshout.com
Brabantia
www.brabantia.com
Jan de Jon Interieur
www.jandejonginterieur.nl
Piet Hein Eek
www.pietheineek.nl
Stedelijk Museum in 's-Hertogenbosch
www.sm-s.nl
Sjoerd Vroonland
www.sjoerdvroonland.com
Studio Ineke Hans
www.inekehans.com
Studio Job
www.studiojob.be
Studio Mae Engelgeer
www.mae-engelgeer.nl
Studio Moooi
www.moooi.com

Find out more about Ben Lambers and Tatjana Quax at www.studioaandacht.nl or www.facebook.com/StudioAandacht

Accelerators and incubators

Accelerators and incubators help young companies grow by providing finance, mentoring, or access to new customers and markets. Some organisations for start-ups provide all three.

Accelerators are all about kick-starting your new business, with the length of stay at the accelerator office around three months. The accelerator invests a small amount into the start-ups it hosts, and provides networks and opportunities for founders to secure more funding.

Incubators involve locating your start-up company in the same premises as other start-ups, where you can stay until you achieve the next level of growth. Incubators often have a common investor for all the start-ups located there, since they often have a thematic interest, e.g. fintech or gaming.

Here's a selection of accelerators an incubators in Amsterdam:

Accelerators

Rockstart
This accelerator runs a 20 week programme for start-ups, providing office space, access to an international network of mentors and investment. Accelerators focus on different industries, such as web, mobile or digital health. Massively involved in the wider world of start-ups and entrepreneurs, Rockstart is often a first choice for start-ups looking for an accelerator in Amsterdam.
www.rockstart.com

Startupbootcamp
This popular accelerator runs programmes of three or six months, grouping together start-ups working in similar fields. Free office space is provided, and participants also have access to an enviable network of entrepreneurs and alumni. The accelerator also provides €15,000 per team to help with living expenses and start-up costs.
www.startupbootcamp.org

Startup in Residence
This joint initiative between StartupAmsterdam and the City of Amsterdam is a four month programme for Dutch and international start-ups working on innovative solutions to social issues, with themes such as 'urban mobility' and 'vibrant city'. The programme includes formal training, workshops, and office space in different locations in Amsterdam to encourage networking with Amsterdam's wider start-up and business community.
www.startupinresidence.com

Open-House
This accelerator programme is specifically for start-ups working in the event, dance and music industries. The accelerator's expertise lies in business modelling, customer development and testing. The programme runs over approximately eight months, and the creative businesses of its alumni include cardboard tents (KarTent) for festivals and the flexible sound systems (Kien).
www.open-house.nl

Incubators

VentureLab
This programme is a cross between an incubator and an accelerator. The programme length is one year — longer than accelerator programmes — and participants have to pay an upfront fee to join the programme (€20,000 as an individual, €30,000 for a team, or other staggered payment options). In return, participants receive intensive coaching and access to a programme of business-related opportunities, and a four years alumnus membership.
www.venturelab.nl

ACE Venture Lab
The Amsterdam Centre for Entrepreneurship (ACE) runs various programmes, one of which is a two year growth programme. The programme kicks off with a three month accelerate section, successful completion of which kicks off the two year growth phase. This accelerator/ incubator combination is for those working in science or tech markets, such as IT applications and sustainable technology.
www.ace-venturelab.org

Learn Dutch

Although the majority of Dutch people speak Dutch and English interchangeably, learning Dutch will only help you increase business opportunities and become more ingrained in local life. There are plenty of opportunities to learn Dutch in Amsterdam, from the more structured language schools to informal language exchanges. Look out for CEDEO certified language training providers, which indicates a higher quality of training and good customer satisfaction. For those who need to prove they have a good command of the Dutch language, there is state-sponsored NT2 examination, which on successful completion, results in an officially recognised diploma of Dutch as a second language.

Language schools

Berlitz
The Amsterdam language centre of this internationally known provider offers a range of courses, including one-to-one sessions, intensive lessons, group sessions for beginners, and phone lessons.
www.berlitz.nl/en/amsterdam

European Language Centre
This language course provider is geared towards business learners, with language training courses available in Dutch and a number of other languages.
www.europeanlanguagecentre.nl

Institute for Dutch Language Education (INTT)
Based at the University of Amsterdam, the INTT offers an array of Dutch language courses, open to anyone regardless of whether or not they're planning to study anything else at the university. Courses include intensive summer courses and preparation sessions for the NT2 exams.
intt.uva.nl

Katakura
This friendly language school has two locations in Amsterdam, and guarantees small class sizes of no more than nine students. There are courses for all levels of learning at various times of the day, meaning there's an option to suit most people.
www.katakura-wblc.nl

Talencoach
This unconventional Dutch language provider runs 'Dutch brainwash' courses for one week, with maximum class sizes of six people. After the week is up, a month-long email course helps participants integrate everything they've learned. The learning approach is based on keeping confidence high and neuro-linguistic programming (NLP) principles. For those who are unsure, Talencoach provides regular free taster workshops.
www.talencoach.nl

Language exchange

Amsterdam Language Cafe
This Meetup group organises 'single language nights' on Wednesday evenings, where participants can come along and practice a language of their choice. On Fridays there are larger gatherings for people to go along and practice any language they like. It's informal, fun and a great way to meet the language lovers of Amsterdam.
www.meetup.com/Amsterdam-Language-Cafe

Gilde Amsterdam
This not-for-profit organisation pairs non-Dutch speakers with native Dutch partners to have informal conversations. It's a great way to practice Dutch and make friends.
www.gildeamsterdam.nl/taalbegeleiding/nederlands-spreken

Online resources

Babbel
This online language course provider runs various Dutch courses, including courses for beginners and those that focus on grammar, words or sentences. Courses are priced per month, at a cost of €9.95 for just one month, to €4.95 for those who want to commit to 12 months. There's an iPhone app that goes with it for those who want to practice on the move too.
www.babbel.com

Duolingo
This online platform and app breaks down Dutch language learning into bite-sized chunks, ideal for busy entrepreneurs who need to multi-task while learning a language.
www.duolingo.com

Learn Dutch
This free online course helps those who want to learn Dutch with vocabulary, grammar and typical Dutch sayings. Those who enjoy the free online resources may be tempted by the annual summer school for more intensive language training.
www.learndutch.org

Livemocha
This online language community by Rosetta Stone gives learners access to a network of native speakers. Write or record yourself completing one of the exercises and submit it to the community for feedback, and connect with an array of native speakers who can help you improve your Dutch.
www.livemocha.com

Taalthuis
This free online Dutch course involves basic grammar, vocabulary and pronunciation. By becoming a member for €10 a year, learners get access to extra exercises to download, as well as a pronunciation programme.
www.taalthuis.com

Networking

Business clubs

American Amsterdam Business Club (AABC)
This club has around 1,000 members and offers informal networking opportunities and 11 events throughout the year in different Amsterdam locations.
www.aabc.nl

Australian Business in Europe: Netherlands
This group is for senior Australian professionals in the Netherlands, and involves a regular calendar of events throughout the year.
www.abie-nl.nl

The British Society of Amsterdam (Britsoc)
This society is free and open to everyone, with the aim of bringing people together based on shared interests. As a result, Britsoc provides a lot of opportunities to network and meet entrepreneurs in the city.
www.britsoc.nl

Canadian International Club of Amsterdam
This club for Canadians and friends in Amsterdam organises bi-monthly meet-ups, with events for networking, business opportunities and friendship.
canadianclubofams.wix.com/home

JCI Amsterdam International
The Amsterdam chapter of this international non-profit organisation is for those aged 18 to 40 who want to develop personally and professionally. The regular calendar of events includes social gatherings and conferences with topics such as social entrepreneurship.
www.jciai.nl

WTC Amsterdam Business Club
This World Trade Center business club is for entrepreneurs and business owners in the Amsterdam Zuidas area. The club provides opportunities for members to get together to discuss ideas and business ventures.
wtcamsterdambusinessclub.com

Professional Women's Network Amsterdam
This network helps connect female professionals in Amsterdam and strengthens opportunities for them to take on leadership roles.
www.pwnamsterdam.net

Toastmasters Amsterdam
This professional club brings together people who want to improve communication and leadership skills, providing ideal opportunities to get together with other Amsterdam professionals too.
www.toastmasters.nl

Networking gatherings

Silicon Drinkabout
The Amsterdam version of this sociable start-up group involves beers, networking and lots of start-up chat.
www.3-beards.com/silicondrinkabout/amsterdam

Open Coffee Amsterdam
This informal Meetup happens on the first Thursday of every month at the Boven de Balie co-working space in central Amsterdam. An eclectic mix of entrepreneurs and investors come along for coffee and a catch up before they head into work.
www.meetup.com/ocamsterdam

Appsterdam
This Meetup group has an event every Wednesday for drinks, bringing together Amsterdam's community of app makers. Wednesday's a busy day for Appsterdam, as the organisation also runs a lunchtime lecture on Wednesday lunchtimes too. On Saturdays, Appsterdam runs a peer lab for start-up owners to come along and get advice on business problems they're facing.
www.meetup.com/Appsterdam

AMS Connected
The mission of this Meetup group is to "get expats out of their fishbowl, and into the ocean called Amsterdam!" The group helps newcomers integrate into the city by arranging opportunities for them to meet Dutch people, visit start-up companies and help out with local charities.
meetup.com/AMS-Connected

Founders Breakfast Club
Enjoy networking over breakfast with start-up founders and those looking for entrepreneurial inspiration. You have to ask to be invited to the event, which usually happens monthly, as there are only a maximum of 16 places available.
www.foundersbreakfastclub.com

Launchpad Meetups
This innovative network is where start-ups pitch their revolutionary business ideas inside the boardrooms of major corporations. You can sign up to pitch or just come along as an audience member to be among like-minded people.
www.launchpadmeetups.com

The Things Network Hackerspace
This group of techies meets up every Friday afternoon to "build cool stuff" on a network.
www.meetup.com/sensemakersams

Photo: Impact Hub

Business events and key dates

Firmly becoming a recognised business and creative centre in Europe, Amsterdam plays host to a number of conferences and business-related events ripe for networking every year.

January

Bitcoin Wednesday's New Year Reception

This annual event involves networking, drinks and presentations about the digital currency revolution.
www.bitcoinwednesday.com

February

Casual Connect

The Amsterdam version of this global event is all about casual gaming. If you want to talk new technologies and mobile and browser gaming, this is the place to go.
www.casualconnect.org

Integrated Systems Europe (ISE)

This huge show is all about AV, electronic systems and connecting new technologies.
www.iseurope.org

Homemakers' Fair

This varied event includes the latest innovations in household products, peppered with fashion, food and beauty stands.
www.huishoudbeurs.nl

March

Insight Innovation eXchange Europe

Find out about the latest insights in innovation, meet new start-ups, and find out about the newest gadgets and tech at this event. There are also TED-style talks and plenty of networking opportunities.
iiex-eu.insightinnovation.org

April

UPRISE Festival

This festival connects start-ups and entrepreneurs with new apps, technologies and the latest trends. There are also workshops, games and chill-out areas with DJs.
www.uprisefestival.co

TALX

This three day event is Amsterdam's leadership exchange, great for networking and inspiring talks.
www.talx.nl

Startupbootcamp Amsterdam

The bootcamp by this accelerator is a three month programme for start-ups working in specific fields, such as smart solutions for the home and environment or e-commerce.
www.startupbootcamp.org

May

BCF Career event

This careers fair focuses on those who want to work in the life sciences and food industries.
www.bcfcareerevent.nl

Ace Venture Lab Bootcamp

This bi-annual bootcamp for tech and science start-ups teaches you how to create a viable business in five days. A concept by the Amsterdam Center for Entrepreneurship (ACE), this is a way to fast-track into an entrepreneur's life.
www.ace-venturelab.org

Amsterdam Art Fair

This fair attracts those working in art, as well as creatives looking for inspiration.
www.amsterdamartfair.nl

June

Startup Weekend Amsterdam

Pitch business ideas, form groups and then spend 54 hours creating a business. It's the perfect way to jump in the deep end as an entrepreneur.
www.startupweekend.org

TheNextWomen Innovation Summit

This summit is for female entrepreneurs looking for inspiration and networking opportunities.
www.thenextwomen100.nl

July

ACE Summerschool

This summer school by the Amsterdam Center for Entrepreneurship (ACE) helps you develop start-up ideas into business plans within a week.
www.ace-amsterdam.org

Development Bootcamp

This bootcamp runs courses for beginner, intermediate and advanced levels, teaching you everything from the basics of programming to deploying web applications.
developmentbootcamp.com

August

International Summer School in Cultural Economics

This annual summertime course is for those working in or interested in creative industries and cultural organisations.

Everything from strategy and entrepreneurship, to marketing and creative financing is on the agenda.
www.crearefoundation.nl/Summer_School

September

Amsterdam Capital Week
A key week in the start-up calendar, start-ups from around the world travel to Amsterdam to pitch more than 500 investors. The week also involves workshops, networking and crowdfunding festivals.
amsterdamcapitalweek.com

International Broadcasting Convention (IBC)
This annual event is for anyone working in the creation, management and delivery of entertainment and news content worldwide. There's also an annual hackfest for those who enjoy a practical challenge.
www.ibc.org

Quantified Self Europe Conference
Hosting a conference in Amsterdam most years, Quantified Self brings together those interested in lifelogging, data visualisation and new technologies of personal science.
www.quantifiedself.com

October

Amsterdam eWeek
This is a special week of events, networking and talks for those working in e-commerce and online media, as well as marketing and technology.
www.amsterdameweek.com

CodeWeekEU
This week has special events for coders running across Europe, including a handful in Amsterdam.
www.codeweek.eu

Tech Startups Job Fair
This international jobs fair provider hosts an event in Amsterdam every year, aimed at those looking for jobs in tech start-ups.
www.techstartupjobs.com

Dutch Design Week
A stalwart in the Dutch design calendar, this week is hosted in Eindhoven, about an hour and a half away from Amsterdam. It attracts those in design related industries from across the Netherlands and further afield.
www.ddw.nl

November

Aquatech Amsterdam
The city of water naturally hosts an annual event about water technology. It's a great place to get design inspiration and talk tech with people who are in-the-know.
www.aquatechtrade.com/amsterdam

Velocity
This conference with international editions is for those working in web operations, IT and mobile platforms.
conferences.oreilly.com/velocity

FuseHack
More than 200 tech entrepreneurs get together at this event to see what they can achieve in 36 hours.
www.fusehack.com

IGNITE! Conference
This conference is all about broadening the application of entrepreneurship into areas such as international development and government.
www.mediamatic.net

Dutch Docker Day
This conference for software developers and those working in IT is full of practical workshops, labs and talks.
www.dutchdockerday.nl

December

ACE Venture Lab Bootcamp
This bi-annual bootcamp for tech and science start-ups teaches you how to create a viable business in five days. A concept by the Amsterdam Center for Entrepreneurship (ACE), this is a way to fast-track into an entrepreneur's life.
www.ace-venturelab.org

ThingsCon Amsterdam
This conference is about the future of hardware, the Internet of Things and the design of new products.
www.thingscon.nl

Ketchum European Food Lab
This competition is for start-ups working in the food industry, with the winner announced at the finale in December.
eufoodlab.ketchum.com

See also: Events and key dates in Amsterdam (page 80)

A really important factor is that the city officials are perfectly aware of the need for the creative scene.

Photo: Peter Rokven

Árpád Gerecsey
Entrepreneur and Chief Innovation Officer of A Lab Amsterdam

Tell us about your background and how it led to you running A Lab Amsterdam.

My father came to the Netherlands in 1956 after Hungary was invaded by the Russians; I was born about ten years later. I studied computer science and worked in that field for a while before joining World Press Photo. It was a very small entity back then but we grew it into a large international organisation; I ran that company as the CEO and was there for almost ten years. Then I moved to Médecins Sans Frontières, working as director on their global fundraising and communications. Then I decided to go back into my field of education; I have an MSc in computer science and got into the start-up world, investing in a start-up which I also ran for a few years. It was shortly after that when I started SocialPeople — a group of experts advising companies on areas of innovation — because I saw that what was happening in technology was going to have a huge impact on what would happen socially and business wise. It was because of all of these past experiences that I was asked by the City of Amsterdam to become a board member of the foundation that was created to run A Lab Amsterdam. I don't like things to stand still, so I embraced the opportunity. So now, with Lucas Hendricks, my co-director and fellow board member, we run A Lab.

What is A Lab?

A Lab is a space where creatives and technologists meet, work, dream and develop. Essentially, it's a breeding place for creativity, run as a foundation. Lucas Hendricks, who is one of the initiators of the Dutch creative industries on a governmental level, and myself, were asked by the City of Amsterdam to run this creative breeding place in partnership with each other. Amsterdam has a long history of supporting creatives; it's been going on for 50 years or more. The idea is to support creatives so they're not pushed to the fringes of the city. There have always been cheap workspaces for artists, but initiatives like A Lab, where we actively connect creatives, technology, business and society, helps to bring creative innovation to the next level. Now we have about 300 members in A Lab and around 80 companies, as well as a range of external members, from freelancers and students, to academies, enterprises and institutions. We strive to develop on the bleeding edge; failure is definitely an option here and we actively let go of people who are not curious.

Tell us about A Lab's building.

A Lab is inside Shell's old laboratory in Amsterdam Noord. The whole
site is 18,000m² and A Lab now offers 5,000 m² of creative spaces. The
building had been bought by the City of Amsterdam but was empty for
ten years, except for a while when the Occupy movement was in the
building. When we arrived, the place was worn out. It's apt that the
building used to be a laboratory because A Lab is a place where creative
experimentation happens. We've kept a lot of the original features in the
building, and each room is set up as a 'lab', where creative experiments of
different types happen. We have some really creative spaces where the walls
and whiteboards can change colour, a huge 'hackathon' and exhibition
space and several technical labs for music, robotics, Internet of Things,
journalism and so on; it's a permanently evolving space.

How is A Lab different from other creative breeding spots?

There are a lot of accelerators and collaborative spaces in Amsterdam,
but A Lab is quite different. The people at A Lab usually come from
creative and technology backgrounds, often having been educated into
creative fields via school, university or other education. Then they start
developing stuff, and they may do a PhD or undertake some research.
They start understanding the ways the creative world works through these
processes. Bleeding edge work starts to come out; things that are not
yet commercialised. What we're doing at A Lab is actually doing it; we're
actually making stuff. This is where the bleeding edge is being defined. We
call A Lab the place where creativity and technology have sex. We don't
know whether it's a one night stand, we don't know whether it will be a
long lasting marriage, but we do know that this is where you try it out. This
is what makes life interesting and what keeps us asking the right questions.

What is the relevance of A Lab at this moment in time?

We live in a super exciting time. The balance is shifting from hierarchical
towards networked, and people are creating new spaces in the world
for themselves. The technological barrier to entry has become so low
and people have a lot more freedom to translate their creative ideas into
solutions than they used to. Ten years ago you would need about €20
million to launch a new start-up and bring a product to market. These days
you can be successful with very little investment, because technology has
become so available and so easy. Everyone is getting involved in technology
without even realising it, using apps and giving away private data without
thinking about it, which is also a little scary. Meanwhile, start-ups are
offering solutions that the incumbents cannot. Big industries are trying to
get to grips with this. I helped initiate the Holland FinTech platform with
KPMG last year, which is where financial technology start-ups get together
with banks, corporates and advisories to discuss what's going on and

where things can go next. As for journalism and media, I was talking to the director of a very big publishing company recently that offers information to a big percentage of Dutch millennials. He feels a huge responsibility on his shoulders of what to offer to them. What does society of the future look like? How do we balance commercial activity with seeing consumers as more than data and clicks? How do we keep a rich and deeply involved society? For me that was one of the drivers for stepping into A Lab. Lucas and I both felt this was a way to move from the talking towards the enabling, the empowering, the inspiring and the doing.

Describe some of the things happening at A Lab at the moment.
We have created actual and virtual 'labs' in every room in our building. We have a journalism lab, where we look at the latest developments in Journalism 3.0. The Correspondent was born at A Lab, and The VJ Movement joined us fairly recently. There is a visual lab, where people get together and experiment with 3D, Virtual Reality and film. We have a social robotics lab looking at how social robots will affect society. There are a couple of professors from VU (Free University) and University of Amsterdam who now have a base at A Lab and they actually have robots there, designed to take care of the elderly. We have a music lab with music studios, looking at totally new ways of producing music. Two of the biggest rappers in the Netherlands go there. Then we have other labs looking at completely new ways of distributing music. There is also an art and culture lab, which is at a much more explorative, early stage. We recently had a neuroscientist come to A Lab who was interested in hosting workshops about the human brain and the computer 'brain'. We hosted the meeting and had a room full of neuroscientists, artists and everyone in between. They were firing off questions to each other for two hours. Of course, artists ask entirely different questions than scientists do; it was wonderful. That sparks all sorts of new things. "Experience the experiment". That's one of our slogans. We don't know what's going to come out of it, but we do know that we touch on things in a changing society. We will invite technology philosophers to discuss the ethical. From this you can see that A Lab is a bit like the odd person out, because we connect everything together. We connect universities, start-ups, creatives, technologists, business and experimentalists. For me, personally, it's all about the transition from a hierarchical to a network society.

What is the A Lab vibe like?
We have specific criteria before anyone can come to A Lab to make sure we continually have the best environment. People need to know what experiment they want to run before they can come to A Lab. When we interview people, we also ask them how willing they are to work with others. If people are inward-looking, they don't belong at A Lab. Even if

Photos: A Lab

someone is doing something very focused or is a techie, coding a great new way of selling music or making music, film or Virtual Reality for example, we still hope they will come to our monthly drinks and 'lunch roulette'. We hope they'll show their work to the community and use the shared platforms we have. A Lab is a very dynamic place where everybody is constantly discussing ideas and asking for and offering help, whether it's building a WordPress site or building a 'coffee-copter' drone that can deliver coffee in the building, which we have actually built. We create these things but we also have a discussion about what it means to have a coffee-copter. Is it good, bad or just a platform for us to talk about what's happening in the world?

A Lab is next door to the Amsterdam University of the Arts. Do you share creative inspiration?

Yes, we not only share the same entrance to our buildings, we share spaces and we invite each other for this 'bleeding edge technology creative sexing'. Our respective film people work together, and we also have a company that works on high-level technology solutions for operas all over Europe, as well as a holographic company. This is a great match for the arts school, since they make dresses that change colour according to the singer's emotional state. We love all that weird stuff and working with others to achieve it. We're here to support the creative scene and to showcase to the world what Amsterdam is capable of in terms of our creativity and technology.

What is it about Amsterdam that makes a place like A Lab work?

Amsterdam has a very accessible and central geographical location, which is why the city has been so successful for hundreds of years. However, a really important factor is that the city officials are perfectly aware of the need for the creative scene. They see it as an integrated part of the fabric of this city. They're not paying me to say that, I promise! This is the city I've lived in my whole life and this is an aspect of the city I've always seen clearly. This kind of outlook creates breathing space. It allows people to come in, find their place and hook up to the readily available creative networks. The academies, universities, start-up hubs, the accelerators, labs like A Lab and Impact Hub, and discussion places like De Waag and Pakhuis De Zwijger, make up the creative and technological fabric of this city. Together with this, humans need philosophical and spiritual creative experiences, which Amsterdam also gives people the freedom to have. As a city to live in, Amsterdam is reasonably affordable, internet penetration is extremely high, and the prevalence of the English language is great — even lectures at universities are in English, making education very accessible. It's an open scene which constantly flows. I think if we keep this up; if we keep mixing business and culture, and keep our eye on the human scale versus the corporate scale, Amsterdam will continue to thrive in the same way.

How have you seen the Amsterdam Noord neighbourhood change?
I actually grew up in the northern part of Amsterdam, although it was considered a no-go area until recently. This is where the shipyards were. There was no culture, hardly any good schools there and no creative scene. As long as 30 years ago they slowly started taking away a few of the shipyards and developing real estate. The stretch of land along the River IJ, separating Amsterdam Noord from downtown, had never really been developed. City officials gradually allowed squatters to take over this area; it was a very conscious decision. They slowly started permitting the squatters to have some rights in those areas and consented to some construction. It was a very well thought-out process that has made the area start to gentrify. At the moment is a high point were the creative scene has taken over. In the next five years we'll start to see more commercial development and I think it will sort of become the new downtown of Amsterdam. There are more ferries coming in to support this, and there will be bridges and tunnels too.

Which developments do you think are most exciting?
I like NDSM, which is further to the west of A Lab. It's a huge area where you can go for art and performances, but there are some early adopters who have had their offices there for ten or 15 years, such as MTV. It's got a very good mix of things. The whole area is moving so fast, particularly the old Shell complex that A Lab sits on. The ClinkNOORD hostel opened up recently next door to A Lab, which is a great creative and low cost place to stay. The Shell Tower was recently converted into A'DAM Tower, a music tower by the renowned dance empire ID&T. There are two 24-hour clubs and a revolving schedule of events; the music industry has basically moved in there, including the famous Nashville guitar brand Gibson. This blend of commercial and creative is what Amsterdam is all about and it's really exciting. We have EYE Film Museum right in front of us, and Tolhuis Tuin on the right, so A Lab is like the connecting fibre between all of them.

Where do you live?
After growing up in Amsterdam Noord, I lived downtown while I was studying at university and during my earlier years of working. I love central Amsterdam. I've recently moved out of the city in the north so my children can grow up with some green space. Interestingly, Amsterdam Noord is connected to large green belts of the country, so in three minutes by car or ten minutes by bicycle, you can travel from the up-and-coming creative hub around A Lab to fields surrounded by cows and lakes. It takes me 15 minutes to get to work on my motorcycle.

How would you sum up your personal life?

I'm an Amsterdammer who loves his city. I have a Canadian wife, four kids and I keep around 500,000 bees. I used to be a skydiver and did a great number of jumps, but I don't do that anymore. I'm also the Chairman of De Melkweg music venue and club. It's where Nirvana had their first gig in the Netherlands, and well-known artists call in if they want to do after-parties or more intimate performances. Prince used to do this when he was in town. It's a great place because it's also where musicians and artists have the freedom to experiment.

Where do you go to enjoy the cultural offerings of the city?

I keep an eye out for anything new coming to the city and interesting-sounding events or performances. For example, I recently saw the National Ballet's Junior Company, with performers from around the world who are just starting their careers. They did performances with short movies and interviews in between, so the audience got to know them a little bit. That was just amazing. For art I like visiting the annual exhibition of the Gerrit Rietveld Academie. The Ilovenoord.nl website is great to find out about things going on in northern Amsterdam. And I still enjoy going to De Melkweg very much. As the Chairman I'm a bit removed from the day-to-day operations, but I'm still always amazed at the variety of what goes on there. We're very well-known for urban performances and music, but we also do a lot of movies, theatre and photo exhibitions. There are 400 performances a year. One day I went there to see what was going on, and it was the national contest for air guitar playing, the winner of which went to the World Series in Finland. It was amazing standing there all night watching these brilliant performances. At the end people had a bit more fun and swapped their air guitars! For those into social entrepreneurship, having a coffee at ImpactHub is a great thing to do. It's conveniently situated in Westerpark, which has lots of other great stuff happening.

Where's a good place to go for a drink in Amsterdam?

I really like the beer bars, such as Gollem in De Pijp which has been there for ages; they always have different beers. I like to go to the Amsterdam brewing company Brouwerij 't IJ on a sunny Friday afternoon. There are also some treasures that hardly anyone knows about, like Brouwerij De Prael, a beer brewery in the red light district. They've been in business for years, but it still feels like a hidden place of Amsterdam.

Where do you like to eat out and why?

Tolhuis Restaurant is a great restaurant near A Lab, right next to the ferry that goes to the Central Station. I used to visit it when I was in high school.

How would you recommend visitors to Amsterdam blend in and live like 'citizens' for the duration of their stay?

Visitors should definitely use the extensive public transport network the city offers or travel by bicycle. Both modes of transport are so easy and are what the locals do. Join the locals at one of the many festivals during the summer too. I would recommend going upstairs in the public library and enjoying the view of the entire city. You can just sit there with a cheap coffee. You could also go to the Hilton DoubleTree next door, which has the same view, but there the coffee will cost you €7 and it's less of a 'local' experience. In general, visitors should talk to people in restaurants and bars, to get a feeling of local life and what people are like. People who need to work should go to a co-working space or a place like A Lab, where you could sit in The Coffee Virus café in the lobby and enjoy the great coffee, free Wi-Fi and being surrounded by interesting creative people. Visiting cultural meeting places such as Pakhuis De Zwijger and De Balie as well, give a great sense of the culture we have in Amsterdam, and an insight into how people think and what people do. The School of Life is another great institution.

What is the current trend in Amsterdam?

The city was awarded the European Innovation City Award, which shows how Amsterdam is in constant transition. At the moment, this takes the form of people moving away from being employees, and moving towards the freelance world instead. This is starting to happen on a wide scale, and you can see it both in the change in demand for office space as well as in the enormous output of new start-ups. People want flexible, state of the art and hip workspaces, so the number of co-working spaces appearing in Amsterdam to meet this need is immense.

How should visitors to the city 'get lost' and discover the city for themselves?

Visitors should cycle outside the city for a real feeling of discovery. Cycling along the dijks (embankments) gives an insight into the real Holland, where the water is higher than the cows. You can see the polders — the areas below sea level that have been built on to increase the amount of land in the city — which are just a stone's throw outside the city. The Muziekgebouw aan het 't IJ is a music hall by the River IJ, which is a great place to lose yourself while enjoying the view and atmosphere. It's great for jazz, excellent performances and interesting experiments; wonderful things happen there. Instead of hanging out very late at night, I would recommend taking an early morning stroll along the canals, when nobody's out on a Sunday morning. De Negen Straatjes (Nine Streets) is a great place to do that too, with all the little shops and pretty streets.

What is the best thing about Amsterdam?
I like the fact it's a small city. You could probably cycle from the far north to the far south in 45 minutes. This gives the city a human scale that is really nice. Even though it's small, it's never boring.

Where's the best place to go people-watching?
I enjoy the Noordermarkt on Saturday mornings, because you see everyone from the elderly people going about their business, to the hipsters and parents with their children in tow. I also like the Westerstraat Market in the Jordaan neighbourhood. Or just stand at the ferry behind Central Station in the morning.

What is your guilty pleasure?
Having a slice of apple pie at Café Winkel 43, which is an apple pie store that has been there for ages, but it's still hip, cool and the pie is amazing.

Árpád's Amsterdam

Places to visit

A'DAM Tower
Overhoeksplein 1, 1031 KS
info@adamtoren.nl
www.adamtoren.nl
Boat/bus: Veer Buiksloterweg

A Lab
Overhoeksplein 2, 1031 KS
+31 (0)20 820 2363
info@a-lab.nl
www.a-lab.nl
Boat/bus: Buiksloterweg

Amsterdam Noord
1020-1039
Boat: Veer Buiksloterweg, Veer
IJplein

ClinkNOORD
Badhuiskade 3, 1031 KV
+31 (0)20 214 9730
reservations@clinkhostels.com
www.clinkhostels.com/
amsterdam/clinknoord
Boat/bus: Veer Buiksloterweg

De Balie
Kleine-Gartmanplantsoen 10,
1017 RR
+31 (0)20 553 5151
www.debalie.nl
Tram: Leidseplein

De Melkweg
Lijnbaansgracht 234A, 1017 PH
+31 (0)20 531 8181
www.melkweg.nl
Tram: Leidseplein

De Negen Straatjes
Bus/tram: Westermarkt

De Waag
Nieuwmarkt 4, 1012 CR
+31 (0)20 422 7772
info@indewaag.nl
www.indewaag.nl
Metro: Nieuwmarkt

Embankments and polders
Take public transport to cities
such as Purmer, Wormer,
Beemster and Schermer

EYE Film Museum
IJpromenade 1, 1031 KT
+31 (0)20 589 1400
info@eyefilm.nl
www.eyefilm.nl
Boat/bus: Veer Buiksloterweg

Ferry near Central Station
Boat: Veer Centraal Station

Gerrit Rietveld Academie
Fred. Roeskestraat 96, 1076 ED
+31 (0)20 571 1600
www.rietveldacademie.nl
Bus/tram: IJsbaanpad

Impact Hub
Haarlemmerweg 10C, 1014 BE
+31 (0)20 427 4283
amsterdam@impacthub.net
www.amsterdam.impacthub.net
Bus: Van Limburg Stirumstraat

Muziekgebouw aan het 't IJ
Piet Heinkade 1, 1019 BR
+31 (0)20 788 2000
www.muziekgebouw.nl
Tram: Muziekgebouw Bimhuis

Nationale Opera and Ballet
Amstel 3, 1011 PN
+31 (0)20 551 8117
info@operaballet.nl
www.operaballet.nl
Bus: Waterlooplein

NDSM
1033
Boat: Veer NDSM Werf

Noordermarkt
Noordermarkt, 1015 MV
+31 (0)20 552 4074
info@noordermarkt-amsterdam.nl
www.noordermarkt-amsterdam.nl
Bus: Buiten Brouwersstraat

**Openbare Bibliotheek
Amsterdam (OBA)**
Oosterdokskade 143, 1011 DL
+31 (0)20 523 0900
klantenservice@oba.nl
www.oba.nl
Tram: Muziekgebouw Bimhuis

Pakhuis de Zwijger
Piet Heinkade 179, 1019 HC
+31 (0)20 624 6380
info@dezwijger.nl
www.dezwijger.nl
Bus: Jan Schaeferbrug

The School of Life
Herengracht 215, 1016 BJ
+31 (0)20 220 0080
amsterdam@theschooloflife.com
www.theschooloflife.com
Tram: Dam/Raadhuisstraat

Tolhuis Tuin
IJpromenade 2, 1031 KT
+31 (0)20 763 0650
info@tolhuistuin.nl
www.tolhuistuin.nl
Boat/bus: Veer Buiksloterweg

Westerpark
Haarlemmerweg, 1014 BE
Bus: Van Hallstraat
(Haarlemmerweg)

Westerstraat Market
Westerstraat, 1015 ML
contact@jordaanmarkten.nl
www.jordaanmarkten.nl
Bus/tram: Marnixplein

Eating and drinking

Brouwerij De Prael
Oudezijds Voorburgwal 30,
1012 GD
+31 (0)20 408 4470
boekingen@deprael.nl
www.deprael.nl
Bus: CS/Nicolaaskerk

Brouwerij 't IJ
Funenkade 7, 1018 AL
+31 (0)20 528 6237
www.brouwerijhetij.nl
Tram: Hoogte Kadijk

Café Gollem
info@cafegollem.nl
www.cafegollem.nl
Multiple locations in the city.

Café Winkel 43
Noordermarkt 43, 1015 NA
+31 (0)20 623 0223
info@winkel43.nl
www.winkel43.nl
Bus: Buiten Brouwersstraat

Hilton DoubleTree
Oosterdoksstraat 4, 1011 DK
+31 (0)20 530 0800
amscs.info@hilton.com
www.doubletree3.hilton.com
Bus: Prins Hendrikkade/CS

The Coffee Virus
Overhoeksplein 2, 1031 KS
+31 (0)6 2819 7012
amsterdam@thecoffeevirus.nl
www.thecoffeevirus.nl
Boat/bus: Veer Buiksloterweg

Tolhuis Restaurant
Buiksloterweg 7, 1031 CC
+31 (0)20 636 6550
info@tolhuisamsterdam.nl
www.tolhuisamsterdam.nl
Boat/bus: Veer Buiksloterweg

See also

Air Guitar playing World Series
airguitarworldchampionships.com
Amsterdam University of the Arts
www.ahk.nl
Holland FinTech
www.hollandfintech.com
Ilovenoord
www.ilovenoord.nl
Médecins Sans Frontières
www.msf.org
SocialPeople
www.socialpeople.nl
The Correspondent
www.decorrespondent.nl
VJ Movement
www.vjmfoundation.org
World Press Photo
www.worldpressphoto.org

Find out more about Árpád Gerecsey at
www.a-lab.nl and on Twitter @arpadg

Photo: A Lab

chapter 3

Live

*Retailers with flair,
a haven for artists
and some nice pillows
to put your head on.*

Live in Amsterdam

Life in Amsterdam is about enjoying a healthy work-life balance. That's just one of the reasons so many people from around the world up sticks and move to the city every year. Together with the distinctive creative flair the city shows in every restaurant, café, bar, shop and hotel, plus the wide open spaces and generally candid way of living, Amsterdam is a city in which to soak up the atmosphere and enjoy every moment of life.

Residential areas in Amsterdam are interspersed with busy localities and neighbourhood centres. This means every street is pocked with eateries, bars and boutiques. Whether in tiny front rooms of old canal houses or in huge industrial style hangars, you're never more than a street away from an interesting amenity or place to grab a snack or drink. Despite its small geographical area and population, Amsterdam is home to a substantial 1,300 restaurants and 1,500 bars and cafés. Amsterdammers love nothing more than stopping for a coffee on the way to work, or for a beer from one of the many Dutch brewers on the way home. Indeed, the Dutch drink more coffee than anyone else in the world, bar the Finnish and the Norwegians, while Amsterdam's brown cafés — wood-clad, smoke stained drinking holes from the olden days — have worldwide recognition, and there seems to be one on every corner. That's not to say there isn't a modern food trend going on in Amsterdam too. In recent years, the city has come along leaps and bounds in the foodie arena, with food innovation and culinary quality now rivalling many of Amsterdam's European neighbours.

An innate design consciousness can be spotted everywhere in Amsterdam's daily life. The city's trend of the concept store is just one way in which this is embodied, where fashion shops become cafés and cafés become design hubs. Every interior of every space makes a design statement, whether it's polished or quirky, industrial chic or Scandi-mellow. That includes the city's 40,000 hotel rooms, where within each one an assured sense of style and an innate Dutch originality is manifested. It's possible to stay everywhere from an old newspaper headquarters and a hotel designed by fashion students with five classes of accommodation, to an industrial crane in the fast-evolving north part of the city and a hotel with vintage video games available to play at your leisure.

This chapter is all about eating, drinking, shopping, sleeping and generally living in Amsterdam. We take you to some of the city's greatest places to stay, from the most elegant hotels to the quirkiest boutique crash pads. If you want your Amsterdam visit to become a more permanent thing, we also help you navigate the world of finding the perfect apartment or house share. When you're hungry, we help you find a meal for every occasion, whether you want a coffee and cake inside a converted theatre, or a meal at a street food hub inside an old tram depot. If you want to shop til you drop, Amsterdam has the ability to keep on giving, and we steer you in the direction of pop-up vintage malls and creative havens for those working in the arts.

Breakfast

Gs

This hipster hangout has locations in the Jordaan and east Amsterdam, but it's gained most notoriety for its 'brunchboat' which sets sail along the canals every Saturday and Sunday. The brunch menu is full of innuendo, with 'foreplay', 'the main act', 'happy endings' and 'tipsy' courses available. Expect oysters and dips, traditional eggs and internationally inspired breakfast burgers, desserts and cocktails, including Gs favourite: the Bloody Mary.
Brunch boat pick up and drop off from Homomonument, Keizersgracht 198, 1016 DW
info@reallyniceplace.com
www.reallyniceplace.com
Bus/tram: Westermarkt

CT coffee & coconuts

This De Pijp coffee house and eatery is inside the former Ceintuur Theatre built in the roaring 1920s. The interior is impressive and the coffee has gained quite a following among the city's coffee lovers, but it's also a great place for a bite to eat any time of day. The breakfasts are particularly inventive and hearty, with an abundance of fresh juices served with the likes of coconut pancakes, shakshuka and overnight buckwheat porridge.
Ceintuurbaan 282-284, 1072 GK
+31 (0)20 354 1104
info@ctamsterdam.nl
www.ctamsterdam.nl
Bus/tram: Ceintuurbaan/F Bolstraat

Bakers & Roasters

Famous for its brunches, the locally known B&R is run by a Kiwi and Brazilian pair who decided to cook everything they missed from their homelands. As a result, the menu is full of items such as the Kiwi Brekkie, Navajo eggs and breakfast burritos accompanied by Ozone coffee, served inside an interior with a Scandi feel.
Kadijksplein 16, 1018 AC
www.bakersandroasters.com
Tram: Stadhouderskade (Ferdinand Bolstraat)

Paper Planes

This travelling all-day brunch spot has popped up in various cool locations across Amsterdam, including Frans in De Pijp and Nacional Amsterdam. Typically serving a combination of healthy and indulgent brunch items alongside tables perfect for a little laptop work and a healthy dose of Wi-Fi, brunch at Paper Planes is the place to become part of Amsterdam's creative concept scene.
www.facebook.com/Paper-Planes-658176414264873

The Meets

This De Pijp breakfast spot only serves sugar-free and gluten-free dishes. Ideal for those on a health-kick or diners who simply don't want to go overboard at breakfast, The Meets is a fab find in a health-conscious city.
Cornelis Troostplein 3, 1072 JJ
+31 (0)61 531 6734
hello@themeets.nl
www.themeets.nl
Bus/tram: Cornelis Troostplein

MOOK Pancakes

This is the place for those who simply can't resist a good pancake breakfast. The breakfast menu even comes with 'starters' offering different combinations of avocado dishes. The main breakfast menu consists of organic pancakes of every variety, from fresh blueberries with grated coconut, to 'The Mancake' with bacon, cheese, onions and maple syrup.
De Clercqstraat 34, 1052 NG
+31 (0)20 334 6995
www.facebook.com/mookpancakes
Tram: Bilderdijkstraat (De Clercqstraat)

Photo: CT coffee & coconuts

Lunch

Loetje aan 't IJ
This restaurant inside the former harbour master's office on the River IJ is an impressive spot for a casual lunch. Popular for steaks or lighter lunches, the wraparound terrace is an ideal place to enjoy a sunny lunchtime. For those who like to combine work and play, the building also has a couple of meeting rooms that can be rented out.
Werfkade 14, 1033 RA
+31 (0)20 208 8000
loetjeaantij.loetje.com
Boat: Veer NDSM Werf
Bus: Stenendokweg

De Foodhallen
One of the most popular hang-out spots in Amsterdam, visit this food hall inside a former tram depot for flavours from across the world via an array of innovative food stands. There's everything from Vietnamese street food, Mediterranean mezzes and Spanish cured meats, to freshly baked pies, fried ravioli and frozen yoghurt.
Bellamyplein 51, 1053 AT
info@foodhallen.nl
www.foodhallen.nl
Bus/tram: Ten Katestraat

Soup en Zo
The Dutch love a hearty soup lunch, and Soup en Zo is a firm favourite, with three locations around the city. Inventive soups such as potato with Roquefort, Indian curry with minced lamb and spicy spinach and coconut are the order of the day.
www.soupenzo.nl

Jodenbreestraat 94, 1011 NS
+31 (0)20 422 2243
Bus: Waterlooplein
(Valkenburgerstraat)

Nieuwe Spiegelstraat 54, 1017 DG
+31 (0)20 330 7781
Tram: Spiegelgracht

Van Baerlestraat 81, 1071 AS
+31 (0)20 354 7497
Bus/tram: Roelof Hartplein

Yamazato Restaurant
For a splash out lunch set to impress, look no further than this Michelin star restaurant found inside the elegant Japanese Hotel Okura. This is a traditional kaiseki restaurant with bento box, sushi and other traditional lunches served by kimono-clad staff. Hotel Okura is home to several other highly regarded restaurants that will also impress.
Hotel Okura
Ferdinand Bolstraat 333, 1072 LH
+31 (0)20 678 7111
sales@okura.nl
www.okura.nl
Bus/tram: Cornelis Troostplein

Zuivere Koffie
This cute spot in a central Amsterdam neighbourhood offers homely lunches of warm Italian rolls, fresh omelettes, savoury pies and various other home-made concoctions depending on the day. There's also a secret courtyard garden ideal for enjoying the fresh air and some of the café's speciality Thai coffee.
Utrechtsestraat 39, 1017 VH
+31 (0)20 624 9999
www.facebook.com/pages/
Zuivere-Koffie/210178892344637
Bus/tram: Keizersgracht
(Utrechtsestraat)

Louie Louie
This east Amsterdam bar and eating spot has cool interior design, a huge terrace and a reasonably-priced, South American inspired lunch menu. Try Cuban tortas, huevos rancheros or the more

locally inspired bread rolls with Dutch cheese.
Linnaeusstraat 11, 1093 ED
+31 (0)20 370 2981
info@louielouie.nl
www.louielouie.nl
Bus/tram: Eerste van Swindenstraat

De Foodhallen:
One of the most popular
hang-out spots in Amsterdam.

Photo: Cyril Wermers

Dinner

Grand Café De Tropen

Found inside the impressive surroundings of the Tropenmuseum, visiting Grand Café De Tropen for an evening meal feels like you've stumbled upon a secret corner of the city. Better known for tea, cake and a bustling atmosphere during the day, the evening takes a more intimate turn, with candlelit tables and fresh Asian-inspired menus. Menu items include the likes of tuna tataki, Suriname peanut bravoe (soup), inventive stir fries and grilled fish with quinoa. Fresh, healthy and original, visit Grand Café De Tropen for an unrivalled dining experience in the city.

Linnaeusstraat 2, 1092 AD
+ 31 (0)20 568 2000
info@amsterdamdetropen.nl
www.amsterdamdetropen.nl
Bus/tram: Eerste van Swindenstraat

Remise47

Part of the popular De Hallen complex filled with food stands, boutiques and bars, Remise47 is a trendy option for a sit-down meal. With exposed brick walls and splashes of colourful furniture, Remise47 is a cool place to spend an evening. The international menu has a varied selection, but the daily changing three course chef's menu offers great value for money at €30, which includes items such as tomato and aubergine bruschetta, decadent burgers and red velvet cake. A decent wine and beer menu washes down the meal perfectly.

Bellamyplein 47, 1053 AT
+31 (0)20 820 8675
info@remise47.com
www.remise47.com
Bus/tram: Ten Katestraat

Graceland BAR-B-Q

If you have a hankering for a barbecued American feast while in Amsterdam, look no further than Graceland BAR-B-Q tucked away in an unassuming residential stretch of Amsterdam West. Surrounded by distressed wood, country-rock music and a saloon bar, Graceland feels like the real deal. The menu offers everything you would expect and more, and in a place like this, it would be rude not to get one of the hedonistic sharing platters. Think super-ribs, pulled pork, brisket, flank steak, crab cakes, jailhouse beans, cornbread, pickles and coleslaw. The cocktail menu is equally impressive, with a range of bourbon spiked concoctions. Head along on a Sunday afternoon for 'Country Sundays' with live music.

Jan van Galenstraat 8, 1051 KM
+31 (0)20 723 1760
gracelandbbq@gmail.com
www.gracelandbbq.com
Bus: Markthallen

Café-Restaurant Amsterdam

Found inside an old power station a little on the Amsterdam outskirts, this huge modern day dining hall with simple decor retains its industrial features. The menu has a penchant for fish such as swordfish, scallops and sea bass, although the steak frites, sweetbread and veal are also local favourites.

Watertorenplein 6, 1051 PA
+31 (0)20 682 2666
www.caferestaurantamsterdam.nl
Tram: Van Hallstraat

The Fat Dog

This trendy and low key eatery serves an eclectic mix of hotdogs and champagne. Conceptualised by the well-known chef Ron Blaauw, hot dog flavours include 'Gangs of New York' with sauerkraut and onion marmalade, 'Chinatown' with pulled pork and pickled bean sprouts, and 'Naughty Bangkok' with red curry mayonnaise and crispy rice.

Ruysdaelkade 251, 1072 AX
+31 (0)20 221 6249
info@thefatdog.nl
www.thefatdog.nl
Bus/tram: Cornelis Troostplein

Hangar

This restaurant in Amsterdam Noord inside a green corrugated iron industrial hangar has a raw and trendy vibe overlooking the River IJ. The menu is full of warm southern European culinary flavours such as risottos, raviolis and carpaccios.

Aambeeldstraat 36, 1021 KB
+31 (0)20 363 8657
www.hangar.amsterdam
Boat: Veer Zamenhofstraat

Yokiyo

This Korean barbecue restaurant in central Amsterdam consistently gets rave reviews from fans of this type of cuisine. The basic interior is well-equipped with grills and extractor fans on every table, and the DIY BBQ menu is a popular choice.

Oudezijds Voorburgwal 67, 1012 EJ
+31 (0)20 331 4562
info@yokiyo.nl
www.yokiyo.nl
Metro: Nieuwmarkt

Cafe-restaurant De Plantage

This restaurant near the zoo, Artis, is a modern bistro with an airy interior. The chef is an alumnus of the popular Amsterdam Noord restaurant, Hotel De Goudfazant, and the menu is full of Mediterranean inspired flavours.

Plantage Kerklaan 36, 1018 CZ
+31 (0)20 760 6800
info@caferestaurantdeplantage.nl
www.caferestaurantdeplantage.nl
Bus/tram: Artis

ctaste
Dine in the dark at this restaurant that is all about flavour. Diners choose their food from set menus in the lit lobby, before being served in a darkened restaurant by blind and visually impaired staff. Diners can choose from fish and fruits de la mer, meat and poultry and vegetarian menus. Or trust the chef and choose the surprise menu.
Amsteldijk 55, 1074 HX
+31 (0)20 675 2831
www.ctaste.nl
Bus/tram: Ceintuurbaan/Van Woustraat

Grand Café De Tropen feels like you've stumbled upon a secret corner of the city.

Photos: Grand Café De Tropen

Splash out

Restaurant Johannes

This pristine restaurant on the picturesque Herengracht canal street attracts a discerning crowd who adore top notch cuisine without pretension and at reasonable prices given the quality. Choose between a four, five or six course meal with optional wine pairings and prepare to be wowed. Fun touches include an upside down amuse-bouche while added extras include freshly baked bread sticks and fragrant breads served with Guernsey butter. Tasting menus include the likes of ceviche, the chef's signature pork belly with king prawns, Dutch cheeses and melting chocolate desserts. Giving a true sense of understated Dutch decadence, Restaurant Johannes is a radiant choice.

Herengracht 413, 1017 BP
+31 (0)20 626 9503
info@restaurantjohannes.nl
www.restaurantjohannes.nl
Tram: Koningsplein

Bussia

This modern Italian restaurant in the Nine Streets area offers four, six or eight course tasting menus. Serving dishes such as roasted celeriac soup, carbonara with bisque and lobster, and Venison fillet, this restaurant serves the freshest cuisines in a chic, romantic interior.

Reestraat 28-32, 1016 DN
+31 (0)20 627 8794
info@bussia.nl
www.bussia.nl
Bus/tram: Westermarkt

supperclub

This sleek venue has a restaurant, club, gallery, cocktail bar and beer café. Part of the etiquette at supperclub involves removing shoes and lying on crisp white beds. In the restaurant, five-course tasting menus include concoctions such as Oreo cookie foie gras, angus steak with cucumber spaghetti and lollipop white chocolate ganache with wasabi and miso.

Singel 460, 1017 AW
+ 31 (0)20 344 6400
amsterdam@supperclub.com
supperclub.amsterdam
Tram: Koningsplein

Librije's Zusje

This two Michelin star restaurant in the Waldorf Astoria is an amazing location for a truly upmarket meal by renowned Chef Sidney Schutte. With a choice of either the chef's menu or the a la carte menu, food served includes young mackerel with smoked haddock liver, Perle Imperial Caviar with oyster, hazelnut and coffee, and milk cow rib-eye.

Herengracht 542-556, 1017 CG
+31 (0)20 718 4643
restaurants.amsterdam@
waldorfastoria.com
www.librijeszusje.com
Bus/tram: Keizersgracht
(Utrechtsestraat)

Salmuera

The place to go for meat lovers, Salmuera is an Argentinian restaurant serving some of the best steaks and ceviche in the city. Offering a variety of beef cuts and all-important side orders such as chimichurri and Inca quinoa salad, this is the place to go for a carnivorous treat.

Rozengracht 106H, 1016 NH
+31 (0)20 624 5752
info@sal-amsterdam.nl
www.sal-amsterdam.nl
Bus/tram: Marnixstraat/
Rozengracht

Blauw aan de Wal

This restaurant tucked away inside an old spice warehouse in the heart of the red light district offers a surprising culinary journey to diners. Three or four course menus with optional matched wines include cuisines such as Scottish razors, oysters, Ibérico pork and Valrhona chocolate.

Oudezijds Achterburgwal 99, 1012 DD
+31 (0)20 330 2257
info@blauwaandewal.com
www.blauwaandewal.com
Metro: Nieuwmarkt

Photos: Restaurant Johannes

Giving a true sense of understated Dutch decadence, Restaurant Johannes is a radiant choice.

Photos: Restaurant Johannes

Snack

Dim Sum Now
This dim sum and gyoza spot offers 'baskets of steamy goodness', ideal for a healthy snack on-the-go. Fillings consist of everything from veal, shrimp or duck, to chestnut, ginger and pak choi. Steamed buns filled with pork or vegetarian options make great fast food at cheap prices.
Ferdinand Bolstraat 36, 1072 LK
+31 (0)20 820 0808
info@dimsumnow.nl
www.dimsumnow.nl
Tram: Albert Cuypstraat

Pho 91
This small Vietnamese eatery at the famous Albert Cuyp Market offers a rich array of small plates and pho, ideal for a fast and delicious meal.
Albert Cuypstraat 91, 1072 CP
+31 (0)20 752 6880
hello@pho91.nl
www.pho91.nl
Tram: Albert Cuypstraat

Salsa Shop
This fast food spot offers fresh, "Mexico-approved" meals to eat in or to go. "Either you like tacos or you're wrong" is just one of the slogans. There are also burritos, burrito bowls, tortilla chips and salads on the menu. With two locations in the city, you're never too far from a spicy fix.
www.salsashop.com

Ferdinand Bolstraat 1, 1072 LA
+31 (0)20 363 7369
Tram: Stadhouderskade
(Ferdinand Bolstraat)

Amstelstraat 32, 1017 DA
+31 (0)20 205 1040
Bus/metro/tram: Waterlooplein

Sir Hummus
This De Pijp eatery serves just three types of its delicious, home-made and 'crap-free' hummus: plain vegan, with egg or with beef. A stop off at this hummus bar is ideal for a snack or even a meal with warm pitta bread and beetroot salad. Sir Hummus is a locally loved stalwart.
Van der Helstplein 2, 1072 PH
+31 (0)20 664 7055
info@sirhummus.nl
www.sirhummus.nl
Bus/tram: Tweede van der Helststraat

STACH food
This organic deli serves small snacks, hams and cheeses, home-made bread and has a rotating menu of home-made cheeses to take away. At the Nieuwe Spiegelstraat location, it's also possible to drink a glass of wine at the bar with small bites to eat.
www.stach-food.nl

Nieuwe Spiegelstraat 52, 1017 DG
+31 (0)20 737 2220
Tram: Keizersgracht (Vijzelstraat)

Van Woustraat 154, 1073 LW
+31 (0)20 754 2672
Bus/tram: Lutmastraat

Mumu
If you have a chocolate craving but want to make it a bit healthy, try Mumu's vitamin chocolates. The dairy-free chocolates come enriched with vitamins B, D3, Chromium and coenzyme Q10.
Eerste Jacob van Campenstraat 33, 1072 BC
+31 (0)6 2123 1255
info@mumuvitaminchocolates.com
mumuvitaminchocolates.com
Bus/tram: Stadhouderskade
(Ferdinand Bolstraat)

Cafés

Latei
Embracing the Amsterdam love of the concept store, Latei is a place where you can grab a coffee and shop for a quirky selection of homeware and trinkets. More or less everything is for sale there. It's a popular place, so be prepared to queue or share a table while you enjoy a slice of home-made apple pie.
Zeedijk 143, 1012 AW
+31 (0)20 625 7485
info@latei.net
www.latei.net
Metro: Nieuwmarkt

White Label Coffee Roasters
Run by an adorable coffee-obsessed duo, White Label hosts regular events such as book readings and gigs and is home to the current Dutch Aeropress champion Floris van der Burg.
Jan Evertsenstraat 136, 1056 EK
+31 (0)20 737 1359
info@whitelabelcoffee.nl
www.whitelabelcoffee.nl
Bus: Mercatorplein

Stooker Roasting Co.
This is not a café in the traditional sense because it's not open to the public during the week, but on Saturdays Stooker Roasting Co. does public cuppings and offers workshops in its gorgeous roastery. So, if you happen to be in town for the weekend, swing by and try some of their expertly-roasted coffees.
Kastanjeplein 2, 1092 CJ
+31 (0)20 737 1714
hello@stookerroastingco.com
www.stookerroastingco.com
Bus/tram: Linnaeusstraat/
Wijttenbachstraat

Hartje Oost

This coffee shop and boutique in eastern Amsterdam's vibrant Javastraat sources everything with painstaking attention-to-detail. The result is top notch coffee in an eclectic and interesting interior, served alongside locally baked goods and cool fashion.

Javastraat 23, 1094 GZ
+31 (0)20 233 2137
info@hartjeoost.nl
www.hartjeoost.nl
Bus/tram: Javaplein

Filter

This no-nonsense coffee spot around the corner from Artis zoo is an ideal quiet spot for coffee, cake and some laptop time.

Valkenburgerstraat 124, 1011 NA
+31 (0)20 261 1434
info@filteramsterdam.nl
www.filteramsterdam.nl
Bus: Waterlooplein
(Valkenburgerstraat)

CoffeeConcepts

This airy coffee bar in Oud Zuid is also a place people go to buy art and gain access to marketing and communications expertise. Combining great coffee and a creative work ethic under one roof, this is the ideal place to spend some time whether it's for work or play.

Jacob Obrechtstraat 5, 1071 KC
+31 (0)20 779 8986
info@coffeeconcepts.co
www.coffeeconcepts.co
Tram: Van Baerlestraat

Photo: Cyril Wermers

Drinks

Café Hoppe
This well-known brown café with its wooden interior and smoke-stained walls dates back to the 1600s, and has even been named a national monument. It used to be a distillery but is now a simple drinking hole with a small food menu.
Spui 18-20, 1012 XA
+31 (0)20 420 4420
info@cafehoppe.com
www.cafehoppe.com
Tram: Spui (Nieuwezijds Voorburgwal)

Jackson Dubois
This bar by the son of a winegrower from the Champagne region of France is an internationally inspired hotspot ripe for trying the best drinks from around the world. Try some of the best beers from Dutch micro-breweries, or travel further afield to grapetails, fire water and of course, an impressive selection of champagnes. There's a tasty selection of street food ideal for munching alongside any tipple.
Spui 10, 1012 WZ
+31 (0)64 636 0044
info@jacksondubois.com
www.jacksondubois.com
Tram: Spui (Nieuwezijds Voorburgwal)

Wynand Fockink
This 17th century distillery and tasting tavern in central Amsterdam serves more than 70 Dutch liqueurs. It's a tiny slice of Amsterdam's long history and an ideal place to taste some alternative alcoholic concoctions.
Pijlsteeg 31, 1012 HH
+31 (0)20 639 2695
contact@wynand-fockink.nl
www.wynand-fockink.nl
Bus/tram: Dam

Bar Oldenhof
This old-fashioned bar in central Amsterdam is a favourite with whiskey lovers given the vast selection of single malts, although there are plenty of other drinks available too. The dimly lit, wood-clad interior with overstuffed armchairs makes it feel like a throwback to times past. Bar Oldenhof also runs regular whiskey tastings with food pairings.
Elandsgracht 84, 1016 TZ
info@bar-oldenhof.com
www.bar-oldenhof.com
Bus/tram: Elandsgracht

Brouwerij Troost
This local Amsterdam micro-brewery brews its own beers in a former monastery in De Pijp and in the cultural venue, Westergasfabriek. Visit either location to try a selection of beers alongside burgers or snacks.
www.brouwerijtroost.nl

Cornelis Troostplein 21, 1072 JJ
+31 (0)20 737 1028
depijp@brouwerijtroost.nl
Bus/tram: Cornelis Troostplein

Pazzanistraat 25-27, 1014 DB
+31 (0)20 737 1028
westergas@brouwerijtroost.nl
Bus: Van Limburg Stirumstraat

Tales and Spirits
This simply decorated bar with a hint of prestige radiating from its giant chandelier is tucked away in a central Amsterdam location. An extensive cocktail menu makes it an ideal spot for an aperitif or some general post-dinner fun. After all, one of the house rules is: "Laugh, giggle and be silly".
Lijnbaanssteeg 5-7, 1012 TE
+31 (0)65 535 6467
info@talesandspirits.com
www.talesandspirits.com
Bus/tram: Nieuwezijds Kolk

Café De Dokter
The smallest café in the city and one of Amsterdam's stalwart brown cafés, this is a great place to stop for a drink inside a tiny, history-steeped and trinket-filled interior. Dating back to the 1700s, this is where doctors and medical students used to relax.
Rozenboomsteeg 4, 1012 PR
+31 (0)20 624 2582
www.cafe-de-dokter.nl
Bus/tram: Spui (Rokin)

Cafe Scrapyard
This western Amsterdam hotspot is home to recycled decor and an environmentally-friendly ethos. The extensive drinks menu is full of inventive cocktails, but the bar is especially known for its boozy shakes. Food to accompany the booze is constantly changing between daily specials, food trucks and kitchen takeovers.
Kinkerstraat 24, 1053 DV
www.cafescrapyard.com
Bus/tram: Elandsgracht

Waterkant
This Suriname-inspired waterfront bar is a fun-loving spot to have a drink and let loose. Drink Surinamese Parbo beers and munch on traditional snack foods. For those who like to party, Waterkant goes on until the early hours at the weekend.
Marnixstraat 246, 1016 TL
+31 (0)20 737 1126
fawaka@waterkantamsterdam.nl
www.waterkantamsterdam.nl
Bus/tram: Elandsgracht

Checkpoint Charlie
This western Amsterdam drinking hole offers a slice of Berlin in the city, with an extensive selection of beers served alongside traditional currywürst. There's a regular

calendar of events to go alongside the pastime of drinking, including DJ sets, spoken word evenings and rock 'n' roll bands.
Nassaukade 48, 1052 CM
+31 (0)20 370 8728
info@cafecheckpointcharlie.nl
www.cafecheckpointcharlie.nl
Tram: Nassaukade

De Prael brewpub
Try the beers from the Brouwerij de Prael, a true Amsterdammer micro-brewery, in its very own brewpub where you can try everything from Prael bitter blonds and wheat beers to barley wine and Scotch ale.
Oudezijds Armsteeg 26, 1012 GP
+31 (0)20 408 4469
boekingen@deprael.nl
www.deprael.nl
Bus: CS/Nicolaaskerk or Amsterdam Centraal

Golden Brown Bar
This cosy bar near Vondelpark is named after an eighties song by The Stranglers. It's a place where Dutch locals, international residents and other visitors meet for Thai food and drinks. Enjoy a cup of coffee or a beer on the front terrace overlooking a busy street, or by the quieter residential street to the side of the bar.
Jan Pieter Heijestraat 146, 1054 MK
+31 (0)20 612 4076
info@goldenbrownbar.nl
www.goldenbrownbar.nl
Tram: Jan Pieter Heijestraat (Overtoom)

Arendsnest
This brown café only serves Dutch beer, with a whopping 100 varieties to try and 30 on tap. There are also tastings held in a room downstairs for those who want to learn to properly appreciate beer.
Herengracht 90, 1015 BS
+31 (0)20 421 2057
www.arendsnest.nl
Bus/tram: Nieuwezijds Kolk

The Golden Brown Bar is a place where Dutch locals, international residents and other visitors meet for Thai food and drinks.

Photo: Cyril Wermers

171

Amsterdam has always been a very open and free city, so everybody who visits should be like that too.

Photo: Oof Verschuren

Yvette van Boven
Recipe writer, food stylist and TV chef

Introduce yourself.
I used to be the co-owner of a restaurant in Amsterdam called Aan de Amstel, which I ran with my cousin, Joris Vermeer, for a number of years. Now I'm a recipe writer and columnist. As well as writing my own cookery books, I write for newspapers, I'm a culinary editor for the biggest women's weekly in Holland — *Libelle Magazine* — and I write for magazines such as *Delicious*, *Elle Food* and *Bon Appétit*. I'm also an illustrator, working on the illustrations for magazines and books. And finally, I have a weekly national television show called *Koken met van Boven*. So that's what I do; it's quite a lot!

How did you get into your line of work?
I went to art school originally, where I studied to become an interior architect. I owned a design studio for about five years with my sister, who is a graphic designer and an artist. I had always cooked as a side job to earn some extra money, and when we had the design studio, both my sister and I missed cooking. So we started working at a fashion magazine, looking after the food pages. We did everything together, including the photography. I particularly enjoyed the visual side of it — now called food styling — but at that time there wasn't even a proper name for it. My boyfriend — now my husband — Oof Verschuren, is a photographer, and he was always asking me to cook things for photos he needed to take for big commercial clients. Cooking for photographs has a strong design element because you have to make a composition. You look at a plate very differently for photographs than when you cook in a restaurant, because you have to look through the lens. When you're writing a recipe you have to bring all of this together, making a composition for taste and texture as well as for a flat canvas. Everything has to be in the right place. I enjoyed doing it so much that I thought I should make it my job. At around the same time, my sister was looking for more freedom to be an artist, so we decided to break up from our joint business venture to pursue our own areas of interest. We're still very good friends; there was no harm done.

You've received awards for Dutch Cookbook of the Year and the ELLE Award for Best Dutch Food Photography, and nominations for accolades such as Best First Cookbook at the Gourmand World Cookbook Awards. Describe your journey from restaurant owner to award-winning cookbook writer.

After branching away from my work with my sister, I opened my own catering company and started working as a full time food stylist and recipe writer. I was cooking from the kitchen in my apartment, and even though my kitchen takes up most of my home, it wasn't big enough for our clients. My cousin Joris was working at a hotel at that time, and he helped me out when we were catering for bigger events and needed a lot of people to help cook and serve. Things were going well and we decided to find a bigger space, so we moved into a great building on the banks of the River Amstel, and started a proper company together. We had the restaurant for nine years in total. Then I injured my back, which is something many cooks suffer from. It was a terrible time; I had to have an operation and stay at home in a corset. It was very sad, but I try to see the positives in life, so I decided to take the opportunity to create the book I'd always dreamed of writing. It was subsequently released in 2010 and it became the Dutch Cookbook of the Year almost immediately. It was translated into English, German, Spanish and French, and it did particularly well in Australia and the United States. Then I was encouraged to make more books, and I was really enjoying it, so I agreed. For me, everything fell into place when I started making books as I could combine all the things I liked to do in one job. Given my background, I could do the design part, the illustrations, and the food styling for the photos that my husband shot. The book could be exactly as I wanted it and I just handed over a PDF file to my publisher. You don't really imagine yourself as cookbook writer; it just happens. It's a tremendous amount of work, but it's so rewarding.

What do readers expect from your cookbooks?

I'm used to making everything myself from scratch, so my books and recipes revolve around the theme of every aspect of a meal being home-made. I was brought up that way. Why would I buy something if I can make it myself? For me it's so normal and logical, but now it's becoming a trend to make everything yourself, which has helped with the success of my books and recipes. I grew up reading the *Time Life* cookbooks, which had photographs showing you step-by-step how each stage of the recipe should turn out, such as the thickness of the sauce or what a cake should look like when you cut it. That's actually how I learned cooking. I wanted to bring this kind of concept into my cookbooks, because it's details like these that people get stuck with. When you're reading a recipe without photos, it will say things like: "the consistency should be like yoghurt." But you wonder if it means thick yoghurt or runny yoghurt! So I have pictures in my books that show you what things should look like in a really explanatory way. We've photographed every technique, whether it's making yoghurt or sour dough, to smoking meat without a smoker.

Tell us about your life in the world of television.
I'd received a number of offers to do TV shows over the years, but I wasn't very interested in doing them because filming is a very different line of work and I wasn't really keen on being a TV personality where people might recognise me in the street! I'm actually quite a private person and I'm very happy to be by myself. So getting into TV was a bit scary at first. But the production company who asked me to do a pilot with them makes such lovely programmes; they're really carefully produced and are in more of an arthouse style than a polished, glamourous style. I love that. The pilot episode went really well and the show took off. Each season has around 12 episodes, but sometimes we end up filming a lot more and I do Christmas specials too. It's a ridiculous amount of work! Every show is about the heritage of food. Sometimes we talk about an ingredient and go to see the producers of that ingredient, whether they are fishermen or vegetable producers. Sometimes we go into a museum to look at a story behind an ingredient or a dish. Then we'll go back to the kitchen in my home and I'll cook something. Once a week we clear out our home so all the people and equipment can pile in, including three cameras pointing at the kitchen from different angles. Making it together with the crew is lovely. I like the fact that it's like making a book, but even more complex. We have a musician who does all the sound, but he also makes all the music himself. And I have a great relationship with the cameraman, the producer and the director. It feels like a family; we're really happy together.

Where did you grow up and which Amsterdam neighbourhood do you call home now?
I was born in Ireland to Dutch parents, and lived there until I was ten years old. Then we moved to Haarlem, which is very near Amsterdam, close to the coast. After I left school I lived in Antwerp and The Hague for a few years while I was attending art school. I moved to Amsterdam at the end of the 1990s and have been there ever since, although my husband and I spend a lot of time in Paris too. The Amsterdam neighbourhood we lived in for many years is Nieuwmarkt, and I'm very fond of that area. It's very near Central Station but it's very quiet. A lot of Amsterdam is very busy; it's a very small city but it's quite crowded, so I really like the peace and quiet of Nieuwmarkt. I loved living there, but our apartment became too small, so we recently moved to the north of the city. To find a bigger house which is affordable, you have to look at the outer parts of Amsterdam nowadays. Amsterdam Noord is still very close to the centre via the ferry and it still has very quiet, village-like areas and green open spaces, but

there is a lot happening in the area too. It's changing into a very modern part of Amsterdam, which I really like. A lot of new adventurous things are happening there and cool restaurants are opening up, which is very inspiring. I'm looking forward to seeing the whole area changing. We have moved to a very old village on a scenic and traditional Dutch street, only five minutes from the ferry. There's also brand new housing being constructed there, and I like that mix. It's not a posh neighbourhood, but instead it has a mixture of all kinds of people, which is great.

Tell us about the time you spend in Paris.
When I had the restaurant, I was so busy, working seven days a week. So when I had time off, I had a strong urge to get away and gain some inspiration from somewhere else. That's when we started going to Paris a lot. It's only a four and a half hour drive, so you can leave Amsterdam after dinner and still be there before midnight. We used to stay with my aunt who lives there, but since we spent so much time in the city, we decided to get our own place. We imagined ourselves being old and having a house in Paris, so we rented one. We thought we'd have it for a year and see how it went, but now we've had it for more than ten years and we've become very close to the house and the life in Paris. For me it's great to be by yourself in another city, soaking up new energy and new ideas. Staying in the same place for your whole life would be too claustrophobic; travel is good for everybody.

Describe Amsterdam's food scene.
It's changed a lot in the last ten years. When we opened our restaurant, I wanted to serve slightly more adventurous things for lunch because I was very disappointed in the way Dutch people ate lunch. Standard lunch places in Amsterdam would serve 'broodjes', which are basically sandwiches or rolls filled with meat or cheese. I hated the way people were eating such basic food. Even when we gave menus to people in the restaurant, they would still ask if we had broodjes. I would say: "No, we only serve real food!" I was designing lunch menus with things like pearl couscous, which wasn't very well known at the time. But now I think a lot of chefs have been looking at the food scene in New York, London, Paris and Berlin, and a lot has changed. Restaurants are getting more and more competitive and it's created a thriving food scene in Amsterdam. Food really has become better in Amsterdam and the standards are quite high nowadays. Chefs are looking at food in a different way. Cuisine that takes into account sustainability, originality and local producers is much more likely to be found on restaurant plates now than it was before. Lots of restaurants are popping up all the time and as well as organic and alternative food markets and festivals, there are also craft beer bars, coffee houses with really good coffee and small projects such as natural wine bars. People are more and more willing to try new things. You can even see it at the supermarket: they too are selling more organic and speciality foods that no-one had even heard of ten years ago.

Where are your favourite places to eat out in Amsterdam?
Restaurant Kaagman & Kortekaas is my absolute favourite. Their culinary
creations have a stroke of genius about them. I like the restaurant because
the interior is very basic and you feel at ease when you go in, yet the
cooking is high-end, modern French. They really know what they're
doing there. They work with funny parts of animals a lot, like roosters'
combs. They don't make a spectacle out of eating weird things; they're
just genuinely inventive and the food is absolutely delicious. Restaurant
Bordewijk, is a restaurant I've been going to for years, and I think it's the
godfather of restaurants with fantastic French food. It's run by Chef Wil
Demant, who is a big inspiration to me. I like Café Modern, which is in
the north of Amsterdam. Sander van Melick is the chef and he changes
the menu every week. It's very original and is inside an old bank; you
really don't expect anything much to be behind the door when you go in.
I like the fact they're brave, and the food, wine and service are all great.
Restaurant As is a fantastic restaurant in the south of Amsterdam. It's built
inside a former church, and they weren't allowed to put the kitchen inside
the church, so they built the kitchen inside a tent in the garden instead.
They have a big wood-fired oven where they bake the best bread ever and
they have a very seasonal, organic kitchen. They have a side project which
is called Vuurtoreneiland (Lighthouse Island) which is in the north of
Amsterdam. It's on a very small island where there are only sheep and a
little house. You buy tickets for the dinner and then all that evening's diners
get into the little boat to go over to the island. On the boat, everyone gets
a little box with nibbles and drinks. Then everyone is served a seasonal, set
menu together on the very scenic island. It's an amazing experience from
start to finish. The island also has a number of bunkers because it used
to be a military fort, so now they use the bunkers to store the wine. It's
only open in the summer at the moment, but they're working on a winter
version and they want to see if they can have a small hotel there, which
would be wonderful.

What do you do in your spare time?
I'm a very big walker and I also have a dog, so I like to walk around the
city a lot. I like to be a tourist in my own city because there's always
something to see; Amsterdam is constantly in motion. I love to go to EYE
Film Museum, the big white building on the River IJ in the north of the
city. They show great movies there and it's lovely to just wander around or
have a drink in the bar. The views over Amsterdam are great. Downstairs
they have small yellow two-person cabins with love seats inside. You can
look through their huge database of films and watch them on a screen.
It's a great thing to do if you have a hangover: just sit there watching films
all day, whether it's Laurel and Hardy or documentaries and arthouse
films. I'm very interested in documentaries so I also love to go to the
International Documentary Festival Amsterdam (IDFA) there every year.

Where do you go for creative escapism?

I really like De Ceuvel in Amsterdam Noord. It's a place for creative and social enterprises consisting of a series of self-sufficient boats on the land. It has a really fun, entrepreneurial and circus-like atmosphere, but the people who run it have a real concern for the environment too, so they also do things like beekeeping. They have really ambitious plans for regenerating the previous industrial plot they are situated on, which is currently quite polluted, into a sustainable and healthy urban development. There is a restaurant and bar there too and it gets very crowded, especially during the summer. It's so inspiring to visit a place like this and to be around people with such important and amazing plans.

What are the most exciting things happening in Amsterdam at the moment?

The Stedelijk Museum and the Rijksmuseum were both closed for a number of years for renovations, but they're finally open again which is great. They're fantastic museums and very good reasons for visiting Amsterdam. Another exciting thing about Amsterdam at the moment is the fact that the smaller neighbourhoods away from the centre of Amsterdam — such as Amsterdam Oost, Amsterdam West and Amsterdam Noord — have got more and more going on. I always think it's a shame if people visit the city just to go to the stupid coffeeshops, which are mainly there for tourists anyway. The neighbourhoods further away from central Amsterdam are getting an increasing amount of attention because there are loads of things happening, such as small artist studios, boutiques and quirky restaurants. That's where people should go for a real flavour of Amsterdam's vibe and innovation. You could compare it to Brooklyn in New York. That's where the small producers and artistic things are happening. On my last visit to New York, I didn't go to Manhattan once!

What is the current trend in the city?

There's definitely a trend for small producers thriving in the city, although I know that is happening elsewhere in the world too. Small producers are popping up everywhere, with butchers such as De Pasteibakkerij or Brandt & Levie, and organic grocery shops. A friend of mine, Simone van Thull, opened up a shop in which she only ferments things; it's called Thull's in the east part of Amsterdam and she makes her own pickled vegetable produce such as kombucha, kefir and sauerkraut. She makes delicious food to take home for dinner or lunch. There are also a lot of craft beer breweries such as Brouwerij 't IJ and Brouwerij Oedipus in Amsterdam Noord.

Is there a smell you associate with Amsterdam?

Fresh air. Despite the fact it's quite a crowded city, it's small, there's a lot of open space and there's an abundance of water that is clean. The canals are looked after very well. We have a boat — lots of people in Amsterdam do — and during the summer everyone jumps off into the canals for a swim.

How should people live like Amsterdammers when they're visiting the city?

The great thing is that it doesn't matter if you don't speak Dutch. I have friends who have lived in Amsterdam for years without speaking a word of Dutch. That's no problem here, which is quite a cool thing. Visitors to Amsterdam blend in if they are simply open-minded. Globally, you still find people are judgemental about things like homosexuality or religion. Amsterdam has always been a very open and free city, so everybody who visits should be like that too. Then they'll fit in fine and have a great time.

Yvette's Amsterdam

Places to visit

Amsterdam Noord
1020-1039
Boat: Veer Buiksloterweg, Veer IJplein

EYE Film Museum
IJpromenade 1, 1031 KT
+31 (0)20 589 1400
info@eyefilm.nl
www.eyefilm.nl
Boat/bus: Veer Buiksloterweg

Nieuwmarkt
1012 CS
Tram/bus: Dam

Rijksmuseum
Museumstraat 1, 1071 XX
+31 (0)900 0745
www.rijksmuseum.nl/en
Tram: Rijksmuseum

Stedelijk Museum
Museumplein 10, 1071 DJ
+31 (0)20 573 2911
www.stedelijk.nl
Tram: Van Baerlestraat

Eating and drinking

Brandt & Levie
Archangelkade 9, 1013 BE
+31 (0)88 044 2100
info@brandtenlevie.nl
www.brandtenlevie.nl
Bus: Koivistokade

Brouwerij Oedipus
Gedempt Hamerkanaal 85, 1021 KP
info@oedipusbrewing.com
www.oedipus.com
Bus: Hamerstraat

Brouwerij 't IJ
Funenkade 7, 1018 AL
+31 (0)20 528 6237
www.brouwerijhetij.nl
Tram: Hoogte Kadijk

Café de Ceuvel
Korte Papaverweg 4, 1032 KB
+31 (0)20 229 6210
info@cafedeceuvel.nl
www.cafedeceuvel.nl
Bus: Mosplein

Café Modern
Meidoornweg 2, 1031 GG
+31 (0)20 494 0684
www.modernamsterdam.nl
Bus: Meidoornplein

De Pasteibakkerij
Hoendiepstraat 2, 1079 LT
+31 (0)6 53 47 5512
info@depasteibakkerij.nl
www.pasteibakkerij.tumblr.com
Bus/tram: Victorieplein

Restaurant As
Prinses Irenestraat 19, 1077 WT
+31 (0)20 644 0100
www.restaurantas.nl
Bus/tram: Prinses Irenestraat/ Beethovenstraat

Restaurant Bordewijk
Noordermarkt 7 /HS, 1015 MV
+31 (0)20 624 3899
www.bordewijk.nl
Bus: Buiten Brouwersstraat

Restaurant Kaagman & Kortekaas
Sint Nicolaasstraat 43, 1012 NJ
+31 (0)20 233 6544
info@kaagmanenkortekaas.nl
www.kaagmanenkortekaas.nl
Bus: Dam/Raadhuisstraat

Restaurant Vuurtoreneiland (Lighthouse Island)
Oostelijks handelskade 34, 1019BN (boat departures)
info@vuurtoreneiland.nl
www.vuurtoreneiland.nl
Bus/tram: C. van Eesterenlaan
Tram: Rietlandpark

Thull's
Pretoriusstraat 69, 1092
+31 (0)20 363 5474
info@thulls.nl
www.thulls.nl
Bus: James Wattstraat

See also

Bon Appétit
www.bonappetit.com
Delicious
www.deliciousmagazine.nl
Elle Food
www.elleeten.nl
International Documentary Festival Amsterdam (IDFA)
www.idfa.nl
Koken met van Boven
www.vpro.nl/koken-met-van-boven.html
Libelle Magazine
www.libelle.nl
Oof Verschuren
www.oofverschuren.com

Find out more about Yvette van Boven at
www.yvettevanboven.com or on
Twitter @yvettevanboven

Photo: Oof Verschuren

Shopping in Amsterdam

General

Nine Streets (De Negen Straatjes)
These nine streets in a central Amsterdam area comprise of a series of small lanes connected together by canals. It's a much-loved pocket of the city for boutique shopping, with shops selling clothing by independent and well-known designers, jewellery, art, giftware and vintage goods. There are also plenty of cosy, independent cafés to stop in for mid-shopping coffee breaks.
Nine Streets, 1016 DT
Bus/tram: Westermarkt

De Bijenkorf
One of the most well-known high-end department stores in the Netherlands, De Bijenkorf (meaning 'the beehive') has its flagship store on Dam Square in Amsterdam. Filled with high-end designer shops and high street stores, it's a popular place for Amsterdammers to peruse the shops.
Dam 1, 1012 JS
+31 (0)800 0818
www.debijenkorf.nl
Bus/tram: Dam

Magna Plaza
This shopping centre is found inside a historical building — the former Post Office — behind the Royal Palace. As well as hosting a range of designer shops, Magna Plaza also has an impressive exhibition space displaying various artworks.
Nieuwezijds Voorburgwal 182, 1012 SJ
www.magnaplaza.nl
Bus/tram: Dam/Raadhuisstraat

Beethovenstraat
This modern shopping street in the Zuid neighbourhood has a range of luxury boutiques, gift shops and high-end cafés, and offers a quieter and more leisurely shopping experience compared to central Amsterdam locations.
Beethovenstraat, 1077 HN
Bus/tram: Beethovenstraat

See also: Spiegelkwartier (p56) and Haarlemmerbuurt (p54)

Markets

Dappermarkt
This traditional and inexpensive market has more than 200 stands selling a vast range of wares. It's popular for serving a spread of exotic foods from Turkey, Suriname and countries in Africa. There is occasionally live music to mark special events.
Dapperstraat, 1093 BS
www.dappermarkt.nl
Bus/tram: Dapperstraat

Bloemenmarkt
The world's only floating flower market, this is where a number of florists and garden shops can be found on a series of barges. It's a colourful place to find souvenirs and soak up local life.
Singel, between Muntplein and Koningsplein, 1017 BE
Tram: Koningsplein or Muntplein

Oudemanhuispoort book market
This market in a covered passage is where second-hand books, prints and sheet music have been sold since the 1700s. Visit the market for a quaint atmosphere and a potential treasure trove of rare finds.
Oudemanhuisport, 1012 CN
Bus/tram: Spui (Rokin)

Pure Market
This travelling market visits Amsterdam once a fortnight, where only goods from sustainable sources can be found. As well as an abundance of foodie items, there is a range of designer, vintage and gift items.
Frankendael Park and Amstel Park
www.puremarkt.nl

See also: Neighbourhoods section (p52)

Fashion

SPRMRKT
This huge store in the Jordaan, found inside a former supermarket, houses some of the most contemporary and progressive fashion in existence. The industrial-esque, artsy space works with a number of designers, and also hosts regular showcase events.
Rozengracht 191-193, 1016 LZ
+31 (0)20 330 5601
info@sprmrkt.nl
www.sprmrkt.nl
Bus/tram: Marnixstraat/Rozengracht

290 Square Meters
This store inside a former bank vault sells a carefully curated concoction of fashions and accessories. Nike even launched a world premiere shoe project with the brand, where people could create their own custom Nike trainers. This is as much a place for keeping up with the fashion world and gaining creative inspiration as it is for shopping.
Houtkopersdwarsstraat 3, 1011 NK
+31 (0)20 419 2525
info@290sqm.com
www.290sqm.com
Bus/metro/tram: Waterlooplein

Tenue de Nîmes is a must-visit in a city famed for denim.

Tenue de Nîmes

Widely cited as being a top store in Amsterdam to procure some of the best quality denim brands from around the world, Tenue de Nîmes is a must-visit in a city famed for denim. The owners really know their stuff, and will happily discuss denim until closing time over an espresso or Heineken.
www.tenuedenimes.com
info@tenuedenimes.com

Elandsgracht 60, 1016 TX
+31 (0)20 320 4012
Bus/tram: Elandsgracht

Haarlemmerstraat 92-94, 1013 EV
+31 (0)20 331 2778
Bus: Buiten Brouwersstraat

By AMFI

This is the showcase store for the Amsterdam Fashion Institute, where fashion-lovers can find the latest creations by the fashion school's students, alumni and teachers. It's the place to find truly original fashion designs and to gain an insight into the up-and-coming designers of the fashion world.
Spui 23, 1012 WX
+31 (0)20 525 8133
www.amfi.nl/byamfi
Bus/tram: Spui (Rokin)

Specialist

Neef Louis

This huge furniture store in the north of Amsterdam is filled with vintage, design and industrial creations. It's ideal for picking out original interiors for your home or office, or for gaining creative inspiration from an eclectic mixture of styles.
Papaverweg 46 - 48, 1032 KJ
+31 (0)20 486 9354
info@neeflouis.nl
www.neeflouis.nl
Bus: Klaprozenweg/
Ridderspoorweg

Lola Luid

This pop-up mall appears in abandoned buildings to put them to good use before they are renovated or let out to permanent new tenants. Supporting creative start-ups, Lola Luid is home to design, fashion and vintage shops, a bicycle store and a café/lunchroom. It's the ideal place to find innovative products and to support fledgling creative entrepreneurs.
hallo@lolaluid.nl
www.lolaluid.nl

Frozen Fountain

This design shop has a loyal following including pretty much every creative individual in Amsterdam. Featuring the works of emerging designers from the Netherlands and internationally, this is the place to find the newest designs for home accessories and art, as well as classical favourites.
Prinsengracht 645, 1016 HV
+31 (0)20 622 9375
enquiry@frozenfountain.nl
www.frozenfountain.nl
Tram: Prinsengracht
(Leidsestraat)

Concerto

This shop is a favourite with music-lovers who love to unearth obscure and vintage CDs, 45s and memorabilia. Taking up several shop-fronts on a favourite shopping street, this is a place where many hours could be lost to the joy of music. There's also a coffee bar and small area for live acts inside.
Utrechtsestraat 52-60, 1017 VP
+31 (0)20 261 2610
info@concerto.nl
www.concerto.nl
Bus/tram: Keizersgracht
(Utrechtsestraat)

De Kaaskamer

This store for foodies has more than 200 varieties of cheese, both from the Netherlands and further afield. Visitors can order cheese to be vacuum packed and shipped to their homes so their Amsterdam experiences can continue long after the end of a trip.
Runstraat 7, 1016 GJ
+31 (0)20 623 3483
www.kaaskamer.nl
Bus/tram: Keizersgracht
(Leidsestraat)

Mail & Female

There's no shortage of sex related shops in Amsterdam, but this one is run for women, by women (although their partners are welcome too). This is the physical store of the popular mail order service for high-quality sex toys and high-end lingerie. If you're planning to go shopping in the city of sex, this probably isn't a bad place to start.
Nieuwe Vijzelstraat 2, 1017 HT
www.mailfemale.com
Tram: Weteringcircuit/
Weteringsch

Peter van Ginkel

A slice of creative heaven for the city's artists and designers, this store sells paints, canvases, brushes and tools for every occasion. There are also several artists in residence for those looking for creative inspiration and some insight into Amsterdam's art scene.
Bilderdijkstraat 99, 1053 KM
+31 (0)20 618 9827
amsterdam@petervanginkel.nl
www.petervanginkel.nl
Bus/tram: Kinkerstraat

Boutique hotels

Hotel V Nesplein

This city centre family-run hotel is the younger sibling of the popular V Frederiksplein in De Pijp. The design is all about the wow factor, with grandiose chandeliers, gold adornments, statement vintage furniture and smatterings of Art Deco inspiration. The loft-style suites are functional with a shabby chic twist, and come with thoughtful extras such as a laptop safe, Nespresso coffee and smart TVs. The Lobby bar and restaurant downstairs is a popular hangout for Amsterdammers, with a roaring fire during the winter, a reading library and a small stage for intimate live events.

Nes 49, 1012 KD
+31 (0)20 662 3233
stay@hotelv.nl
www.hotelvnesplein.nl
Bus/tram: Dam

Morgan and Mees

With just nine individually designed rooms, Morgan and Mees offers a contemporary style inside one of Amsterdam's most traditional buildings. There's a room to suit any personality, whether you like split level living or terraces with far-reaching city views. Oak floors, vintage furniture and original artwork give a feeling of personality, while the downstairs restaurant and bar provides a place close to bed to hang out with chic Amsterdammers.

Tweede Hugo de Grootstraat 2-6, 1052 LC
+31 (0)20 233 4930
reservation@morganandmees.com
www.morganandmees.com
Tram: Hugo de Grootplein

Hotel IX

With just five suites and located in the popular Nine Streets shopping area, this hotel feels more like a home from home than a hotel. Rooms are spacious, particularly given the central spot and location squirrelled away inside a traditional 17th century building. Each suite has an inspiring design, with exposed brick walls, black and white photos and an individual touch, whether it's a private terrace or separate bedroom and sitting room. Other welcome extras include a free mini-bar and a keyless entry system.

Hartenstraat 8, 1016 CB
+31 (0)20 845 8451
info@hotelixamsterdam.com
www.hotelixamsterdam.com
Bus/tram: Westermarkt

Photos: INK Hotel

INK Hotel: the former home of the Dutch newspaper 'De Tijd'.

Design hotels

INK Hotel Amsterdam
The former home of the Dutch newspaper 'De Tijd', INK Hotel celebrates the fact this is a place where stories were brought to life, with vintage typewriters peppered throughout the building and the all-day PRESSROOM bar and restaurant. The bright lobby has skylights, dominant greenery and a snack cart, making you feel at home as soon as you step off the street. Rooms come in all shapes and sizes, with fun touches such as hand-drawn depictions of the city and hotel amenities described on crisp newspapers. While the library keeps the building's dedication to the printed word alive, the courtyard terrace provides another tranquil spot to spend time. With so many nooks and crannies to explore, this is a good-looking hotel that gives travellers an unpretentious home from home.
Nieuwezijds Voorburgwal 67, 1012 RE
+31 (0)20 721 9178
H1159@accor.com
www.ink-hotel-amsterdam.com
Bus/tram: Nieuwezijds Kolk

Hotel The Exchange
This original hotel comes complete with rooms designed by fashion students and five levels of room type to suit all budgets. While one star rooms come with basic amenities and smatterings of whimsical design touches, five star rooms are found on the upper floors of the hotel, with more spacious accommodation and great city views. Quirky communal areas include access to sewing machines and piles of reading material about Amsterdam, while a vending machine comes stocked with important goods such as wine, beer and late-night snacks. A fun and design-conscious hotel, this is a place to lay your head and become part of the fabric of the city for a while.
Damrak 50, 1012 LL
+31 (0)20 523 0080
post@hoteltheexchange.com
www.hoteltheexchange.com
Bus/tram: Nieuwezijds Kolk

citizenM
This Dutch hotel brand has made quite a name for itself across the world since opening its first hotel in Amsterdam in 2008. Tech savvy, design conscious and living room style communal areas set the hotel apart. Guests can check themselves in via the electronic terminals in the lobby within a minute, and can use iMacs free of charge in communal areas. Suites come with ambient lighting, blackout blinds, free movies and international plug systems. canteenM in the lobby is a popular place for visitors and locals to meet for breakfast or drinks. There's a citizenM at Schiphol Airport too for those on-the-move.
Prinses Irenestraat 30, 1077 WX
+31 (0)20 811 7090
www.citizenm.com/destinations/amsterdam
Bus/tram: Prinses Irenestraat/Beethovenstraat

Hotel The Exchange comes complete with rooms designed by fashion students.

Photo: The Exchange

Luxury hotels

Conservatorium

This hotel's historic Museumplein building was originally built as a bank, and was later the home of a music conservatory. Nowadays a grand hotel in a Neo-Gothic facade, a sweeping, light-filled lobby paves the way for further opulence and elegance within. Rooms and suites range in size, but all come with added extras such as a Nespresso coffee machine and access to the hotel's holistic centre. For those truly splashing out, suites come with spectacular interiors and private butlers. The hotel's facilities are top notch too, with various restaurants and bars, and a spa and gym offering an array of treatments and wellbeing classes.

Van Baerlestraat 27, 1071 AN
+31 (0)20 570 0000
info@conservatoriumhotel.com
www.conservatoriumhotel.com
Tram: Van Baerlestraat

Andaz Amsterdam

This hotel in the city's previous library is all about modern rooms, splashes of colour and luxurious details. While rooms have all the creature comforts you could crave, little touches such as complimentary snacks and non-alcoholic drinks from the mini-bar are a real bonus. There are also on-site bars and restaurants, a spa, and a video art collection showcased in different areas of the hotel. On Wednesday mornings, guests can even join the hotel manager for a morning run through Amsterdam.

Prinsengracht 587, 1016 HT
+31 (0)20 523 1234
amsterdam.prinsengracht@
andaz.com

amsterdam.prinsengracht.andaz.
hyatt.com
Tram: Keizersgracht
(Leidsestraat)

Hotel De Hallen

This industrial chic hotel is found inside a former tram depot, and is filled with impeccable interiors and statement furniture pieces. 'Indoor' rooms can be found off the sweeping central lobby, while other rooms have views over this western Amsterdam neighbourhood. Coffee machines, smart TVs and designer in-room amenities make for an even more comfortable stay, while the hotel can also organise babysitting services, bicycle rental and flower services.

Bellamyplein 47, 1053 AT
+31 (0)20 820 8670
info@hoteldehallen.com
www.hoteldehallen.com
Bus/tram: Ten Katestraat

Work-stay spaces

Zoku

Designed to be a second home-office for travelling entrepreneurs and business people, Zoku — Japanese for 'tribe' or 'clan' — provides apartment workspaces and opportunities for collaboration with like-minded locals and travellers. Rooms and loft spaces all come intelligently designed and with comfort in mind, including desks with city views, pull-up rings for keeping fit, screened off sleeping areas and luxury beds with organic linen. Guests can even personalise their room via a vast collection of wall art, and grab extra supplies from the guest pantry in the hall. It's the social places in Zoku that guests love even more than

the rooms, with a living room, kitchen, co-working spaces, green spaces, a games room, an (almost) everything store and a bar. There are plenty of opportunities for interaction, and Zoku 'Sidekicks' are never far away to give you a helping hand too. In a nutshell: staying in Zoku gives you more than just a room; it creates a whole creative lifestyle in Amsterdam.

Weesperstraat 105, 1018 VN
+31 (0)20 811 2811
hello@livezoku.com
www.livezoku.com
Bus/metro/tram: Weesperplein

CityHub

This high tech hotel has capsule style rooms, known as 'hubs', and co-working style communal areas for interaction with locals and travellers. Everything in CityHub is operated with a wristband activated after a three-click check-in process. The wristband acts as a key and a charging card for on-site purchases; guests can even swipe their wristbands in the bar to pour their own beers and cocktails. Hubs come with luxurious beds, app-controlled lighting and kimonos, while generously stocked shared bathrooms come with shampoo and hairdryers. Local hosts are also on-hand 24/7 for tips of great places to go out and general questions. A combination of an upmarket hostel and local lifestyle hotspot, CityHub is a cool place to hunker down.

Bellamystraat 3, 1053 BE
ask@cityhub.com
www.cityhub.com
Bus/tram: Ten Katestraat

Zoku is designed to be a second home-office for travelling entrepreneurs and business people.

Photo made for Zoku and concrete by Ewout Huibers

Quirky

The Arcade
This retro hotel in the trendy De Pijp neighbourhood offers practical and design-conscious rooms near the locally loved Sarphatipark. Attracting video game lovers from across the world, various vintage consoles are available for guests to play in the lobby, whether it's Space Invaders on the Atari or Street Fighter II on the Gameboy. Particularly avid gaming guests can also rent consoles and arrange deliveries of beer and crisps to complete the experience, as well as access a special gaming room and attend events. Extra touches make the hotel feel truly welcoming, including a welcome drink of your choice on arrival, late check-out and free loose tea and Earth coffee from the bar. Individually designed rooms offer pop-retro design and all the mod cons. The hotel also plays host to a range of special events guests can get involved in, such as gin and tonic evenings, Mexican breakfasts and poutine nights.
Sarphatipark 106, 1073 EC
+31 (0)20 676 0310
info@arcadehotel.nl
www.arcadehotel.nl
Bus/tram: Tweede van der Helststraat

Hotel Not Hotel
This eccentric hotel consists of 15 rooms scattered inside oddball constructions throughout the hotel lobby. Among others, there's a room in an Amsterdam tram cart, bedrooms in secret bookcases, and an intricately wooden carved 'Crisis Free Zone'. The spaces inside mostly just consist of beds, while communal bathrooms have excellent amenities. The bar, Kevin Bacon, is also a popular hangout for guests and locals alike.
Piri Reisplein 34, 1057 KH
+31 (0)20 820 4538
hello@hotelnothotel.com
www.hotelnothotel.com
Tram: Postjesweg/de Withstraat

Faralda Crane Hotel
This hotel is found inside a crane in the emerging industrial-chic neighbourhood of north Amsterdam. With just three carefully designed suites, guests at Faralda can enjoy all the mod cons, access to an elevated picnic area and spa pool, and of course, sweeping views of the city. Visitors may even catch a glimpse of bungee jumpers plummeting from the top of the crane. A hotel for thrill-seekers and daredevils, Faralda makes for an unforgettable overnight stay.
NDSM-plein 78, 1033 WB
+31 (0)20 760 6161
info@faralda.com
www.faralda.com
Boat: Veer NDSM Werf

Sweet Dreamz
Each of the three rooms in this hotel have been given stereotypical Dutch names: Maarten & Bas, Herman & Tania, and Kiki & Joost. Rooms have a fitting dated style and are peppered with random trinkets, giving the feel of a bedroom at an older relative's house. Each room booking comes with two bicycles thrown in for no extra cost. Downstairs is Café Modern, offering hearty breakfasts and lunches in similarly vintage surroundings.
Meidoornweg 2, 1031 GG
+31 (0)20 494 0684
mail@sweetdreamz.nl
www.sweetdreamz.nl
Bus: Meidoornplein

Hotel Droog
A design company, studio, gallery, bar and shop, Droog also has one hotel room, perfect for design lovers who love an immersive experience that's more than just about sleeping. The impeccably designed bedroom by Droog also comes with a fully equipped kitchen, dining table and chill out area separate from the bedroom. Bright and airy on the top floor of the 17th century building, Hotel Droog offers an unrivalled overnight experience in Amsterdam.
Staalstraat 7B, 1011 JJ
+31 (0)20 523 5059
reservations@hoteldroog.com
www.hoteldroog.com
Bus/metro/tram: Waterlooplein

The Arcade hotel is attracting video game lovers from across the world.

Photo: *The Arcade*

Outdoors

Camping Zeeburg

Given the abundant waterways of Amsterdam and the proximity of green spaces on the city outskirts to the city centre, camping in nature is a surprising accommodation option in the city. Camping Zeeburg in the east of Amsterdam is a great option. As well as an abundance of camping and campervan pitches, there are also eco-cabins and quirky waggonettes. There's also a huge communal living room for socialising, bicycles and canoes available to rent, and access to an abundance of nature nearby. It's city and country living at its best.
Zuider IJdijk 20, 1095 KN
+31 (0)20 694 4430
info@campingzeeburg.nl
www.campingzeeburg.nl
Tram: Flevopark

Urban Campsite

Every summer Urban Campsite creates an open-air exhibition of artworks on Blijburg Beach that doubles as an unusual campsite. Guests can stay inside the installations, which look like anything from space pods to unusual tribal homes. A 'superfire' campfire keeps the campsite warm, while the Tribal Toilet Tower provides access to toilets and showers.
Blijburg Beach, 1087 LA
info@urbancampsiteamsterdam.com
urbancampsiteamsterdam.com
Bus: Pieter Oosterhuisstraat

Other hotels

**Mövenpick Hotel
Amsterdam City Centre**
This central hotel with
impressive and far-reaching
views of the city and the
water is a practical and clean-
cut accommodation option
for visitors to Amsterdam.
The rooms are modern and
have all the mod-cons city
travellers could wish for,
including tea and coffee
making facilities, luxuriant
organic bed linen and
complimentary minibars for
those in superior or executive
rooms. The real focal point
of the rooms, however, is
the spectacular views over
the city or the River IJ —
definitely some of the best
in Amsterdam. Guests also
have access to the on-site
health and fitness club, while
executives can access the
Executive Lounge, which
includes an extensive and
delicious buffet breakfast and
complimentary snacks and
drinks early evening.
Piet Heinkade 11, 1019 BR
+31 (0)20 519 1200
hotel.amsterdam@movenpick.com
www.movenpick.com/amsterdam
Tram: Muziekgebouw Bimhuis

Photos: Mövenpick Hotel

Volkshotel

This trendy hotel is popular with co-workers due to the on-site 'workplace' and cosy café ripe for working on a laptop. The style of the rooms themselves is all about exposed concrete, distressed wood and an industrial feel; all of them come with a distinct hint of cool mingled with comfortable amenities. Hotel guests also have access to the sauna, yoga and other sport classes, a travelling hairdresser and masseuse, and of course the Canvas club and cocktail bar on the seventh floor.

Wibautstraat 150, 1091 GR
+31 (0)20 261 2100
info@volkshotel.nl
www.volkshotel.nl
Bus/metro: Wibautstraat

Hotel Dwars

This cute hotel with wooden-beamed rooms inside a traditional building combines modern amenities with a classical feel. Ideally located for many of Amsterdam's central attractions, Hotel Dwars is homely and convenient.

Utrechtsedwarsstraat 79, 1017 WD
+31 (0)61 955 5651
www.hoteldwars.com
Bus/tram: Prinsengracht (Utrechtsestraat)

Sir Albert

Inhabiting the premises of a former diamond factory, this luxury design hotel offers rooms of homely, muted tones decorated with statement furniture pieces. Complete with Illy coffee machines, iPod docking stations and laptop safes as well as an abundance of luxurious accessories, a stay at Sir Albert is all about understated elegance. Guests also have access to The Study, ideal for reading, working and coffee catch-ups.

Albert Cuypstraat 2-6, 1072 CT
+31 (0)20 305 3020
hello@siralbert.com
www.siralberthotel.com
Tram: Ruysdaelstraat

The Student Hotel

An affordable accommodation option in Amsterdam, The Student Hotel is ideal for travelling creative workers and global nomads on a budget, as well as students. Rooms come in all shapes and sizes, some with private kitchens, while a myriad of communal spaces are ideal for working, socialising and cooking. Guests also have access the on-site gym and group exercise classes. The Student Hotel has two locations in Amsterdam, and it's possible to stay short term or for a whole semester.

info@thestudenthotel.com
www.thestudenthotel.com

Wibautstraat 129, 1091 GL
+31 (0)20 214 9999
Bus/metro: Wibautstraat

Jan van Galenstraat 335, 1061 AZ
+31 (0)20 760 4000
Metro/tram: Jan van Galenstraat

Cocomama

Described as a boutique hostel, guests can stay in private rooms or small dorms. Each room or dorm has its own bathroom and access to sociable common areas, including a kitchen and movie corner. The atmosphere is warm, with a strong community spirit.

Westeinde 18, 1017 ZP
+31 (0)20 627 2454
info@cocomama.nl
www.cocomama.nl
Tram: Stadhouderskade (Westeinde)

City apartments

Amsterdam City Apartments

For those who prefer their own city crash pad for the duration of their stay, Amsterdam City Apartments has a number of short stay rentals on its books, scattered throughout the city. Most only have a two night minimum stay, and come impeccably furnished with all the amenities travellers could need. It's a great way to become ensconced in proper Amsterdam life.

www.amsterdamcityapartments.com

House-boat Hotel

For those who want to truly engrain themselves in Amsterdam life, house-boats moored along the city's many canals are available as short term rentals. Smaller narrow-boats can accommodate just one or two people, while larger house-boats can accommodate up to six people. If you're not au fait with on-board living, owners are usually more than happy to tell you the basics.

www.houseboathotel.nl

Amsterdam is fast becoming the epicentre of the developing coffee movement in mainland Europe.

Richard Jones
Founder and Managing Director of
Jones Brothers Coffee Company

How did you become a coffee guru?

It was a happy accident, to be honest. I'm originally from Wales and part of
a very entrepreneurial family. From around 2002, we had become frequent
travellers to Dubai, linked to property investment, and we spotted a gap
in the coffee market, in particular the availability and access to premium
quality 'on the go' coffee in convenient locations. Together with a friend
Matthew, who I met in Dubai, and my younger brother Rob, we put the
idea into practice in 2004 with just a single coffee machine. And so our
adventure in the coffee world began! We found a pretty decent super-
automated bean to cup coffee machine from the USA and some excellent
coffee from London and gave it a go. We had tried the machine in a few
locations without much impact when we came into contact, and eventually
a contract, with the Government of Abu Dhabi's petrol station operator
ADNOC. This was the start of a very successful partnership for placing our
machines and delivering premium fresh bean, fresh milk coffees in less
than 30 seconds per drink. Our machines were in petrol stations across
Abu Dhabi and eventually the whole of the United Arab Emirates. By 2007
we had a pretty significant business going. The coffee market in the region
wasn't particularly discerning at this time, but it was massively expanding
along with the rest of the economy.

Have you always been interested in coffee?

I'd always been interested in coffee, but never a huge fan, probably because
the only real options for coffee when I was young were instant coffees. It
was only at this point in Dubai that I started properly learning about coffee
— real coffee, that is. My commercial and marketing background up to
that point and my growing passion for coffee helped me to approach and
think about coffee from a different angle. I wasn't strictly a 'coffee person'. I
hadn't come from the coffee industry and had no pre-conceived ideas about
what I could or couldn't do. I just thought that we could do better than
what I saw around me. Oh, and we didn't have the money to open a chain
of cafés, so we always knew we had to do it differently from Starbucks!

How did you develop your business further?

With the confidence we gained from seeing our volumes grow, we invested
in a small roasting facility and began roasting our own coffee in 2008. We

immediately started visiting coffee plantations in Ethiopia, other parts of Africa and eventually all around the world. This was the eye opener for me: the light bulb moment. It was amazing to see with my own eyes where the beans came from, how they were grown and harvested, processed and 'cupped' — the coffee term for taste testing. By 2012 the business was really motoring along. We had expanded the roastery and our range of coffees, we had 150 people working for us, we were supplying into every part of the market and we had started franchising and distributing our coffee into six countries. We'd also built a few cafés by then too!

How did this take you to Amsterdam?

In 2012, there was another happy accident. I had met a Dutch guy at a food show in Barcelona where my brother and I were showing our coffee. He'd suggested setting up in the Netherlands. It came at a time when my wife and I were thinking about moving back to Europe anyway, and Amsterdam seemed very appealing. Good luck doesn't knock on your door twice, so they say, and after some discussions and a lucky break with a big retailer in the Netherlands who liked my ideas for a new coffee brand on their shelves, I set up Jones Brothers Coffee Company in Amsterdam in mid-2013. My complete passion now, after my wife and baby daughter of course, is coffee, and it's become a big part of my life.

What is the concept behind Jones Brothers Coffee Company?

I believe that most coffee we get served — particularly at home, in our offices and in a lot of restaurants and hotels — is generally quite bad. And it doesn't have to be. I think this is partly because the actual coffee bean is not taken seriously enough by the big players who only see volume and profit, and so they are creating a big mismatch, because there are a lot of consumers who do take coffee quite seriously, and whose knowledge of what makes and tastes like a good coffee is growing. There are so many possibilities with the humble coffee bean around taste which are still being explored. It starts from the growing and harvesting processes, from new regions of the world bringing better quality and more consistent coffees to the market, to the roastmasters who are pushing the boundaries with better blending and roasting to maximise the flavour in every bean. I just think with all these possibilities, it isn't too difficult to provide a decent coffee at a pretty reasonable price for everyday drinking. So this is where Jones Brothers comes in; in essence to offer better quality and better tasting coffee to a broader group of consumers who are out there looking for it.

<u>Tell us about your products and where they fit into the broader coffee industry spectrum.</u>
We provide coffee as whole beans or in Nespresso compatible capsules, which are big growth areas. We work with supermarkets and wholesalers, we supply coffee and coffee equipment to a number of hotels, offices, restaurants and cafés in the Netherlands, Belgium, Germany and the UK, and we have a growing online business, which I am finding particularly fascinating. We try to reach as many people as we can with a really premium product at a smart price. And to me, there's a gap in the market between those massive coffee corporations and their multitude of overly polished brands and the local microroasters. The larger corporations are desperately trying to find ways to attract more consumers, yet consumers are leaving them in droves because they're looking for brands and products which are more authentic and a bit more 'local'. On the other end of the scale, the microroasters and the independent coffee houses are fantastic and innovative, but they only really appeal to people within a very small geographical area, often within a few streets around them. So our aim is to fill that space in the middle for premium quality coffee, available to lots of people, and to talk about coffee in a fairly normal, jargon-free way. There are plenty of coffee 'experts' and coffee snobs around, and that's not really us. We do have expertise and knowledge but we just try to be normal about how we communicate that knowledge, and try to make a pretty decent quality product.

<u>What is it about Amsterdam that makes it a great place to have a coffee company?</u>
I just knew as soon as I came to the city in late 2012 that it would be a great place to live, work and bring up our daughter. Amsterdam is fast becoming the epicentre of the developing coffee movement in mainland Europe. London is the real beacon for the independent specialist coffee sector, but the coffee scene in Amsterdam has grown massively, especially in the last few years and it has 'infected' the whole of the Netherlands as well. There are a lot of fantastic microroasters and small independent concepts popping up, which is driving interest in coffee and increasing consumers' understanding. That helps coffee companies like mine, since we're trying to appeal to a really wide audience. A lot of consumers now know what good coffee is and they have greater expectations of the coffee they're buying, wherever they are buying it.

Amsterdam is home to a lot of coffee innovation, whether it's in terms of more interesting origins, preparation methods and ways of drinking coffee. 'Slow coffee' options are very in vogue, as are food and coffee pairing cafés and mixed use coffee bars, which join up with barbers, fashion shops or bicycle repair shops: very important places in Netherlands! There are a lot of small-scale but very unique things going on. I really feel Jones Brothers Coffee Company is in the right place at the right time and that the very dynamic city of Amsterdam is giving us an opportunity to grow our business, our brand and our reputation within and beyond the city's borders.

Describe the Dutch love affair with good coffee at this moment in time.
The Dutch are well known for their consumption of coffee. They're the third or fourth largest consumers of coffee per capita in the world, after those very cold northern European countries. But they've grown up on very traditional dark roasted filter coffee from one particular traditional brand, which just isn't brilliant quality. I think Amsterdam's sense of dynamic entrepreneurial adventure has really helped the coffee industry grow. The increased awareness that has resulted from the influx of start-up microroasters and independent coffee bars has made Amsterdam coffee consumers more discerning and even more in love with coffee than they previously were. There is a lot of change happening, and fast.

Have you noticed any coffee related trends in the city?
A coffee trend in Amsterdam that I haven't seen in many other cities yet is the mixed use premises idea; a very entrepreneurial way of delivering coffee in a completely different environment to what you might expect. One example is a very nice little fashion shop called KOKO Coffee & Design. It's a tiny little place where they mainly sell fashionable clothes and accessories, but on one side of the shop they have a beautiful little coffee bar. The two girls who run it are both very knowledgeable about coffee; they buy great coffee from a local roaster and they know how to get the best out of every blend or origin when they make it. They care about it. It's on a canal street and they just have a few seats where a handful of people can sit inside or out. It's a perfect little coffee package. There's another place called the Cut Throat Barber & Coffee, where you can get your hair cut in the environment of a traditional barber shop, or you can have a fantastic espresso or cappuccino from a trained barista. This dual concept idea where different things are happening inside small spaces is hugely popular in Amsterdam and is growing into other cities in the Netherlands as well. I have even been to a vintage bike shop and café in Utrecht! You can get coffee in every single kind of environment or store you could imagine. Even normal high-street clothing shops are putting in very decent coffee machines and hiring trained coffee makers, just as a part of their service.

What is life like as an entrepreneur in Amsterdam?
In general, being an entrepreneur has its ups and downs; I think we probably have lower lows and higher highs. Any start-up business has its challenges — and this is my fourth start-up now, so I know! You have to

rely on your intuition, what you have learned and your ability to fund your business operationally for the first couple of years. We're still in that relatively early phase, where cash is king and occasionally a problem. But the opportunity to be an entrepreneur in Amsterdam is a great one. The city provides an environment in which we have plenty of customers, both in their homes and offices. There's also a very dynamic freelance culture, so you have access to every kind of service to support your business. I only employ four people full time right now, but I have about ten freelancers supporting me. We control the product design, the brand and the marketing, and I have outsourced support for everything else to individuals and small companies. They are also entrepreneurs who provide the support we need to function effectively, or even at all. Amsterdam has this real ability to provide networks of people and small businesses, who join together and work with each other. That's something I really enjoy in Amsterdam; you can always find somebody to do something that you need at a fairly competitive price that is reasonable for both parties. And there's a willingness to share and help others. There's a certain amount of help from the government too; it's quite easy to set up a company and there are tax breaks if you're from overseas.

Where do you work?
I work in a co-working space building where we have a small office — this is a huge trend in Amsterdam and across Europe at the moment. I think it's going to become an even more pronounced trend in the next ten to 20 years, where many more people like me — small companies and even big companies — will move into shared working spaces. My office building is called Rokin 75, which is home to about 40 companies across six floors. There's a great community there and once a quarter there's a champagne and croissant breakfast on the roof terrace — a nice gathering put on by the building's owner. The street, Rokin, is a very lively place and during the spring and summer, the pavement is packed with people from late afternoon enjoying a beer and food in the sunshine.

Where is your favourite place to work in the city outside the office?
My favourite alternative place to work is The Lobby bar and restaurant in Hotel V, a boutique hotel, right in the city centre. You can usually find me imprinted into the soft couch in the corner by the lovely fireplace which is suspended from the ceiling, working on Friday mornings to do my creative writing, since I write all of the blog articles, packaging and marketing material texts and other communications for the company. I find the environment very conducive to writing and feeling at ease. It's calm, not too quiet but it's not overly noisy either. The staff are really great; very service-minded and they really get to know their customers. They keep me well fuelled with coffee and croissants and the food that comes out of the

small kitchen is amazing and great quality. It has a lovely feel to it and it's always busy. It's a little bit off the beaten track; you have to be in the know to find it. I would honestly recommend it for a drink, for food at all times of the day — their breakfast pancakes with blueberries and cream is my favourite — for chilling and for meetings. And of course, the coffee there is excellent, as they take it seriously.

Tell us about your life as 'The Espresso Hunter' blogger.
I write and blog about espresso, which takes me around the city and the rest of the Netherlands looking for and trying out all sorts of espresso bars. I have even written about new coffee places in Antwerp in Belgium! I do a lot of biking around Amsterdam, just getting to know coffee places and the people behind them. I take an interest in the coffee and what they're doing, and I write about it if it's good. I don't write negative reviews as there's no value in that and I actually really want people to serve good coffee, so I share a little bit of knowledge if they want to listen, but I don't push it onto anyone. Most people I meet this way are really receptive and happy to talk about any aspect of the coffee or their business. Plus, I want to have a reason to go back! I also use the various espresso bars around Amsterdam as more alternative environments to work in.

Where are your top recommendations for drinking coffee in Amsterdam?
I like a place called CT coffee & coconuts which is inside a converted theatre. It's beautiful inside. It's fairly new and is bustling all the time. The coffee — always my principle concern —is fantastic. They really know what they're doing when it comes to choosing and making the right coffees. The kitchen there produces some fabulous food too. For pure coffee experiences, there are quite a few: but my favourites include Toki, opened by an ex-advertising agency guy Jeff Flink in 2015, which is small, super cosy and uses some excellent coffees; and Quartier Putain in the red light district, which is a pretty, stripped back joint, run by Erik de Koch. It's a cool hangout place with a small range of great tasting coffees. White Label is another small roaster producing high class coffees. The place has a strong reputation and I loved the Ethiopia Sidamo coffee they served me recently. Sweet Cup close to Leidseplein also roasts on the premises on a small roasting machine, but you can tell that there's a lot of love being poured into their coffee. Paul, the roastmaster, is a little bit outshone by his now famous Bassett Hound! They have a nice menu in slow and drip brew coffees as well. I also like Lot Sixty One Coffee, which is a tiny place, but has a big reputation. The two guys who started it have done a great job in roasting excellent coffees on the premises and their coffees are very popular across town now. Scandinavian Embassy on Sarphatipark has won awards for its coffee — they focus a lot on slow and filter coffee options — but it's

also become famous for its food pairing menu. One of the partners, Rikard, from Sweden, brings a really innovative Nordic approach to the food. On the other hand, Nicolas is from Argentina with some Swedish heritage, and focuses on the coffee purity. He is pretty scientific about it: ask him about solubility! It's a small space but offers a great experience. Caffenation close to both the Rembrandtpark and Vondelpark is run by Bert, who is a super experienced coffee guy and very, very chilled...like, horizontally so! He knows a thing or two about his coffee, I can tell you. His filter coffees are my favourite in Amsterdam.

Tell me about the neighbourhood where you live.
I live in the Jordaan, which is in the central part of the canal district of Amsterdam. I think all of Amsterdam's neighbourhoods, particularly those within the canal belt, are fabulous. It's like a series of intertwined villages. They've all got their distinctive qualities. The Jordaan is lovely, it's full of beautiful little streets and it has every kind of shop, bakery and boutique you could want, hidden away in nooks and crannies. You know you're in the city centre, but you could be in a village in the middle of the countryside too. Amsterdam manages to combine that sense of always knowing you're in a city, but always feeling like you could be miles away from it as well. I love the fact I live on a canal street and that I can get up in the morning and cycle alongside the canal for five minutes to get to work. I think that's a wonderful way to live your life. I don't even own a car. Apart from the main tourist hubs such as Dam Square, the Leidseplein and Rembrandtplein — where all the bars and touristy stuff is — everywhere else is really residential. Yet even along these wonderful little streets you can still find every kind of shop, restaurant, small supermarket, butcher or bakery. Every single street seems to have something along it where you would want to spend time. There's such a street behind where we live called the Elandsgracht, which is a relatively small street, but it has got everything you can imagine on it. I love the idea that everything you need is on your doorstep. I'm a city dweller naturally and this is the perfect environment for me.

How would you describe the Amsterdam vibe?
The vibe that describes the whole city is one of calmness. Compared to most other major cities, it doesn't feel too hectic to me. I think the bicycle to car ratio has a lot to do with that. It's funny that as a 40-something year old man, I'm travelling to work and to meetings and to restaurants across the city on a bicycle. It seems ludicrous if I stop to think about it — and my friends from home find it particularly amusing — but it is easily the best, fastest and most productive way to get around the city, and I think that contributes hugely to the overall feel. You don't feel out of place — everybody is on a bicycle. My overall sense of the city is that it hasn't got

a craziness about it that cities like London, Paris and New York do. It's all about quality of life in Amsterdam, and it's an enjoyable place to live. I don't hear too many people complaining about it. In many other cities you notice people have a reason to complain about something, but it's not like that in Amsterdam. I feel privileged to live there.

What is it like to have a family in Amsterdam?
Brilliant. My daughter is still very young, but I'm really looking forward to her growing up in the city. There are a lot of parks and play areas, and many opportunities to have a very busy, interesting and culturally based family life. You don't have to go to a museum every day of the week to feel you're in a city steeped in culture. The education and healthcare systems are highly rated too. Amsterdam has all the positive qualities and amenities of a world city, wrapped up in the size of a slightly large village. I love it for that.

Where do you go most frequently for a meal out with friends?
One of our favourite places that we visit frequently, especially on the weekends, is De Hallen. It's an old tram station that has been converted into a huge gourmet food hall, full of different food stands where they cook fresh food of every variety. The Vietnamese rolls are particular favourites of mine. It also has a couple of bars within it, which are great for a drink, as well as a library-café-shop called Belcampo and a cinema complex called Filmhallen. We hang out there in the late afternoon and early evening with friends to eat, drink and chat. It's absolutely fantastic and there's a brilliant atmosphere; it's buzzing.

Where do you like to go for a low-key meal in Amsterdam?
There are a lot of fabulous restaurants in Amsterdam for every kind of budget. I really like Gartine. It's a tiny family-run restaurant on a side street off the Rokin — it can't have more than 15 or 20 places to sit down — and it's a real gem. They've got their own garden up in the north of the country and they serve mainly organic food. It has a fantastic range of desserts too; I especially like the cheesecakes. My wife and I also really like Cucina Casalinga in Amsterdam Zuid. It's a small Roman inspired living room of the chef-owner Giovanni Carmelitano. They serve unusual regional Italian fare with great wines by the glass, and we love the hand-made pasta and gnocchi. It's a hidden gem. Vasso, close to the Rokin is also a great little Italian place. Restaurant Oud Zuid is another restaurant that feels like home. It's really cosy with a great terrace, while the food is French brasserie style with a twist. There's a big Indonesian influence in Amsterdam, so there are a lot of great Asian restaurants. Izakaya Asian Kitchen & Bar is a really good one, and Rakang on Elandsgracht is a great Thai restaurant. For low key Thai food that is freshly cooked in front of you, Warie's Thai is

also great. We also like De Vondeltuin at the end of Vondelpark; it has an amazing combination of a play garden perfect for my daughter, while we can indulge in some good food and drinks!

Where are the best places to go for a special meal out?
So far, my favourite high-end restaurant is The Duchess, which is part of the W Hotel. It has a fabulous interior inside an old banking hall. The food is of a very high standard and is all based on sharing plates. The chocolate bomb experience at the end is just one of many reasons to go. There are some great concept restaurants in the city too. There's one called Bak Restaurant, which is to the west of Central Station. There's a set tasting menu every day and they use some really unusual ingredients. Another one I like is called C, short for 'Celsius', and they cook their food according to very specific temperatures. Each dish takes you on a culinary journey through different temperatures. There's a great website called *Your Little Black Book*, which is a guide to the more innovative things going on in Amsterdam, and that's a good website to check for new restaurant openings.

Where do you go for a foodie treat?
There's a bakery I like called Lanksroon, which is pretty well-known for its excellent croissants and cakes. There's also a small fresh cookie shop called Van Stapele around the corner which is a bit of a hidden gem and is the perfect pit stop for a sweet treat!

Where do you like to go for a drink in the city?
Amsterdam has little pubs and bars in every neighbourhood and almost on every street corner to choose from. The Toren, Café De Eland, Papeneiland, Louis and Waterkant are all favourite watering holes. There's a great rooftop bar called Canvas on top of the Volkshotel, which is great for an after-dinner drink. It's nice on the weekends and very chilled out; it becomes a club with DJs a little bit later on. The W Hotel is relatively new in Amsterdam, and there's a great restaurant and bar area there called Mr Porter. The bar at the top of the Hilton DoubleTree has spectacular views over the city from a big outside terrace area. I also like Bubbles and Wines, who serve a big range of wines and champagnes by the glass. It's one of those places a little off the beaten track, even though it's right in the centre, doing something slightly different. That's the kind of thing I really like. There's a growing craft micro-brewery scene going on in Amsterdam, which mirrors what is happening on the coffee scene. Amsterdam is all about craft beers and specialist coffee at the moment! That just demonstrates the trend for things that are local, authentic and different. One craft beer place I like is Bier Fabriek, which is on the ground floor of my office building — very handy! They make their own delicious craft beers

that you can pour yourself from taps on the tables. They also serve chicken and chips and they use their beer in the cooking too. Amsterdam is also famous for its 'brown bars' — very local, traditional drinking holes— and I really like The Pilsner Club, also known as Engelse Reet. There is sand on the floor, no music, an intellectual audience, very well served beers and great old fashioned waiters. What more could you want from a brown bar? It's also a great place to try the Dutch cheese and delicious sausages.

Where's the ideal place to spend an afternoon chilling out?
I really like Pllek in the north of the city, which you get to by a free ferry from behind Central Station, within a few minutes. It's a very chilled out place made with recycled shipping containers, a man-made beach and great views back towards the city. There's a fabulous organic food restaurant there and it's great for kids to run around. We really like going there during the spring and summer. I really like De Ysbreeker — this is a famous place on the Amstel River and as well as great service, it has a really nice casual dining feel to it in a really beautiful and airy, Art Deco interior. Another great thing to do during the summer is to go to the zoo, Artis, in the Plantage area. I've never been a huge fan of zoos, but Artis is a really lovely one I must say — we take our daughter there a lot. During the summer they have musicians playing on the bandstand on Saturday evenings and people sit around with their kids and have picnics. It's very chilled. It's something only the locals really know about because they don't really advertise it. Nearby there is a fantastic restaurant and brasserie called De Plantage; I really love it there.

Which of Amsterdam's markets do you most enjoy?
We have a particular favourite in Amsterdam Oud Zuid called ZuiderMRKT, which is an organic market near Museumplein. It's actually in the middle of a roundabout! We go there on Saturday mornings for the lovely range of organic meats and vegetables. The market also has a great little space to sit down and eat some food, whether it's from a lady cooking up fresh Indonesian dishes, the guy doing crêpes, the guys making hotdogs from homemade sausages or the Pieman stand for pies. ZuiderMRKT is a great example of these little community markets that are popping up all over. There's generally a big push towards organic produce in Amsterdam at the moment. One of the city's most famous markets that we also like is the Albert Cuyp Market in the De Pijp neighbourhood. It's huge and most renowned for its fresh fish. It's a big tourist attraction, but they say the best fish in the Netherlands comes to the Albert Cuyp Market. As well as being a great market, all the streets in the surrounding area are fantastic to explore. It's an artier part of the city and there are loads of little places to eat, drink and discover.

How would you encourage people to blend in and live like locals during their visit to Amsterdam?

Try not to wear a woolly hat that says Amsterdam on it! My top recommendation would be to get a bicycle. Although if you want to blend in, you need to understand the rules. When you're a local, tourists are often the most dangerous people to come across on a bike! But there's no doubt: there isn't a better way to see the city than by a bicycle. It's very easy to hire one too and a lot of hotels even have their own to rent out. If you've got young children, you can hire a bakfiets, which are bicycles with a box on the front that you stick the kids in. Another typical Amsterdam pastime is to visit the city's main park, Vondelpark. It's beautiful with big cycle lanes to cycle around, then you can throw down a blanket and have a picnic and wine. On Sunday afternoons during the summer, the park is really bustling and there is live music on the bandstand. Amsterdam's parks are where the city breathes a little; Sarphatipark and Erasmuspark are also nice. There's so much to see in Amsterdam, so visitors shouldn't limit themselves to the city centre only. You can travel for just five minutes on a bicycle and be in a completely different part of the city. Stay away from the tourist traps of Leidseplein and Rembrandtplein, and instead go to the Jordaan and the little canal streets. Go to the north of the city across the River IJ on the ferry and enjoy places like the EYE Film Museum, where there is also a lovely restaurant, café and great views across the city.

What do you think surprises people about Amsterdam?

The red light district is not to be feared — it is an unexpectedly pretty part of town during the daytime and it's not as seedy as you'd expect it would be. If you wander around during the day, you'll see a lot of couples and families. There are really pretty canals, lovely boutiques and cafés, and Chinatown is just around the corner. Oddly enough, some of the best espresso bars of the city are found there, such as Quartier Putain. It's somewhere you can't ignore because Amsterdam is famous for the red light district. But it's been scaled back a lot over the last few years, so it's only a relatively small part of the city now. It's also easy to avoid if you can resist the curiosity.

What does Amsterdam smell like?

Fresh air! The air feels really clean, which is surprising for a city. I've lived in other cities which seem quite polluted in comparison.

What sound do you most associate with the city?

The 'ding ding' noise the trams make as they're coming along. That's a very common sound and definitely reminds me of Amsterdam if I hear something similar when I'm elsewhere.

<u>What is the most unusual Amsterdammer habit you have come across?</u>
Amsterdammers sometimes call themselves sunflowers because at the
first sight of sun, they head straight outside. For people who don't have
their own garden or terrace, you see people put their sofa or chair on the
pavement outside their front door and sit there, sometimes eating dinner!
It's something I could imagine my grandparents doing 50 years ago when
there was more of a community feeling on the streets, but you wouldn't see
it happening in the UK nowadays. Dutch people don't find it strange at all,
they're very relaxed about things like that. You also notice this when you
walk along the streets and you can see straight into people's kitchens, living
rooms and bedrooms. In the UK, we'd have netting and curtains up for
privacy. But the Dutch viewpoint is that if you want to look inside, then go
ahead and look! I cycle past and see unmade beds and think: "I would have
at least made the bed knowing that people can see inside!" Dutch people
are pretty 'straight', but have liberal ways as well. It makes for interesting
observations and conversations!

Richard's Amsterdam

Places to visit

Albert Cuyp Market
Albert Cuypstraat, 1072 CN
www.albertcuyp-markt.
amsterdam
Tram: Albert Cuypstraat

Amsterdam Noord
1020-1039
Boat: Veer Buiksloterweg, Veer
IJplein

Natura Artis Magistra (zoo)
Plantage Kerklaan 38-40, 1018 CZ
+31 (0)900 278 4796
info@artis.nl
www.artis.nl
Bus/tram: Plantage Lepellaan

De Hallen
Hannie Dankbaarpassage 33,
1053 RT
+31 (0)20 705 8164
www.dehallen-amsterdam.nl
Bus/tram: Ten Katestraat

De Pijp
1073
Tram: Albert Cuypstraat

Elandsgracht
1016
Bus/tram: Elandsgracht

Erasmuspark
1056 LE
Bus/tram: Jan van Galenstraat
(Hoofdweg)

EYE Film Museum
IJpromenade 1, 1031 KT
+31 (0)20 589 1400
info@eyefilm.nl
www.eyefilm.nl
Boat/bus: Veer Buiksloterweg

Filmhallen
Hannie Dankbaarpassage 12,
1053 RT
+31 (0)20 820 8122
info@filmhallen.nl
www.filmhallen.nl
Bus/Tram: Ten Katestraat

Hilton DoubleTree
Oosterdoksstraat 4, 1011 DK
+31 (0)20 530 0800
amscs.info@hilton.com
www.doubletree3.hilton.com
Bus: Prins Hendrikkade/CS

Hotel V
Nesplein 49, 1012 KD
+31 (0)20 662 3233
stay@hotelv.nl
www.hotelvnesplein.nl
Bus/tram: Spui (Rokin)

Jordaan
1015-1016
Bus/tram: Nieuwe Willemsstraat

Pllek
Tt. Neveritaweg 59, 1033 WB
+31 (0)20 290 0020
info@pllek.nl
www.pllek.nl
Boat: Veer NDSM Werf

Rokin 75
Rokin 75, 1012 KL
info@rokin75.com
www.rokin75.com
Bus/tram: Spui (Rokin)

Sarphatipark
1073
sarphatipark.wordpress.com

Toki
Binnen Dommersstraat 15, 1013 HK
+31 (0)20 363 6009
hello@tokiho.amsterdam
www.tokiho.amsterdam
Bus: Buiten Oranjestraat

Vondelpark
Vondelpark, 1017 AA
www.hetvondelpark.net
Tram: J.P. Heijesstraat or Rhijnvis
Feithstraat

ZuiderMRKT
Jacob Obrechtstraat, Johannes
Verhulststraat, 1071 MR
info@zuidermrkt.nl
www.zuidermrkt.nl
Bus: Jacob Obrechtstraat/ de
Lairessestraat

Eating and drinking

Bak Restaurant
Van Diemenstraat 408, 1013 CR
+31 (0)20 737 2553
info@bakrestaurant.nl
www.bakrestaurant.nl
Bus: Houtmankade

Belcampo
Hannie Dankbaarpassage 10,
1053 RT
+31 (0)20 303 2886
cafebelcampo@cafebelcampo.nl
www.cafebelcampo.nl
Bus/tram: Ten Katestraat

Bier Fabriek
Rokin 75, 1012 KL
info@rokin75.com
www.rokin75.com
Bus/tram: Spui (Rokin)

Bubbles and Wines
Nes 37, 1012 KC
+31 (0)20 422 3318
info@bubblesandwines.com
bubblesandwines.com
Bus/tram: Dam

C
Wibautstraat 125, 1091 GL
+31 (0)20 210 3011
info@c.amsterdam
www.c.amsterdam
Bus/metro: Wibautstraat

Café De Eland
Prinsengracht 296, 1016 HW
+31 (0)20 623 7654
https://www.facebook.
com/pages/cafe-de-
eland/388474804553168
Bus/tram: Elandsgracht

Caffenation
Warmondstraat 120, 1058 KZ
www.facebook.com/
CaffenationAmsterdam
Bus: Haarlemmermeerstraat

Canvas
Wibautstraat 150, 1091 GR
+31 (0)20 261 2110
hell@volkshotel.nl
www.volkshotel.nl/canvas
Bus/metro: Wibautstraat

CT coffee & coconuts
Ceintuurbaan 282-284, 1072 LR
+31 (0)20 354 1104
info@ctamsterdam.nl
www.ctamsterdam.nl
Tram: Ceintuurbaan/F Bolstraat

Cucina Casalinga
Stadionweg 271, 1076 NZ
+31 (0)20 679 1592
info@casalinga.nl
www.casalinga.nl
Bus/tram: Olympiaweg

Cut Throat Barber & Coffee
Beursplein 5, 1012 JW
+31 (0)6 25 343 769
www.cutthroatbarber.nl
Bus/tram: Dam

De Plantage
Plantage Kerklaan 36, 1018 CZ
+31 (0)20 760 6800
info@caferestaurantdeplantage.nl
www.caferestaurantdeplantage.nl
Bus/tram: Artis

De Vondeltuin
Vondelpark 7, 1075 VR
+31 (0)6 27 565 576
info@vondeltuin.nl
www.devondeltuin.nl
Tram: Overtoomsesluis

De Ysbreeker
Weesperzijde 23, 1091 EC
+31 (0)20 468 1808
info@deysbreeker.nl
www.deysbreeker.nl
Tram: Wibautstraat/Ruyschstraat

Gartine
Taksteeg 7 BG, 1012 PB
+31 (0)20 320 4132
www.gartine.nl
Bus/tram: Spui (Rokin)

Izakaya Asian Kitchen & Bar
Albert Cuypstraat 2-6, 1072 CT
+31 (0)20 305 3090
info@izakaya-amsterdam.com
www.izakaya-amsterdam.com
Tram: Ruysdaelstraat

KOKO Coffee & Design
Oudezijds Achterburgwal 145, 1012 DG
+31 (0)20 626 4208
info@ilovekoko.com
www.ilovekoko.com
Metro: Nieuwmarkt

Lanksroon
Singel 385, 1012 WL
+31 (0)20 623 7743
info@lanskroon.nl
www.lanskroon.nl
Tram: Spui (Nieuwezijds Voorburgwal)

Lot Sixty One Coffee
Kinkerstraat 112, 1053 ED
+31 (0)6 42 613 394
info@lotsixtyonecoffee.com
www.lotsixtyonecoffee.com
Bus/tram: Bilderdijkstraat/ Kinkerstraat

Louis
Singel 43, 1012 VC
+31 (0)20 752 6328
info@louis-amsterdam.nl
www.louis-amsterdam.nl
Bus/tram: Nieuwezijds Kolk

Mr Porter
Spuistraat 175, 1012 VN
+31 (0)20 811 3399
www.mrportersteakhouse.com
Tram: Dam (Raadhuisstraat) or Dam (Paleisstraat)

Papeneiland
Prinsengracht 2, 1015 DV
+31 (0)20 624 1989
info@papeneiland.nl
www.papeneiland.nl
Bus: Buiten Brouwersstraat

Pieman Bakery at ZuiderMRKT
Jacob Obrechtstraat 44, 1071 KN
info@piemanbakery.nl
www.piemanbakery.nl
Bus: Jacob Obrechtstraat

Quartier Putain
Oudekerksplein 4, 1012 GZ
+31 (0)20 895 0162
contact@quartierputain.nl
www.quartierputain.nl
Bus: CS/Nicolaaskerk

Rakang
Elandsgracht 29-31, 1016 TM
+31 (0)20 627 5012
reservation@rakang.nl
www.rakang.nl
Bus/tram: Elandsgracht

Restaurant Oud Zuid
Johannes Verhulststraat 64, 1071 NH
+31 (0)20 676 6058
info@restaurantoudzuid.nl
www.restaurantoudzuid.nl
Bus: Jacob Obrechtstraat/de Lairessestraat

Scandinavian Embassy
Sarphatipark 34, 1072 PB
+31 (0)6 19 518 199
info@scandinavianembassy.nl
www.scandinavianembassy.nl
Bus/tram: Tweede van der Helststraat

Sweet Cup
Lange Leidsedwarsstraat 93HS, 1017 NH
+31 (0)20 370 3783
info@sweetcupcafe.com
www.sweetcupcafe.com
Bus/tram: Leidseplein

The Duchess
Spuistraat 172, 1012 VT
+31 (0)20 811 3322
info@the-duchess.com
www.the-duchess.com
Tram: Dam/Raadhuisstraat

The Pilsner Club
Begijnensteeg 4, 1012 PN
+31 (0)20 623 1777
www.kroegenweb.nl/cafe/10924/
De_Pilsener_Club
Bus/tram: Spui (Rokin)

The Toren
Keizersgracht 164, 1015 CZ
+31 (0)20 622 6352
info@thetoren.nl
www.thetoren.nl
Bus/tram: Westermarkt

Van Stapele
Heisteeg 4, 1012 WC
+31 (0)6 54 241 497
info@vanstapele.com
www.vanstapele.com
Tram: Spui (Nieuwezijds
Voorburgwal)

Vasso
Rozenboomsteeg 10-14, 1012 PR
+31 (0)20 626 0158
www.vasso.nl
Bus/tram: Spui (Rokin)

Warie's Thai Food
Rozengracht 235, 1016 NA
+31 (0)20 622 3638
www.wariesthaifood.nl
Bus/tram: Marnixstraat/
Rozengracht

Waterkant
Marnixstraat 246, 1016 TL
+31 (0)20 737 1126
fawaka@waterkantamsterdam.nl
www.waterkantamsterdam.nl
Bus/tram: Elandsgracht

White Label Coffee
Jan Evertsenstraat 136
+31 (0)20 737 1359
info@whitelabelcoffee.nl
www.whitelabelcoffee.nl
Bus: Mercatoplein

See also

Your Little Black Book
www.yourlittleblackbook.me

Photo: CT coffee & coconuts

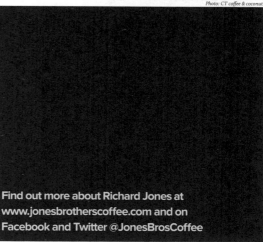

Find out more about Richard Jones at
www.jonesbrotherscoffee.com and on
Facebook and Twitter @JonesBrosCoffee

chapter 4

Getting away and getting lost

*Wandering aimlessly without a plan
sometimes brings unexpected inspiration.*

Away for a day

Get away from Amsterdam for a day to explore traditional Dutch communities and to experience yet more water-side life.

Zandvoort aan Zee

This fun-loving seaside retreat just half an hour on the train from Amsterdam is the ideal spot to relax, explore and enjoy the plentiful beach clubs. It's a place where Dutch people enjoy their holidays, but it's equally accessible for Amsterdammers who want to enjoy beach life for a day or two. Even during the winter it's perfect for a cosy hot chocolate inside one of the beach pavilions. Enjoy a long walk along the beach, catch some rays and have a swim; the sea at Zandvoort is said to be very clean. Chill out for a while in one of the beach clubs, do some water sports if you're feeling adventurous, and be sure to try some herring from the Vis van Floor food truck, and some fries from Fritures d'Anvers.
www.vvvzandvoort.com
Transport: Regular Sprinter service from Amsterdam Centraal to Zandvoort aan Zee.

Zaanstad

Reaching the city this area is known for — Zaandam — takes just 15 minutes from Amsterdam by train. Zaandam has a colourful history of industry, milling and shipping, so be sure to check out the windmills and the house of Czar Peter I of Russia, who stayed in the city to study ship-building. Claude Monet also made 25 paintings of the area. Be sure to stop off for a drink in The Black Smith, a typical brown café inside a former blacksmith's workshop. Many people visit Zaanstad to see the conservation area of Zaanse Schans, with its traditional green houses and still-functioning windmills. From there, cross the Zaan river to Zaandijk, to experience a lesser-known but charming Dutch village.
www.zaanstad.nl
Transport: Regular Sprinter and Intercity train services from Amsterdam Centraal to Zaanstad.

Giethoorn

It takes a couple of hours to get to Giethoorn by public transport from Amsterdam, but it's well worth the journey to visit the 'Venice of the North' for a day. Holland's water village has no roads, and is only served by small canals and a few pedestrian and cycle routes. Even the postman delivers the mail by boat. Rent a 'fluisterboot' (silent electric boat) from one of many canal-side restaurants and explore the beautiful waterways. This is a place to truly get lost in the Netherlands. Go on a bright, dry day to make the most of it; the town tends to hibernate when it rains. If you're looking for a little more adventure, rent an inflatable ball instead, so you can literally walk on water.
www.giethoorntourism.com
Transport: Regular Intercity train service from Amsterdam Centraal to Almere, to connect to the Intercity service to Steenwijk. Then take the number 70 bus to Giethoorn.

Away for a weekend

Discover the variety of what the Netherlands has to offer with a weekend trip away from Amsterdam.

Utrecht

Just half an hour south-east of Amsterdam, Utrecht is a city that blends history with a bohemian vibe. The ancient city, dating back to the Middle Ages, is surrounded by a medieval canal and is the perfect place for idle wandering and soaking up a feeling of the past. Hundreds of canal-side wharves and wharf cellars have now been inhabited by quirky cafés. Try Wijnlokaal Aal on the Oudegracht, or for an alternative experience, sample the beer at Stadskasteel Oudaen, inside the city castle that has its own brewery. After dark, follow the Trajectum Lumen light art trail, where artworks and notable buildings have been dramatically lit-up. Enjoy the history of the city further by staying in a boutique hotel, such as the Mother Goose Hotel, whose building dates back to the 14th century.

www.visit-utrecht.com

Transport: Regular Intercity train service from Amsterdam Centraal to Utrecht.

Terschelling

The most cultural of the West Frisian Islands in the North Sea, Terschelling makes for a rugged setting to find peace and to get lost. The journey takes more than four hours from Amsterdam whether travelling by car or public transport, but it's well worth the journey. Rent a bike, ride through the dunes and experience the amazing and calm atmosphere of the island. Visit the annual Oerol Festival for theatre performances that use the whole island as a stage, and visit the transmitter house on the highest part of the island, used during World War II. Hang out at the beach pavilions, and go seal spotting, surfing and horseback riding. By night, there are a surprising number of bars and clubs, although chilling out by a campfire is the preferred pastime of many too.

www.terschelling.org

Transport: Regular Intercity and Stoptrein services from Amsterdam Centraal to Harlingen Haven. From there, catch the ferry to West Terschelling, then the 120 bus to get around.

Twente

This region in the far east of the country is close to the German border, and is a two and a half hour journey from Amsterdam. Larger cities are Almelo, Hengelo and Enschede, and the region is well known for its textiling history. As well as vibrant festivals, nowadays the area is famous for its scenic countryside and 'green living'. For the ultimate away-from-it-all experience, rent a lodge on a farm from Droste's. They have an inn near the village of Tubbergen, which is a cosy place to stop for organic and local food and a drink, and the farm lodges are spread around the surrounding area.

www.beleeftwente.nl

Transport: Regular Intercity trains from Amsterdam Centraal to Almelo. Then take the 64 bus to Droste's inn.

Away forever

Sometimes it's simply time to say goodbye. Here are our top recommendations of where Amsterdam-lovers should travel to next.

Rotterdam

This up-and-coming Dutch city is reachable in just over half an hour from Amsterdam, thanks to the high-speed Thalys train service that passes through both stations. Rotterdam is the second city of the Netherlands, and is increasingly considered to be Amsterdam's cooler younger sibling. Judging by looks alone, the city is modern and inviting, with futuristic architecture peppered across the city along with inventive art installations. The modernistic focus couldn't be more different from Amsterdam's traditions, and is rooted in the necessity of wide-scale rebuilding after World War II. The constant redevelopment means the city has an energetic and creative personality, which is ideal for entrepreneurs and those in creative industries. Hire a desk at a co-working space such as The Rotterdam Startup Port or The Rotterdam Collective, or grab a desk by the hour at Meetz!. Network at the Erasmus Centre for Entrepreneurship, and partake in 'Get in the Ring', known as the 'Olympics for Startups'. Get around by bicycle as the locals do, and join them for brunch in places such as the idyllic Bertmans by the water. Enjoy the art scene at venues such as the Witte de With Center for Contemporary Art and go along to the annual International Film Festival Rotterdam. Drink at The Suicide Club, on an eighth floor roof terrace, and get a food stall fix at Markthal and Fenix Food Factory.

www.rotterdam.info

Berlin

This city of creativity, culture and entrepreneurialism is a haven for those who want to try out start-up projects in Berlin's historical localities alongside fun-loving city-dwellers. Just like in Amsterdam, Berliners flock outside when there's even a little bit of sun, and they love festivals and outdoor spaces. Tempelhofer Flughafen — an abandoned airfield and now a park — is to Berliners what Vondelpark is to Amsterdammers. Cycling everywhere is almost as much a way of life in Berlin as it is in Amsterdam. Hire a desk at a co-working space such as the trendy St. Oberholz, or the grandmother of European co-working, betahaus. Attend entrepreneurial networking events such as (likemind) bln and NetParty, and enjoy coffee at 5 Elephant and Café Anna Blume. Drink beer by the River Spree with the locals, or join them at a beer garden stalwart such as Prater Garten. And when it's time to eat, join Berliners at Street Food Thursday or visit locally-adored eateries such as Il Ritrovo, complete with the hand-drawn graffiti on the walls. Although the cost of living is increasing in Berlin, it's still more affordable than many other European cities. Together with its unique history and post- Berlin Wall pioneering spirit, Berlin is an intoxicating city to call home for a while.

www.carlgoes.com/berlin
www.visitberlin.de

Antwerp

A smaller city than Amsterdam in terms of population, although similar in size geographically, Antwerp makes an ideal home from home for those who love a village-like city feeling. The city is by no means a Belgian backwater, however, and is widely considered to be Belgium's city of cool, attracting a cultivated combination of creatives, fashionistas and entrepreneurs. A medieval centre, cobbled lanes and a majestic fortress sit alongside modern coffee bars, cool vintage furniture and lots of the latest fashions. Visit Barnini for great coffee, find antique and vintage stores on Nationalestraat, and go shopping around Schuttershofstraat and Graanmarkt. Just like Amsterdam, Antwerp is small enough to get around on foot or by bicycle. Hire a desk in a co-working space such as Floating Desk or Burooz, and meet the city's entrepreneurs at Conversation Starter events. For downtime in the evenings, browse in the Copyright Art & Architecture Bookshop for creative inspiration, visit traditional Belgian restaurants such as Chez Fred, and enjoy the city's summer bars such as Summer Josephines.

www.visitantwerpen.be

Cape Town

The Dutch were a notable part of Cape Town's history, although today the connection mostly only remains in the vague similarity between the Dutch and Afrikaans languages. Like Amsterdammers, however, Capetonians can't get enough of their outdoorsy lifestyle and the feeling of freedom they experience in the city's open spaces. With a flourishing start-up scene in a city that enjoys a great work-life balance, Cape Town is a vivacious city to call home for a while. Rent a desk at one of the city's many good-looking co-working spaces, such as The Cape Town Garage or Daddy.O, and network with like-minded people at events such as Startup Grind Cape Town. Make the most of everything the city has to offer by visiting the beach and bars of Camps Bay, surf or go horse-riding in the rugged but idyllic Kommetjie, and have a hike and a braai (barbecue) by the Silvermine Dam in Table Mountain National Park. Enjoy summertime open air music performances in the Kirstenbosch National Botanical Gardens, and eat and drink in open-air restaurants at the V&A Waterfront. With so much going on, it may be difficult to re-join life in the northern hemisphere...

www.capetown.travel

Getting lost

Wandering without having a destination in mind is becoming a lost art in cities today. Paying no attention to street names and directions, the ticking of time and 'having a plan', is a liberating way to authentically experience a locality and a moment in time.

'Getting lost' is not a new concept. Flâneurs — idle strollers — were first talked about in the 16th century. A concept with no exact English translation, flânerie is all about aimless wandering, losing yourself and urban exploration.

We urge you to get lost in the waterway-pocked urban jungle of Amsterdam, to experience the rhythm of the city without thought or direction. Our suggestions in this section are simply starting points for the adventures you'll create in the city. Whether you decide to jump on a tram and travel six stops, or make a beeline for something that looks interesting before sitting down and observing your surroundings, that's up to you.

Wandering aimlessly without a plan sometimes brings unexpected inspiration. We challenge you to give it a try.

Photo: Cyril Wermers

2

Photos: Cyril Wermers

5

Photo: Cyril Wermers

5

Photo: Cyril Wermers

6

Photo: Cyril Wermers

Getting lost

Wandering aimlessly can bring some of the best discoveries. Here's some inspiration for how to 'get lost' in Amsterdam:

1. Saunter amid the crowds of Amsterdam's buzzing markets such as the Albert Cuyp Market.
2. Hire a motor boat or pedal boat and meander along the canals, or take an early morning walk along the canal-side when no-one else is around.
3. Amsterdam is full of parks and green spaces with corners still left to explore: Vondelpark, Hortus Botanicus and the city's 2,500 acre forest Amsterdamse Bos are all local favourites. Or make the most of the quiet in northern Amsterdam's Schellingwouderpark,

accessed by pull ferries.
4. Explore the narrow lanes and antique stores in the Spiegelkwartier, or wander through the 300 stalls at the Waterlooplein Flea Market.
5. Two-person film booths, in the basement of the EYE Film Museum, are small hideaway spaces for visual escapism.
6. Get lost in the arts: inside a room away from the crowds in the Rijksmuseum, at a free concert in the National Opera and Ballet building, Het konijnklijk Concertgebouw, or check out who's performing for free at the Conservatorium van Amsterdam (CvA).

Flâneur, from the French noun flâneur, means "stroller", "lounger", "saunterer", or "loafer". Flânerie refers to the act of strolling, with all of its accompanying associations.

About Carl Goes

Travel guides for curious and creative people

Whether you travel to a city for three days, three weeks or three months, we know it's increasingly important to you to become part of the fabric of the city you visit. As a result, we see it as our job to give you an insight into how residents live, work and play in the city, with cherry-picked recommendations from locals of where you can find collaborative workspaces and homely city crash pads, or where you can meet up with like-minded people and find places you can visit to get away from the crowds. Perhaps you want to stay for longer than the length of a vacation or work trip, or want dream about the possibilities at least, in which case you might be curious to find out how to hire office space or gain work as a freelancer, where you can learn the language, and which neighbourhood would suit you best to live in.

Carl Goes wants you to become a citizen of the cities you visit

This is why we think *Carl Goes* is different from other travel guides. It's not about highlighting the well-trodden backpacker trails and tourist sites everyone already knows about, nor is it about featuring the most visually impressive sites of a city without any substance behind it. You want to know about the river barge doubling as a spa, the art gallery hiding away in a concrete car park on the edge of town, and how to discover the city for yourself. You want to know how local residents experience the city, where you can take your laptop to work for a day among like-minded professionals or creatives, and where you can sample cuisines prepared by trailblazing chefs.

Wandering aimlessly without a plan sometimes brings unexpected inspiration

Carl Goes guides are about presenting cities from local viewpoints: our guides are driven by insights from the people who actually live in a city. Juxtaposing our hand-picked recommendations of things to do and places to go with interviews giving the spotlight to a range of the city's residents, *Carl Goes* helps you become part of the city scene. Whether you're travelling for three days, three weeks or three months, a *Carl Goes* guide makes a destination a place to call home.

If you have any questions, ideas or suggestions then please e-mail us at info@carlgoes.com